North Korea
After Kim Il Sung

NORTH KOREA
AFTER KIM IL SUNG

edited by
Dae-Sook Suh
Chae-Jin Lee

LYNNE
RIENNER
PUBLISHERS

BOULDER
LONDON

Published in the United States of America in 1998 by
Lynne Rienner Publishers, Inc.
1800 30th Street, Boulder, Colorado 80301

and in the United Kingdom by
Lynne Rienner Publishers, Inc.
3 Henrietta Street, Covent Garden, London WC2E 8LU

Library of Congress Cataloging-in-Publication Data
North Korea after Kim Il Sung /   edited by Dae-Sook Suh and Chae-Jin
   Lee.
        p.   cm.
     ISBN 1-55587-763-X (alk. paper)
     1. Korea (North)   I. Suh, Dae-Sook, 1931–   II. Lee, Chae-Jin,
   1936–
   DS932.N665   1998
   951.93—dc21   97-32958
                                                              CIP

British Cataloguing in Publication Data
A Cataloguing in Publication record for this book
is available from the British Library.

Printed and bound in the United States of America

       The paper used in this publication meets the requirements
 ∞ of the American National Standard for Permanence of
       Paper for Printed Library Materials Z39.48–1984.

     5 4 3 2

CONTENTS

TABLES AND FIGURES

Tables

Figures

PREFACE

In October 1994, more than four decades after the Korean War, the United States and North Korea signed an agreement designed to prevent North Korea from developing nuclear weapons. The Agreed Framework was the first constructive measure that the United States and North Korea had taken to ease tensions on the Korean peninsula. During the Cold War, North Korea was firmly ensconced in the socialist camp in alliance with the Soviet Union and China, while the United States supported South Korea. In an effort to stave off a recurrence of North Korean aggression, U.S. troops have been stationed in South Korea for nearly fifty years. Since the collapse of the Soviet Union and its allies in Eastern Europe, North Korea has been searching for a place in the community of nations. It joined the nonaligned movement and has succeeded in establishing diplomatic relations with more than one hundred countries, but it is completely isolated from the technologically advanced and industrialized countries of the world.

In the eyes of the world community, in particular the industrialized countries, the image of North Korea is unfavorable. The country is so isolated that few hard facts about its people and politics are known to the outside world. It has been accused of practicing state terrorism and has been labeled a rogue state that cannot be trusted.

The U.S. perception of North Korea is especially bad. Because of its long-standing ties with South Korea, the United States has maintained an adversarial relationship with the North. During the Korean War, the United States placed North Korea in the rank of enemy state, a move that prevented U.S. citizens from transacting business with North Korea. (The United States has not rescinded that statute.) Even after the war, encounters between the United States and North Korea were military confrontations, such as the *Pueblo* incident and the ax murders in the Demilitarized Zone. These incidents did not help the North Korean cause in the United States, nor did the North's constant and often vitriolic propaganda campaigns to denounce the United States as the enemy of the Korean people. The United

States views North Korea as a militant state that threatens the security of South Korea, and it has deployed its troops to maintain peace on the Korean peninsula. North Korea is also considered an aggressive state that can disturb the peace and security of its neighbors when and if it develops and acquires weapons of mass destruction.

When North Korea was suspected of developing nuclear weapons, the United States began to negotiate in earnest to persuade North Korea to remain a member of the Treaty on the Non-Proliferation of Nuclear Weapons and to dissuade it from further developing nuclear capabilities by providing alternative energy sources. In cooperation with Japan and South Korea, the United States organized the Korean Peninsula Energy Development Organization to implement this approach. The United States is working to establish a liaison office in Pyongyang and will allow North Korea to establish the same in Washington, D.C. These tentative first steps of diplomatic negotiations may or may not lead to normalization of diplomatic relations. However, U.S. initiatives in this regard represent the most significant progress any country has made to bring North Korea into the community of the industrialized countries of the world.

North Korea was ruled by Kim Il Sung, often referred to as the supreme leader, for fifty years until his death in July 1994. Although Kim prepared his son, Kim Jong Il, as successor, the country seems to have fallen into disarray since his death. It has yet to convene its Supreme People's Assembly to elect a new president of the republic; and the ruling party, the Workers' Party of Korea, which has not held a party congress in seventeen years, has not elected a new general secretary. The people seem to be loyal to Kim Jong Il, who controls the North Korean military as commander-in-chief, but they suffer from food shortages and general economic hardships. North Korea has recorded negative economic growth ever since the collapse of the Soviet Union, and the severe floods of 1995 and 1996 depleted whatever savings it had in food reserves. To prevent mass starvation, North Korea sought approximately two million metric tons of grain to cover the food shortage until the harvest of 1997.

The number of North Korean refugees fleeing to the South has increased since the death of Kim Il Sung. The most significant defection occurred in February 1997, when Hwang Chang-yop, secretary of the Workers' Party of Korea and chairman of the Foreign Affairs Committee of the Supreme People's Assembly, turned to the South seeking political asylum. Hwang's defection is a sign of disintegration among the old leaders loyal to Kim Il Sung, but it also signifies the rise of new and younger political leaders of Kim Jong Il's generation. More important than Hwang's defection is the resignation, also in February 1997, of Premier Kang Song-san, an architect of the North Korean economic reform. It was Kang who in the 1980s introduced joint-venture laws to attract foreign investment and who tried to create the special economic zone in Najin-Sonbong in the

1990s. Although Kang has been replaced by Vice-Premier Hong Song-nam as acting premier, his economic programs seem to have survived the change.

Since the death of Kim Il Sung, many other important leaders of the older generation have also passed away. Marshal O Chin-u died in February 1995; Marshal Ch'oe Kwang, who replaced O Chin-u as minister of the People's Armed Forces, died in February 1997; and one week after Ch'oe's death, his deputy, Kim Kwang-jin, vice-minister of the People's Armed Forces, also died. Approximately 10 percent of the 270 individuals who constituted the top leadership at the time of Kim Il Sung's death have since passed away.

Kim Jong Il compares the current North Korean difficulties with his father's "march in distress" in the winter of 1938 and the spring of 1939, which the Korean guerrillas made during their revolutionary struggle for independence from Japan. The hardship the North Korean people suffer today may be similar to the suffering the guerrillas experienced in the Manchurian plains without food, adequate clothing, or warm shelter. The guerrillas had to fight the pursuing Japanese expeditionary force to survive; and despite their share of defectors and traitors who betrayed the cause of the revolution, Kim Il Sung persisted and fought for Korean independence. Like his father, Kim Jong Il claims that his "march in distress" will be victorious.

This book is an effort by U.S. scholars, longtime observers of North Korea, to introduce readers to a country in transition after the death of Kim Il Sung. True to the U.S. tradition, the contributors' views vary, but collectively they represent our current understanding of this long-hidden, enigmatic, and impoverished state.

The book grew out of two workshops held at the Keck Center for International and Strategic Studies of Claremont McKenna College in 1995 and 1996. We express our appreciation for the able assistance of Mary Anderson, administrative officer of the Keck Center, and the editorial recommendations of John C. Thomas.

The Editors

Introduction

Robert A. Scalapino

For those who enjoy a mystery, North Korea is an ideal subject of study. Where else does a state exist without an officially designated head and with a political system that operates with scarcely any visible institutions? Is there any other nation where the paucity of data regarding the economy is so great or outside estimates of intentions regarding future economic policies so diverse? Even in the strategic realm, external opinions vary greatly regarding both the capabilities and intentions of the Democratic People's Republic of Korea (DPRK), and for good reason. Only with respect to the North's relations with other nations are the data sufficient to permit reasonably assured analyses, but this is also an area where unexpected changes can occur, subject to leadership decisions.

Yet it would be a serious mistake to assume that because there are many lacunae in our knowledge, we know nothing about the DPRK. The chapters in this volume are testimony to the fact that much *is* known, and even when the available data do not permit precision, they enable perimeters to be created or varying degrees of probability to be assigned to alternative scenarios.

One should start with the North Korean domestic scene because in the final analysis domestic conditions, political and economic, are likely to be the decisive factor in determining the North's relations with others and, indeed, the crucial question of its survival.

It seems clear that the political operation of the DPRK is not dependent upon those formal institutions embedded in the constitution. When was the last time the Supreme People's Assembly met or the Central Committee of the Workers' Party was convened? Personal relationships, operating through certain institutional frameworks but above all dependent upon informal ties, especially ties to the supreme leader, are the essence of governance in this society. Today, "the great leader" is Kim Jong Il, and in Chapter 1 Dae-Sook Suh gives us an informed analysis of this enigmatic man and his present political role.

1

The decision to transmit power from father to son was made long ago, and young Kim was steadily groomed for his role, albeit through indigenous training. His personal interests appear to have been in making motion pictures, and being an introvert, he has never relished the public role that his father played so effectively. Yet, to partially compensate for this lack of charisma, the succession has been suffused with a religious aura: The father is not truly dead; he is being reborn in the son. Kim Il Sung is eternal.

There may be practical reasons why the formal inauguration of Kim Jong Il as president or party general secretary has been delayed. The people had to be adjusted to a new era after decades of regarding the first great leader as the source of all wisdom, especially in this period of great economic hardship. Thus, mourning—and with it the full panoply of tradition—remains in effect as North Korea moves into the fourth post–Kim Il Sung year, but with growing signs that with the third anniversary duly commemorated, the son will assume one or more high offices in addition to his command of the armed forces.

Meanwhile, the evidence strongly suggests that Kim Jong Il is without challenge at this point. His primary attention has been directed toward the military, and in this realm, he is taking care to pay due homage to those remaining of his father's generation while elevating a younger group in whom he has confidence. Several key generals of the older generation have recently passed away, making this task easier. At the same time, a few civilian contemporaries of Kim Jong Il, including certain relatives, have that all-important access that gives them power. Whether there are three separate channels through which information flows to the top—military, party, and government—or whether such information is often synthesized before reaching the great leader remains unclear.

Spotty evidence suggests that differences among leaders of North Korea have existed, at least over timing and tactics, some of them requiring very high level decisions. Indeed, North Korean sources have recently made such assertions to the United States, but to what extent this information is a part of the bargaining game—with the implication that "moderates" must be supported lest "hard-liners" gain greater authority—is unclear. Stronger evidence points to sharp rivalry for turf and recognition at horizontal levels, for example, between party and governmental agencies. In sum, the power structure is undoubtedly tight but less than monolithic.

Since the capacity of the DPRK to survive—or, if one prefers, the length of its survival—depends heavily upon the economy, it is vitally important to weigh this factor as carefully as possible, as Marcus Noland has done in Chapter 2. On the broad facts, there is wide-ranging agreement; even North Korean spokespeople acknowledge that the economy is in crisis today. Naturally, they place primary emphasis upon the recent floods. More detached observers point to the intrinsic flaws in the command economy that have been operative since its establishment: an autarky that has precluded keeping pace with the technological revolution; scanty foreign trade and access to foreign exchange; a strong imbalance between heavy industry and consumer goods and a military quotient that has constituted a crushing burden; overbureaucratization, with ever-increasing reliance upon exhortation in an effort to raise production. The list of defects could be extended.

Then came the deluge, literally and figuratively. The collapse of the Soviet Union largely removed North Korea's chief source of vital trade and economic aid in the form of postponed debt payments and "friendship prices." These benefits had been of crucial importance to the DPRK economy. China also toughened its terms of trade. Suddenly, *chuch'e* (self-reliance) became all too real. The floods of 1995 and 1996 were the final blow.

The evidence strongly indicates that from 1989 to 1996, the gross domestic product (GDP) of the DPRK declined yearly, between roughly 2 to 5 percent per annum. Despite efforts to obtain energy supplies from the Middle East through military sales, shortages in North Korea have had a serious effect upon the ability of industrial plants to operate at or near capacity. Agriculture has also been affected by inadequate fertilizer and weak mechanization. Trade has probably represented only 12 percent of total GDP, and while estimates of per capita GDP vary widely, most analysts believe that it is somewhere between one-fourth to one-tenth that of the South.

For these reasons, a number of observers are prone to argue that the collapse of the DPRK is inevitable, the only uncertainties being those of timing and consequences. Others are more cautious, emphasizing that this society has long known hardship, that it is governed by a tough elite intent upon survival at whatever price, and that external influences can be kept far more minimal than was the case with Eastern Europe and the USSR. Nonetheless, it is extraordinarily difficult to maintain that the status quo is tenable. Indeed, the evidence accumulates that a growing portion of the North Korean elite, recognizing this fact, is exploring economic reforms. This group is taking cautious steps because it recognizes the hazards that a process of opening up can have upon a political system. Yet the exploration of change gathers momentum.

It has been more than a decade since the first joint venture law was promulgated in the North, but limited progress has been made in inducing foreign investment despite heightened efforts. The International Investment and Trade Forum held in Najin-Sonbong in September 1996 represented a major effort to attract outside investors. However, other than the funds from the Choch'ongnyon adherents (pro–North Koreans living in Japan), investments have been sparse, most of them small scale and generally for processing, taking advantage of the North's cheap and efficient labor force. Groups of foreign entrepreneurs continue to be invited to inspect the North's sites; special attention is being directed toward the South Korean *chaebol* (business conglomerate). And the DPRK actively participates in the Tumen River Area Development Project under United Nations Development Programme (UNDP) auspices. Pessimists say that these efforts, even if they go forward, are too late. Optimists give the DPRK a chance of following a modified Chinese or Vietnamese path and, by this route, achieving a "soft landing."

The DPRK's advantages lie in an educated, effective labor force, important natural resources, and political stability (up to date). Yet in a highly competitive field, when the quest for foreign capital and technology is growing ever more acute, can the DPRK hold its own? Or if it needs external assistance, which seems inescapable, will agencies like the Asian Development Bank and the World Bank—together with South Korea and Japan—be available? Recently, North Korea's prospects for joining these organizations have brightened somewhat.

As noted by Edward Olsen in Chapter 7, one cannot separate the North's economic difficulties from its high level of militarization. With some 25 percent of its population enlisted in military or militia forces and military expenditures taking more than one-fourth of the total budget, the DPRK is truly a garrison state. Although much of the North Korean military is utilized for civilian purposes—construction, road building, harvesting, and various other activities—there are also legitimate questions about its qualitative aspects. The evidence suggests that while there are areas such as missile production where advances are significant, much of the North's conventional forces are antiquated and certainly no match for those of the South. Indeed, it is for this reason that the DPRK is currently seeking external assistance in upgrading its military equipment.

With the nuclear field off limits for the present, will this lead to moves toward chemical and biological weaponry in an effort to achieve balance? And will advances in missile production constitute a growing regional threat, with repercussions for Japan's security policies? Given these questions and the fact that the great bulk of the DPRK military is in the vicinity of the Demilitarized Zone (DMZ), it is not surprising that strategic-military issues have loomed large in the evolution of U.S.–North Korean relations.

In Chapter 3, Selig Harrison goes beyond these concerns, setting forth his views on a full range of issues confronting the United States in its relations with both North and South Korea and suggesting specific proposals that will evoke varied responses and serious reflections. B. C. Koh follows in Chapter 4 with a discerning analysis of the North's approach to the United States. As Koh underlines, the DPRK leaders, using brinkmanship tactics, have made the most of their meager bargaining chips. By inducing a crisis and exhibiting toughness as both parties move toward the edge of confrontation, North Korea has done remarkably well in bringing the most powerful nation in the world to the table and ultimately obtaining an outcome, the Agreed Framework of October 1994, that is favorable to the

DPRK. Doug Bandow details the difficult and painful steps in reaching this agreement in Chapter 6.

As Kenneth Quinones points out in Chapter 5, however, North Korea's bargaining skill should not be overrated. For profoundly important reasons, the United States has been moving from policies of containment regarding traditional foes to those of engagement. Such a move has been most clearly exemplified with respect to China, but it has also been applied elsewhere. After the collapse of the USSR, the United States found that containment attracted limited international support, pushing the United States into an increasingly isolated position. Further, containment strengthened extremism, whereas engagement encouraged reform—both economic and political—in authoritarian states, making them a more integral part of the ongoing global revolution and pushing them into the stream of rapid change. As Patrick Morgan sets forth in Chapter 8, in North Korea, there is an added factor: Policies designed to induce stagnation and collapse could exact a heavy penalty on the South and create a potential crisis for the region. Failing or failed states in strategically important regions can easily induce multiple forms of external intervention.

U.S. policies toward North Korea have been constructed with both general and specific considerations in mind, and the DPRK's priorities have also clearly been in evidence, though on occasion the tactics used to achieve those objectives have not always seemed well chosen. The North's principal goal has been to establish a full range of relations with the United States, using the nuclear card as the initial ploy. The DPRK hopes that recognition and reparations from Japan will follow. Official North-South relations will be given the most minimal attention possible, though various unofficial ties will be cultivated. This strategy is eminently logical from Pyongyang's perspective. It also represents a silent tribute to the South's earlier *nordpolitik*. If Seoul could induce Moscow and Beijing to establish a two-Koreas policy, should the North not seek a similar outcome from Washington and Tokyo?

The strengths in the North's strategy have been considerable. First, the United States has always taken the issue of nuclear proliferation very seriously despite the argument of some that it is less consequential than the rapid advances being made in sophisticated conventional weapons—weapons that, unlike nuclear bombs, will be used in the event of conflict. Other bargaining chips available to Pyongyang include such issues as soldiers missing in action (MIA), an end to terrorism, and the replacement of a precarious armistice. But Washington's concern about a "rogue state" having nuclear weapons and the impact this would have upon the region as a whole has proved of the greatest consequence.

The North's strategy has major weaknesses as well. Unlike China, the DPRK has had no U.S. business constituency; the United States has shown scant interest in economic opportunities in the North. Indeed, virtually all

U.S. pressure groups, both those in the private sector and those in the public domain, have seen the DPRK in a very negative light and have frequently questioned whether any concessions made have not been excessive.

More important, however, the North's effort to relegate the South to the position of an outsider is totally unrealistic. Such a stance is unacceptable to the United States and is regarded negatively by Japan and by China and Russia as well. As Chong-Sik Lee indicates in Chapter 11, North Korea's efforts to separate the United States and the Republic of Korea (ROK) have borne some fruit; U.S.–South Korean relations have been troubled from time to time over the issue of how to handle the North. However, as the arrangement with the Korean Peninsula Energy Development Organization (KEDO) clearly demonstrates, while some face-saving may be permitted, the North must accept the South as a principal actor in determining the future of the Korean peninsula both strategically and economically. No amount of vitriol directed at Kim Young Sam or other South Korean leaders can alter this fact.

The immediate case in point is the ROK-U.S. proposal for a four-party dialogue, to include the United States, the ROK, the DPRK, and China, possibly arranged so as to accommodate various combinations of the parties in the course of the meetings. Pyongyang has been reluctant to officially respond to the proposal, which clearly constitutes a dilemma. To accept would advance a series of desired economic and political agreements with the United States and others, but it would also constitute recognition of the ROK as a full dialogue partner, equal to the United States and China, however camouflaged for purposes of face-saving.

Meanwhile, the United States has responded to North Korean provocations such as DMZ violations in a low-key fashion. The predominant assumption is that these maneuvers are bids for attention, not a prelude to conflict. The decibel level of DPRK propaganda is so continuously high that it ceases to have effect. Thus, when *Nodong sinmun* (*Workers' Daily*) declares that there is "an imminent risk of war," the external response is a stifled yawn. Certainly, a risk of conflict does exist, as the statement in April 1997 of defector Hwang Chang-yop indicates. Yet given the certainty of being pulverized by U.S. and ROK power, will DPRK leaders elect suicide? Conflict might more logically emerge from the fallout that could accompany a weakening or collapse of the North regime.

Indeed, it is precisely because the costs and risks of DPRK collapse are so high that the United States has been able to construct an ad hoc coalition of major powers among the countries directly involved in the Korean issue. While no consensus has been achieved, the United States, Japan, China, and Russia have been in frequent consultation, with subsequent actions, at a minimum serving to contain further deterioration and, on occasion, advancing the cause of tension reduction.

At the same time, the United States has maintained its alliance with the

South—despite recurrent doubts in some South Korean quarters—including the commitment to regular consultation on all critical matters. In South Korea, as elsewhere in East Asia, nationalism sometimes takes anti-U.S. form, especially among younger generations. The shift from patron-client relations to demands for partnership is a general trend. But the U.S.-ROK alliance still commands the support of a strong majority of each country's citizenry and the overwhelming portion of the elites. And it can be argued that even when Korea is unified, there is likely to be a desire for a continued U.S. presence of some type as a balancing force to much nearer neighbors.

North Korea's current predicament is more complicated than that of the South. Today it is bereft of trusted allies. Relations with Russia fell to an all-time low after 1990, with the DPRK feeling betrayed by Russian policies at home and abroad. In recent times, Russia has sought to reestablish normal relations with Pyongyang so as to regain some leverage on the Korean issue. The North listens, hoping to obtain Russian military assistance and aid in updating its obsolescent Soviet industrial plants. But whence will come the funds? The North owes a large debt to Russia, a debt that hard-pressed Moscow is reluctant to cancel. Progress in rebuilding Russian–North Korean relations is likely to be slow.

As Chae-Jin Lee clearly indicates in Chapter 9, North Korea retains its closest relations with China. Beijing is eager to maintain a relationship with the North that keeps it from straying toward others—Japan or, more likely, the United States. Thus, effusive pledges of an eternal friendship sealed in blood are repeated on ceremonial occasions. Moreover, China has recently given signs of a willingness to increase its assistance, particularly with respect to food. Privately, however, the Chinese not only insist that their influence upon Pyongyang is limited but indicate a strong aversion to the North Korean system, regarding it as chauvinistic and traditional—far from true socialism. More important, the imbalance in China's economic relations with the South and North steadily grows. By the mid-1990s, the trade difference (some $11.7 billion versus $623 million) was massive. With this trend, cultural interaction between China and the ROK grew as well and included nonofficial dialogues on political and strategic matters. Signaling its annoyance, Pyongyang has twisted the tail of the dragon slightly by encouraging Taiwan's investment and tourism and by agreeing to accept Taiwan's nuclear waste for much needed money. In sum, while the China–North Korea relationship will always be of great importance to both parties—as it has been throughout history—true intimacy has given way to heightened apprehensions by each side.

Richard Halloran brings North Korea's relations with Japan into focus in Chapter 10. In this relationship, rationality clashes with emotion, leaving the picture confused. Logically, Japan could be of great assistance to the North, both in making available its capital and technology—as it has done to other developing Asian states—and in serving as a balance to the other major powers, including the United States. Further, good relations with Tokyo would make even more useful the services of Choch'ongnyon. The role of the pro–North Koreans living in Japan has been significant. Although figures on remittances from this source vary widely, when such remittances were at their peak, they may have totaled $700 million. Fully 70 percent of foreign investment in the DPRK appears to have come from Japanese Koreans.

Japan has no interest in seeing either a nuclear North or a collapsed North. Thus, a variety of Japanese political leaders have periodically shown an active interest in normalizing relations with the DPRK. Moreover, Tokyo, together with South Korea and the United States, has recently indicated a willingness to provide a substantial quantity of food. However, it is questionable whether Japan wants a unified Korea given the clouds that are destined to hang over the relationship. Why would Tokyo want to see a greatly strengthened, still antagonistic Korea?

In their respective attitudes toward Japan, the North and the South are brought closer together than on any other issue of foreign policy, with a full array of suspicions and antagonisms revealed. Thus, efforts to achieve DPRK-Japan normalization have foundered on a range of issues: nuclear inspections; reparations; "comfort women"; the mysterious case of Yi Un-hye, the Japanese woman who was supposedly kidnapped and used to tutor a North Korean terrorist in Japanese; and more recently kidnapping cases involving Japanese youth. Despite the fact that Japan is currently the North's largest trading partner, the prospects for a positive relationship between Tokyo and Pyongyang can scarcely be considered bright. A combination of history and ethnic prejudice impinge heavily upon this scene.

In the final analysis, one must return to the issue of North-South relations because these two governments and peoples will determine the future of Korea. As Chong-Sik Lee points out in Chapter 11, within the South, advocates of containment and engagement vie with each other, and at times it appears that individuals shift position on this crucial matter.

Current animosities between North and South are high. The North's vulnerability and its deep feeling that the South is preparing to absorb it, coupled with the emotionalism that surrounds the issue of Southern leaders having offered no condolences at the time of Kim Il Sung's death, have caused Pyongyang to unleash a steady stream of violent rhetoric against the Seoul government. On the part of the South, resentment of these vitriolic attacks and of the effort to keep all knowledge of the South's aid from the North Korean people stimulates those who argue for tougher policies.

Despite the high level of verbal hostility and the absence of any meaningful dialogue at official levels, however, economic contacts are gradually expanding. The South is beginning to penetrate the North through small-scale investment and trade, including such operations as the Daewoo joint venture in textiles at Namp'o. Moreover, as the KEDO operation unfolds, the ROK presence will expand irrespective of measures to keep it controlled. Thus, whatever the future holds, it seems highly unlikely that a return to total isolation between the two Koreas can take place.

As one surveys the North Korean scene, there is room for hope despite the grim domestic picture. Indeed, the very grimness of that picture is causing some flexibility of policy at home, however begrudging. The DPRK quest for external economic involvement is genuine if limited. Furthermore, on the international front, there is a significant consensus among the major powers about desired policies and results. Most important, despite internal divisions of opinion over the desirable course of action, South Korea is committed to the effort to bring the North into the regional and international arena. One must expect the unexpected, but the risks of conflict appear less at present than at many points in the past, and a road map toward an evolutionary course exists.

PART 1

Political and Economic Development

1

Kim Jong Il and New Leadership in North Korea

Dae-Sook Suh

Three years have passed since Kim Il Sung died, and Kim Jong Il has ended the three-year mourning period. Kim Jong Il was recommended to take over the helms of the party and the government. The 1997 New Year's editorial of *Nodong sinmun* replaced the familiar New Year's message of Kim Il Sung with a joint editorial of three North Korean newspapers, *Nodong sinmun* (*Workers' Daily*), *Choson inmin'gun* (the *Korean People's Army*), and *Nodong ch'ongnyon* (the *Working Youth*). The three newspapers represent the three most powerful organizations in North Korea after the death of Kim Il Sung: the Workers' Party of Korea, the Korean People's Army, and the Kim Il Sung Socialist Youth League.[1]

The editorial claimed that the North Korean people are making progress in dealing with the setbacks they suffered after the death of Kim Il Sung. It compared the current difficulties with Kim Il Sung's "march in distress" (*konanui haenggun*) in the winter of 1938, during which Kim's partisan guerrillas had to march for five months from the northeastern part of Manchuria to the southeastern region to escape the Japanese expeditionary force. They often marched without food for three or four days at a time, fighting the cold and hunger without adequate shelter. They also suffered the defection and betrayal of their comrades who surrendered to the Japanese, but they claim their revolution persisted. Kim Jong Il characterizes the current difficulties as his "march in distress" and claims that his march will also end in victory. The editorial also hinted that the transitional period will come to an end in 1997. It proclaimed that the North Korean people will carry on with pride the revolutionary task of the previous generation and that the present generation will honor Kim Il Sung as its supreme leader of the country under the leadership of the great leader, Kim Jong Il.[2]

The real situation in the North is quite different from what has been propagated. The North Korean people are starving. Food shortage is so severe that the Flood Damage and Rehabilitation Committee of North

Korea made an international appeal for food. It is difficult to comprehend how North Korea, once a proud and self-reliant state that often boasted its people had nothing to envy in the world, has been reduced to mendicancy. Kim Jong Il's problems are not confined to economic woes alone. In February 1997, Hwang Chang-yop, one of the top ideologues, defected to the South, an indication of serious discord among the top leaders of North Korea. More important than Hwang's defection is the resignation of Kang Song-san, premier of the Administration Council, for health reasons. Kang is the economic reformer who advocated the joint venture laws and the development of the Najin-Sonbong special economic zone. In addition, some of the very top military leaders have passed away. Following the death of Marshal O Chin-u in February 1995, Marshal Ch'oe Kwang and Vice-Marshal Kim Kwang-jin, who headed the Ministry of People's Armed Forces as minister and vice-minister respectively, died in February 1997.[3]

Few would dispute that today North Korea is undergoing a difficult time. Some even argue that it may not overcome the current crisis; still others contend that its political regime as we understand it may not survive the current emergency. North Korea, however, is a resilient state, and it will most likely endure the current "march in distress" and recover from the setbacks, but much depends on the leadership capabilities of its new leader, Kim Jong Il, and his new generation of leaders in North Korea. The reason for serious concern is that Kim Jong Il is an unknown leader who may not be able to manage the current difficulties to a successful conclusion.

It is quite clear that the North Korean people and their mass media do not refer to Kim Jong Il as their supreme leader, *suryong,* but as their great leader, *widaehan yongdoja.* The fine line dividing these titles may not mean anything to the uninitiated, but it is important in terms of North Korean ideology, *chuch'e,* which requires a supreme leader in a country that claims to be self-reliant. According to Kim Jong Il's interpretation of *chuch'e,* a self-reliant country must have a supreme leader, a functioning party, and the people.[4]

When Kim Jong Il was selected as heir to Kim Il Sung in the 1980s, North Koreans said that they were blessed with *suryong* generation after generation, implying that Kim Jong Il would eventually become the supreme leader of the next generation. It seems logical that when Kim Jong Il assumes his position as general secretary of the party or president of the republic, or both, he will be called *suryong.* Although *suryong* is a ceremonial rather than a legal title, it seems that one must obtain one or both of the top positions (i.e., of party and government) in order to become one. Obviously, the title of the commander-in-chief of the North Korean armed forces is not sufficient to make one a *suryong.* According to the definition of a self-reliant state based on the idea of *chuch'e,* North Korea is still, even after the death of Kim Il Sung, ruled not by Kim Jong Il but by his deceased father. However, Kim Jong Il seems to be in firm control of the transitional period as the supreme commander of the armed forces of North Korea.

The delay in convening the party congress or the Supreme People's Assembly seems to be more an expression of deference to the death of Kim Il Sung than a result of political dissatisfaction or dispute about the succession. Kim Jong Il could have assumed the top positions of the party and the government at the time of the death of Kim Il Sung, and it does not seem that he will have any trouble in taking over the power anytime in the future. There is no way to ascertain the state of his health accurately, but there is evidence that he was seriously ill in 1993 and 1994. He seems to have regained his health gradually, and he will be officially elected to the top positions of the party and the government in the near future.

Background

It has often been alleged that Kim Jong Il is an incoherent, short-tempered, reclusive person of little consequence, and it was predicted that when his father died, the succession scheme would come to an abrupt end. Many disparaging remarks have been made about his personality: He is a playboy, a philanderer, and a movie and video fanatic who enjoys not Korean but Western films. These reports are similar to the false allegations lodged against his father when he first took office in North Korea. It is important to recognize that Kim Jong Il is now the top leader of approximately 22 million people, one-third of the entire Korean population, and there is no political group that can challenge his leadership.

Like his father, Kim Jong Il shows a tendency to paint a glorious and patriotic picture in order to make his true record of meager accomplishments look more resplendent. It is not important to refute every detail of his claims, but it is important to ascertain his true record. Compared with his father, who fought the Japanese under difficult conditions, Kim Jong Il seems to have enjoyed a normal life.

Kim Jong Il was born on February 16, 1942, the eldest of three children (two sons and a daughter) of Kim Il Sung and his first wife, Kim Chong-suk. North Koreans claim that he was born in an armed guerrilla camp on the Korean side of Paektusan, the legendary mountain on the border of China and Korea. This claim seems to emanate from the desire of North Koreans to locate the birthplace of their leader within Korean territory, but this is not true. Both his father and mother were guerrilla fighters in the northeastern part of China, formerly Manchuria, and they fled from there into the Russian Maritime Province of the Soviet Union as early as March 1941. Their first son was born in a special forces camp in Vyatsk, near Khabarovsk. Because he was born in Russia he was given a Russian name, Yura, and a Korean name, Chong-il (Jong Il, meaning Correct Sun).

Their second son was also born there, and he was named Shura (Alexandr) in Russian and P'yong-il in Korean.[5]

The family returned to North Korea after the end of World War II, and the couple gave birth to a third child, Kyong-hui, a younger sister to Kim Jong Il. He and his sister are the only surviving members of the family today. His brother and mother died soon after they returned to North Korea. Shura drowned in a large water fountain in Pyongyang while playing with his friend, a son of Major General N. G. Lebedev, executive officer of the Soviet occupation authority. In September 1949, when Kim Jong Il was seven years old, his mother died while giving birth to a stillborn baby. His father, Kim Il Sung, died in July 1994.

Unlike his father, who lost both of his parents early and had to scramble for his sustenance, Kim Jong Il seems to have enjoyed a fairly normal family life and an affluent childhood. He was close to his sister when they were young, and he grew up under the watchful eyes of his powerful father. Early in the Korean War, when Kim Jong Il was eight years old, he and his sister were evacuated to northeastern China along with many children of Kim Il Sung's guerrilla comrades, and there he attended a school specifically designed for the children of North Korean leaders. Kim Jong Il is said to have written a number of letters to his father from there. Except for this short period in northeastern China, Kim Jong Il has spent all of his life in North Korea.

When he returned to Korea from China, Kim Jong Il was enrolled in Samsok Elementary School, and he later transferred to the Fourth Pyongyang Elementary, where he graduated in 1954, when he was twelve years old. He advanced to the First Pyongyang Intermediate School that year and went on to Namsan High School in Pyongyang. He graduated from this high school in July 1960 at the age of eighteen. Thus, he received the regular elementary and secondary school education that North Korea offered at the time.

North Koreans highly praise Kim Jong Il for his academic achievements during this period. They assert that he had already read and understood the writings of Marx and Lenin and had mastered the theory of dialectical materialism and his father's idea of *chuch'e* when he was in secondary school. Such attributions are without foundation. It is not clear how well Kim Jong Il understood Marxism and Leninism or mastered dialectical materialism, but his understanding of his father's *chuch'e* could only be cursory at best. Kim Il Sung first expounded on the idea of *chuch'e* in December 1955, when Kim Jong Il was only thirteen years old, one year after his elementary school graduation. There are no significant stories of his high school days or of any teacher or close friends who influenced him. Perhaps it is more important to note that Kim, as a son of the most powerful political figure in North Korea, went through his elementary and secondary schools without any fanfare.

Unlike his father, Kim Jong Il graduated from college. The university he attended bears his father's name, Kim Il Sung University, and it is the premier institution of higher learning in North Korea. Kim Jong Il entered the university in September 1960 and graduated in 1964, majoring in political economy. It has been mentioned in North Korean writings that Kim Jong Il was given the opportunity to go abroad for his college education, but out of patriotism and national consciousness, he refused, staying home to learn more about Korea. There is also a false story that he studied in East Germany; Kim Jong Il did travel to Eastern European countries, but he did not stay there any length of time. North Korean writers also claim that Kim Jong Il was a brilliant student who authored articles on many different topics—about party policies on local economy, tradition of the party, loyalty to the supreme leader, and others—throughout his college years. However, such articles have not yet been published in their entirety. These writers also assert that Kim Jong Il had good personal relations with his friends and that he was a leader among his peers.[6]

North Korean writers acknowledge that Kim Jong Il spent his college years preparing himself for the future of North Korea. He was apparently active in campus politics during his college days and often accompanied his father to inspect factories and collective farms in North Korea. For his graduation, he wrote a thesis titled "The Position and the Role of the County in Socialist Construction," about the role of the county in solving agrarian problems in North Korea. He allegedly studied the problem of the gap in urban and rural developments and tried to bring the earnings of the farmers in rural areas to the level of industrial workers in urban areas. For this study, it is claimed, Kim Jong Il closely followed his father's theses on the issue.

This is an incredible claim. Kim Il Sung's *Theses on the Socialist Rural Question in Our Country* was first made public on February 25, 1964, at the time of the Eighth Plenum of the Fourth Central Committee.[7] Kim Jong Il's graduation thesis was submitted on March 18, 1964. This means either that the father and son coauthored the theses or that Kim Jong Il got his father's draft in advance. The choice of this thesis topic was excellent because the county-centered solution for agrarian problems was an innovative idea unique to North Korea, but the timing of its announcement in the party by the father and its submission by the son for graduation was somewhat too close to be taken seriously. To be sure, Kim Il Sung seems to have had the idea of solving North Korean agrarian problems, and Kim Jong Il seems to have claimed credit for understanding it.

Regardless of these exaggerated claims, it is important to note that Kim Jong Il did receive a four-year college education; although he may or may not have shown brilliance, he successfully concluded his formal education from elementary school through college, something his father was not able to accomplish. Kim Il Sung remarried in 1963 while Kim Jong Il was in college. Kim Jong Il hated his stepmother, Kim Song-ae, and his bond with his sister grew stronger. She later married a man named Chang Song-t'aek; both his sister and her husband exercise significant influence over Kim Jong Il today.

The Plot of 1967

Unlike his classmates, Kim Jong Il was not drafted to serve in the North Korean armed forces. Instead, he was assigned to work in the party on June 19, 1964, soon after his graduation. In June 1994, shortly before the death of Kim Il Sung, North Koreans celebrated the thirtieth anniversary of the work of Kim Jong Il in the party.[8] Kim Jong Il was first assigned to work in the Organization Section, one of the most powerful sections of the party Secretariat. He was transferred in 1965 to the office of his father, the prime minister's office, and from there he was reassigned to the party post in the office of his uncle, Kim Yong-ju, who was then the head of the party's Propaganda and Agitation Section. Kim Jong Il showed great interest in promoting cultural and artistic works, and he worked closely with Kim Kuk-t'ae, son of the famous partisan comrade Kim Ch'aek. He also showed interest in ideological works within the party, and he worked closely with Yang Hyong-sop in developing his father's idea of self-reliance. From the rapidity with which he was assigned to various important offices within and outside the party, it is not difficult to see that Kim Jong Il was given treatment worthy of a son of Kim Il Sung.

North Koreans claim that Kim Jong Il made "an important contribution" to the party in 1967 by uncovering a plot by bourgeois and revisionist elements within the party who conspired to overthrow his father. After Kim Jong Il purged these traitors, he is said to have helped establish the unitary ideological system and elevated his father to the position of *suryong*. The plot was taken up in secret at both the Fifteenth Plenum of the Fourth Central Committee on May 4–8, 1967, and the Sixteenth Plenum on June 28–July 3, 1967. These two plenums addressed what the North Koreans referred to as "antiparty activities" by Pak Kum-ch'ol and Yi Hyo-sun, who, along with their supporters, allegedly promoted individual heroism and regionalism against the party. Pak Kum-ch'ol, who had been imprisoned during the Japanese colonial period, commissioned a film titled *Ilp'yon tansim* (*One-Track Mind*), which depicted the passionate devotion of his wife not to the party or to the cause of the revolution but to Pak himself. Thus, he had promoted individual heroism. He also commissioned a play titled *Naegohyang* (*My Hometown*), which praised the people from Hamgyongdo, home of both Pak Kum-ch'ol and Yi Hyo-sun. Yi Hyo-sun supposedly heavily favored party cadres from the northeastern region of Hamgyongdo, thus trying to create a regional faction favorable to the people from that region. Kim Jong Il purportedly uncovered this plot, purged the two, and identified their co-conspirators.

This version of events is incredible. These incidents occurred only three years after Kim Jong Il graduated from college and joined the party, and the people who were purged were leaders of the party with impressive records and credentials. But the episode is important enough to warrant closer examination, and to understand it, we must examine the political scene of North Korea in 1967, a time when Kim Il Sung was having trouble with China's Red Guard and its Cultural Revolution.

In 1965 Kim Il Sung had just restored normal relations with the Soviet Union and declared an independent, self-reliant policy for North Korea by expressing his interest in joining the ranks of nonaligned nations. Kim was tired of revisionism in the Soviet Union as well as dogmatism in China, and he wanted to chart his own self-reliant course for North Korea. Instead of blindly following the course of the Chinese Cultural Revolution, Kim wanted to establish a self-reliant North Korea with himself as *suryong*. However, the Chinese Red Guard began to attack him personally, and some North Korean leaders expressed doubts about his policy and about elevating him to the position of supreme leader.

The persons identified as the leaders of the opposition were Pak Kumch'ol and Yi Hyo-sun, heads of an organization known as the Kapsan Operation Committee (KOC). The KOC was organized in the 1930s to support the Korean independence movement, and it supported Kim Il Sung and his most illustrious raid into Korea, the Poch'onbo battle of June 1937. Members of the KOC and another anti-Japanese organization, the Korean Fatherland Restoration Association in Manchuria (KFRAM), provided Kim Il Sung and his partisans with local information about the Japanese police movement and its security arrangements. The battle of Poch'onbo was one of Kim Il Sung's most successful guerrilla raids; however, after Kim and his guerrillas retreated, the local informants from the KOC and the KFRAM were arrested. They were tried, and those identified as informants were found guilty and executed, including such loyal supporters as Kwon Yong-byok, Yi Che-sun, Chi T'ae-hwan, and So In-hong.[9]

Pak Kum-ch'ol was one of a few informants who survived the Poch'onbo raid. He was arrested and found guilty of helping the guerrillas, but he was not executed. Instead, he was sentenced to life imprisonment and sent to Seoul to be incarcerated. He remained in jail at Sodaemun prison until the end of World War II, and when he was released he returned to North Korea and was reunited with Kim Il Sung and his partisans. Yi Hyo-sun was a brother of Yi Che-sun, who was found guilty and executed after the Poch'onbo raid. Yi Hyo-sun himself was engaged in anti-Japanese revolutionary activities in the region of Hamgyongdo, but he did not participate in the Poch'onbo raid. During the time Kim Il Sung was consolidating his power, he identified all former members of the KOC and the KFRAM as partisans and as members of the partisan group. However, by the mid-1960s, when leaders of other competing groups were purged and when the partisan group was the only group that remained, some leaders began to distinguish between the guerrillas who had fought in the front against the Japanese and those who had supported them in the rear. They also began to distinguish among units within the Northeast Anti-Japanese United Army that had operated in different regions in northeast China. The KOC was a rearguard organization of partisans, and although members of this group were in powerful positions within the party and the government, they were no match for the guerrilla fighters of the partisan group.

At the time of the Fourth Party Congress in September 1961, some members of the KOC held high positions. Pak Kum-ch'ol, for example, ranked fourth in the Political Committee of the party behind Kim Il Sung, Ch'oe Yong-gon, and Kim Il. Yi Hyo-sun was not far behind; he ranked sixth behind these four and Kim Ch'ang-man. Five years later, at the Second Party Conference in 1966, Pak Kum-ch'ol and Yi Hyo-sun ranked fourth and fifth, respectively, in the Political Committee as a result of the purge of Kim Ch'ang-man. Pak Kum-ch'ol was in charge of the Organization Section of the Secretariat, and Yi Hyo-sun was in charge of North Korean operations within South Korea.[10]

In addition to Pak Kum-ch'ol and Yi Hyo-sun, other leaders were implicated in the conspiracy. These included Kim To-man, who ranked tenth and was appointed a secretary of the party in October 1966; Ko Hyok, who was in charge of the culture and arts section of the party; and Ho Sok-son, who was in charge of the party's education section. Others were Kim Wal-yong, chairman of the General Federation of Trade Unions; Ho Hak-song, chairman of the Hwanghae Provincial Party Committee; and Yi Song-un, procurator-general of the Central Procurator's Office.[11]

All of these individuals were powerful, but they were never a threat to Kim Il Sung, because none of them had been fighting men in Kim's guerrilla units. They had not organized a separate group to challenge Kim. The KOC had become more an organization to commemorate its support for Kim Il Sung and his Poch'onbo raid than a political organization that plotted to challenge him. Yi Hyo-sun was in charge of North Korean underground operations in South Korea, and his operations were not going well. Yi was replaced by Ho Pong-hak, a partisan fighter who instituted a new militant policy toward the South, including an attempt to assassinate the president of South Korea in January 1968. Also, members of the Chinese Red Guard spread a rumor during the Cultural Revolution that North Korean general Kim Kwang-hyop, a partisan who had operated in the northern region of Manchuria under the direction of the Fourth Route Army of the Northeast Anti-Japanese United Army, was planning a coup to overthrow Kim Il Sung. This allegation proved false.

It is commonly alleged that Pak Kum-ch'ol and his group cautioned

Kim Il Sung about his policy toward the Soviet Union and China, particularly in view of the fact that South Korea had been taken over by a professional soldier who understood the military balance between the North and the South. They reminded Kim that South Korea was modernizing its armed forces by sending troops to Vietnam and making significant strides in economic development by normalizing diplomatic relations with Japan. Pak Kum-ch'ol and Yi Hyo-sun seem to have had reservations about supporting the campaign to make Kim Il Sung the supreme leader of the Korean people. It was also said that Pak Kum-ch'ol, who headed the Organization Section of the Secretariat, favored people from his own region, Hamgyongdo, over other areas in recruiting officials for the party. Yi Hyo-sun was supposedly not doing his job to promote the national liberation movement in South Korea. It is clear, however, that the members of the KOC and those officials recruited into the party by Pak and Yi did not constitute a powerful enough political force to challenge Kim Il Sung and his partisans.

It is ludicrous to claim that Kim Jong Il uncovered a plot by these men and purged them. Even if the claims about the plot had been true, it would have taken Kim Il Sung and all his fighting partisan guerrillas to purge these men. Kim Jong Il joined the party in June 1964, and it would have been virtually impossible even for the son of Kim Il Sung to purge these men in 1967. This tale seems to be an effort on the part of North Korean writers to give credit to Kim Jong Il for something he was not able to do. *Choson nodongdang yoksa,* the official history of the Workers' Party of Korea, which was published in December 1991 to commemorate Kim Il Sung's eightieth birthday, mentions the antiparty activities of Pak Kum-ch'ol, Yi Hyo-sun, and their supporters at the time of the Fifteenth and the Sixteenth Plenums of the Fourth Central Committee, but it does not mention any role played by Kim Jong Il. It was after the purge that the North Korean people began to call Kim Il Sung *suryong* of the Korean people. Kim Jong Il may have contributed to the campaign to promote Kim Il Sung's cult of personality to a higher level, but he did not play an important role in uncovering the plot of 1967.[12]

Works in the Party

Had he uncovered a plot and saved the party, Kim Jong Il would have attained a prominent position within the party after the antiparty elements were purged, but when the Fifth Party Congress was convened in November 1970, Kim Jong Il was not elected as a member of the Central Committee. Nor was he elected to any official post within the party organization. Instead, he was assigned to work in the Propaganda and Agitation Section of the party's Secretariat, and he began in earnest to make films to glorify his father's revolutionary guerrilla activities of the 1930s. In this endeavor, Kim Jong Il did outstanding work. Films representative of this work include *P'ibada* (*Sea of Blood*) in 1969, *Han chawidanwon ui unmyong* (*Fate of a Member of the Self-Defense Corps*) in 1970, and *Kkotp'anun ch'onyo* (*Flower Girl*) in 1972. He made many other films as well, and his frequent contacts with the film industry earned him a reputation for flirting with actresses and dancers.

It is claimed that the films were artistic productions of high quality that contributed to the cultural life of the North Korean people and that the films aroused the national consciousness of the people and renewed their appreciation of Kim Il Sung's past revolutionary activities. Kim Jong Il made a deliberate effort to link his films with the tenets of his father's *chuch'e* idea by emphasizing and promoting a close relationship among the people, the party, and the supreme leader, and his films are said to have expressed his loyalty to his father. The films entertained the people and enhanced the position of the party and its propaganda and agitation, but most important, they won the approval of Kim Il Sung, who was apparently extremely pleased with the quality of his son's work. Kim Jong Il worked hard to impress his father and to gain recognition as a pious and able son who could be trusted. The films were widely distributed within North Korea as well as abroad.

It was not until September 1973, at the Seventh Plenum of the Fifth Central Committee, that Kim Jong Il was elected to the Secretariat as a secretary; five months later, at the Eighth Plenum of the Fifth Central Committee, he was elected as a member to the Political Committee.[13] Of course, such "important" elections were not made public at the time. The agenda of the plenums dealt with the task of the three revolutions (ideological, technical, and cultural) that had been initiated at the Fifth Party Congress in 1970. There were reports by Kim Il Sung on general mobilization for construction and a report by Yang Hyong-sop on the complete abolition of taxes, but neither plenum addressed the election of new members to the Secretariat or the Political Committee.

However, it does seem that at these meetings serious questions were raised about Kim Jong Il, the three-revolution movement, and possibly the succession, because the Ninth Plenum of the Fifth Central Committee was held in secret. Even its exact date was unknown: It was held sometime after February 1974 and sometime before February 1975, when the Tenth Plenum was held. Kim Jong Il's election as a member of the Secretariat and the Political Committee was unusual to say the least; no one had ever been elected to the top leadership organization of the Central Committee without first being elected to the Central Committee. Such extraordinary personnel actions and the secret meeting of the plenum signaled that the larger issue of selecting Kim Jong Il as the successor to Kim Il Sung was imminent.

It is assumed that the selection of Kim Jong Il was made at the Ninth

Plenum of the Fifth Central Committee and that the meeting of the plenum was most likely held in April 1974. It was not Kim Il Sung who recommended Kim Jong Il as successor but his old partisan comrades such as Kim Il, Yim Ch'un-ch'u, and O Chin-u. At first, Kim Il Sung was supposedly not in favor of the idea, citing the fact that his son was still too young for the job. Indeed, at the time, Kim Jong Il was only thirty-two years old, younger than Kim Il Sung was when he took power in 1945 at the age of thirty-three. It may have taken some persuasion on the part of the leaders of Kim Il Sung's own generation to convince him that a successor must be chosen not from the older but from the younger generation. Kim Il Sung supposedly acquiesced to such a demand from the leaders of his generation only after careful deliberation.[14]

There is speculation that a number of high party officials at the Ninth Plenum opposed the selection of Kim Jong Il as successor. For example, Kim Tong-gyu, who ranked third behind Kim Il Sung and Kim Il in the Political Committee of the Central Committee at the time, suddenly disappeared from all public functions shortly after the Ninth Plenum, and he was never mentioned again in the North. It was also after the Ninth Plenum that North Korean media began to use a mysterious term, "party center," to refer to Kim Jong Il. The succession of Kim Jong Il was implied in a *Nodong sinmun* article to commemorate the forty-second anniversary of the founding of the Korean People's Army on April 25, 1974. The article mentioned that the people should support the "party center" generation after generation.[15]

It was not Kim Il Sung who tried to force the mantle of power onto his reluctant or indifferent son; it was Kim Jong Il who actively sought to succeed his father. To gain his father's blessing, Kim Jong Il worked hard throughout the 1970s under his father's tutelage. In addition to making films for his father, Kim Jong Il led various campaigns to increase industrial and agricultural production by mobilizing young people. He took charge of the Three-Revolution Team Movement and later developed it into the Three-Revolution Red Flag Movement to improve the sagging economy. Kim Jong Il and the young people of his generation went out to the factory and farms to encourage tired old workers to increase production by using new methods and new technology. In the beginning, Kim Jong Il failed miserably in the campaign. Many older workers resented working under the watchful eyes of the younger cadres, who knew nothing about the work. Their new methods were unworkable and their new technologies needed explanation and proper application. Industrial as well as agrarian production dropped sharply in the mid-1970s. Kim Il Sung made serious efforts to teach his son and the young people how to conduct mass campaigns to increase production. At the same time, he had to encourage the tired workers to continue the pace they were used to and gradually to adopt new methods whenever possible.[16]

Toward the end of the 1970s, it was claimed that the Three-Revolution Team Movement and the Three-Revolution Red Flag Movement were successfully concluded, and in December 1979 Kim Jong Il was awarded the highest medal in North Korea, the Kim Il Sung Medal, First Class, for his accomplishments. In addition to the production campaigns, Kim Jong Il launched a campaign to compile the complete works of his father into a new series called *Kim Il Sung chojakchip* (*Works of Kim Il Sung*). This effort to compile all of Kim Il Sung's writings, including his earlier collection of selected works, has thus far filled thirty-four volumes.[17] Kim Jong Il began to refer to his father's idea as "Kimilsungism," in line with such terms as "Marxism" and "Leninism."

Kim Jong Il worked hard to impress his father that he was a pious son who would honor his father. He built several landmark monuments to his father, including a tower for the *chuch'e* idea and an Arch of Triumph to commemorate his father's triumphant return to North Korea from Manchuria. There were celebrations for his father's seventieth and eightieth birthdays on a scale larger than any other tribute ever made to Kim Il Sung. Through these efforts, Kim Jong Il also wanted to prove to his father that he was an able person who could meet his father's expectations. Kim Jong Il wanted the job, and Kim Il Sung seems to have acquiesced and supported his son's quest.

New Leadership in North Korea

It was at the Sixth Congress of the Workers' Party of Korea, on October 10, 1980, that Kim Jong Il was first introduced as an important officer of the party. His earlier elections to the Secretariat and the Political Committee in 1973 and 1974 were never publicly announced, and his rise to power was only implied through obscure terminology. However, by the time of the Sixth Congress, all unofficial references to Kim Jong Il were dropped, and his photograph was displayed alongside his father's to indicate that he would be the successor. Kim Jong Il was elected to the Secretariat as a secretary, ranking second only behind his father, who was the general secretary. He was also elected to the Presidium of the Politburo, ranking fourth behind Kim Il Sung, Kim Il, and O Chin-u. He maintained his fourth-place rank in the Central Committee, and he was also elected to the Military Commission of the party, ranking third behind Kim Il Sung and O Chin-u. No one else had been elected to these organizations, and no one ranked higher than Kim Jong Il except his father, who ranked first in all important party leadership organizations. Kim Il and O Chin-u, for example, ranked higher than Kim Jong Il in the Politburo, but neither one had been elected to the Secretariat. This was a clear indication that Kim Jong Il had won the approval of his succession from both his father and the party.[18]

Even after the Sixth Party Congress, when his selection as successor was publicly proclaimed, Kim Jong Il moved cautiously within the party. From October 1980 to August 1982, he held Central Committee meetings frequently under his father's direction. During this time the Central Committee held six plenums and its Politburo held five joint meetings with the members of the Central People's Committee of the government to coordinate party activities with those of the government. It was not until the Sixth Plenum of the Central Committee in August 1982 that Kim Jong Il began to replace officers and members of the Central Committee and its leadership organizations with people of his own generation to build new leadership in North Korea.

From that time until the Twenty-First Plenum in December 1993, Kim Jong Il was busy replacing leaders from his father's generation with leaders from his own generation. A total of 261 personnel actions were taken during this period. These actions represented a significant change in the Central Committee, which consisted of only 248 members, of whom 145 were full members and 103 were alternates. Seventy-nine full members and 111 alternate members were either promoted or demoted from the Central Committee (see Table 1.1). The plenums were held an average of twice a year from 1980 to 1984 and in 1986 and 1990, but no meetings were held in 1985 or 1987. There were three plenums in 1988, but in 1989 and from 1991 to 1993, the Central Committee held only one meeting per year, usually in December. A great number of personnel actions took place in plenums in 1986 and 1988. Of course, no plenums of the party and no sessions of the Supreme People's Assembly have been held since the death of Kim Il Sung in July 1994. The ruling party of North Korea, the Workers' Party of Korea, has not convened its party congress since 1980, although the bylaws of the party stipulate that a party congress must be held every four years.

In addition to his work in the Central Committee, Kim Jong Il took control of the military of North Korea. As early as December 1991, Kim Jong Il was made commander-in-chief of the Korean People's Army. This event was timed to commemorate the sixtieth anniversary of the founding of the army on April 25, 1992. On this day in 1932, Kim Il Sung is said to have organized his first guerrilla unit in Antu to begin his anti-Japanese guerrilla fighting. On this day sixty years later, Kim Jong Il took over his father's army, now one million strong, and honored old comrades of his father by promoting them to a higher rank. At the same time, Kim Jong Il also promoted 524 young colonels to the rank of general. Assuming control of the military was the method his father had used to secure power when he returned to Korea in 1945, placing all his partisan guerrillas in military organizations, the police, and the security forces so that no one could challenge him with force.

Throughout 1995 and 1996, Kim Jong Il made monthly visits to

Table 1.1 Changes in the Central Committee, 1980–1993

Plenum of the Central Committee	Dates	Politburo	Secretary	Central Committee Member	Central Committee Alternate Member	Auditing Committee Member	Other	Total
1–5	1980–1982	0	0	0	0	0	0	0
6	August 1982	4	0	0	0	0	0	4
7	June 1983	0	4	2	0	0	0	6
8	November 1983	4	0	1	7	2	0	14
9	July 1984	0	0	4	2	1	0	7
10	December 1984	0	1	3	6	2	0	12
11	February 1986	5	6	8	15	2	1	37
12	December 1986	2	7	13	17	2	0	41
13	March 1988	1	0	13	21	1	0	36
14	November 1988	2	2	1	5	1	0	11
15	December 1988	1	2	1	0	0	1	5
16	June 1989	0	0	5	2	1	0	8
17	January 1990	0	1	1	8	0	0	10
18	May 1990	5	2	1	3	0	0	11
19	December 1991	0	0	8	9	0	0	17
20	December 1992	2	2	9	9	1	0	23
21	December 1993	3	0	9	7	0	0	19
Total		29	27	79	111	13	2	261

Notes: Other indicates editors of *Nodong sinmun*.

various armed forces camps to ensure their support for him. On September 13, 1995, he even visited a guard post in the Demilitarized Zone. These personal visits, along with numerous military rallies to support him, reaffirmed his strong relationship with the military establishment. The North Korean constitution was amended in April 1992 to strengthen the position of the military, and it also gave Kim Jong Il a legal basis for his position as the supreme commander of the armed forces. When O Chin-u, minister of the People's Armed Forces, died in 1995, Kim Jong Il gave an elaborate funeral service for this long-time supporter who had controlled the North Korean armed forces after the death of his father. Kim chose to replace O Chin-u with still another general of his father's generation, Ch'oe Kwang, on October 10, 1995, the fiftieth anniversary of the founding of the Workers' Party of Korea. Ch'oe Kwang was a strong supporter of Kim Jong Il, and when Ch'oe died in February 1997, Kim replaced him with another supporter, Yi Ul-sol. In so doing, Kim Jong Il reaffirmed his strong ties with the military establishment. Although he did not serve in the North Korean military, Kim Jong Il is surrounded with military officers who pledge their loyalty to him.

On the fiftieth anniversary of the founding of the Workers' Party of Korea, Kim also promoted Yi Ul-sol to the rank of marshal, and he promoted three other generals, Cho Myong-nok, Yi Ha-il, and Kim Yong-ch'un, to the rank of vice-marshal. Other military leaders who are often seen in his company are Kim Pong-yul, Yi Pong-won, and Kim Myong-guk—all generals who pledged their loyalty to Kim Il Sung and continue to support Kim Jong Il. In April 1997, on the sixty-fifth anniversary of the founding of the Korean People's Army, Kim Jong Il promoted four generals (Kim Il-ch'ol, Chon Chae-son, Pak Ki-so, and Yi Chong-san) to vice-marshal and promoted some fifty generals. Together with selected party and government leaders, these military men seem to constitute an ad hoc emergency council with Kim Jong Il as its head, and they are helping him govern North Korea under some sort of an undeclared martial law or emergency decree during the transitional period. However, the generals represent the older generation, and Kim Jong Il undoubtedly will replace them with generals of his own generation.

On the political front, top North Korean political leadership at the time of Kim Il Sung's death can be ascertained from the composition of Kim's funeral committee. There were 273 members in the committee, and they seem to have been listed in order of rank. Approximately 240 top members of Kim's funeral committee constituted O Chin-u's funeral committee in February 1995, indicating that there had been no significant leadership changes in the seven months after the death of Kim Il Sung. The members of the two funeral committees were of two kinds: One group consisted of old leaders Kim Jong Il had inherited from his father, and the other group contained new, younger leaders whom Kim Jong Il had promoted in the

1980s. Members of the funeral committees represented important political organizations, including the Politburo, the office of the vice president, the Secretariat, the Central People's Committee, departments of the Secretariat, the provincial party committees, the Administration Council, the military, and the Central Committee of the party.

It is noteworthy that only 80 of the 145 full members, 53 of the 103 alternate members, and 5 of the 15 members of the Auditing Committee of the Sixth Central Committee were selected to Kim's funeral committee (see Table 1.2). However, 100 of the 190 new members of the Central Committee elected since 1982 were selected. A group of 35 members of the funeral committee represented other leaders of political and social organizations. They included Chief Justice Ch'oe Won-ik of the Central Court, Chairman Yi Yong-sop of the Central Procurator's Office, Chairman Kim Pyong-sik of the Social Democratic Party, President Pak Kwan-o of Kim Il Sung University, Director Yi Chi-su of the Chuch'e Academy, Chairman Yu Mi-yong of the Ch'ondogyo Young Friends' Party, and the scholar Pak Si-hyong of the Academy of Sciences.

Table 1.2   Composition of the Funeral Committee, 1994

Position in Central Committee	When Elected	Total Number	Funeral Committee
Full member	October 10, 1980	145	80
Alternate member	October 10, 1980	103	53
Auditing Committee member	October 10, 1980	15	5
New member	June 1983–December 1993	190	100
Others	June 1983–December 1993		35
Total		453	273

The funeral committee for O Chin-u consisted of 240 members, 33 fewer than the committee for Kim Il Sung, and consisted of the same leaders except for those who had died. Only minor changes in its composition hinted at political stability under Kim Jong Il after the death of Kim Il Sung. The funeral committee for Ch'oe Kwang, who died in February 1997, consisted of only 85 members, mostly military men. Approximately one-third, 26 members, were new to the funeral committee of Ch'oe Kwang, but more than two-thirds, 59 members, had served in the funeral committees of Kim Il Sung and O Chin-u. There are a few other important leaders who have died since July 1994, including Kang Hui-won, Ch'oe Pok-yon, Kim Ch'ang-ho, Yi Sok, Paek Pom-su, Kim Pong-yul, Kim Kwang-jin, Paek Ch'ang-sik, and Yi Sung-gi.[19]

There are many ways to analyze new leadership under Kim Jong Il.

Those remaining leaders of the older generation, such as the partisans (e.g., Pak Song-ch'ol, Paek Hak-nim, Yi Ul-sol, Chon Mun-sop), and those members who were elected to the Central Committee of the party three or four times (e.g., Yi Chong-ok, Kim Yong-ju, Yi Chi-ch'an, Chong Tu-hwan, Kim Chung-nin), will undoubtedly yield their positions of power to the younger generation of new leaders and retire into ceremonial positions. Those leaders who are marked for demotion, such as Hwang Chang-yop, will either defect or be purged, and still others will resign for political and health reasons.

New leaders we must observe with care are those who were appointed to the Central Committee after the Sixth Plenum of the Sixth Central Committee in August 1982. There are 130 full and alternate members of the Central Committee, but even more important are those who were selected to the funeral committee of Kim Il Sung. Of course, the most important among these new leaders are those who rank within the top 100 of the 273 members of the funeral committee, including Ch'oe T'ae-bok, Hong Sok-hyong, Kim Pok-sin, Pak Nam-gi, Chong Ha-ch'ol, Kim Ki-ryong, Pak Sung-il, and Kim Hak-bong. More detailed analyses can be made by examining the roster of the funeral committees of Kim Il Sung, O Chin-u, and Ch'oe Kwang in Appendix 2.

Current North Korean political leadership consists of a mixture of old leaders of the Kim Il Sung generation and new, young leaders of the Kim Jong Il generation. All leaders, the old and the new alike, are in full support of Kim Jong Il. In view of the fact that Kim Jong Il has been preparing for his rule for nearly two decades, there is little doubt that he will become the next supreme leader of North Korea. It is most likely that at the time of the Seventh Congress of the Workers' Party of Korea, a number of old-generation leaders will remain in positions of power, but a majority of the members of the Central Committee will be leaders from the younger generation. Given the political climate after the death of Kim Il Sung, it is inconceivable that any individual holds a prominent position in the party or that the government plans to organize a political or social group opposed to Kim Jong Il and his leadership in North Korea. The takeover of political leadership by Kim Jong Il has been in progress for a long time, and there have been ample opportunities to deal with any opposition to his leadership.

North Korean political leadership has been changing since the mid-1980s with the blessing of Kim Il Sung. Kim Jong Il may use leaders from both generations during the transitional period, but he will eventually replace the old leaders with new leaders who will take over North Korean politics. At the time of the Ninth Supreme People's Assembly in May 1990, for example, it was claimed that nearly 60 percent of the 687 representatives to the North Korean legislature consisted of men and women younger than fifty-five years.

Notes

1. In January 1996, on the fiftieth anniversary of its founding, the League of the Socialist Working Youth decided to change its name to Kim Il Sung Socialist Youth League. *Nodong sinmun,* January 20, 1996.

2. *Nodong sinmun,* January 1, 1997.

3. Hwang Chang-yop and Kang Song-san are leaders of the old generation and Kim Jong Il will replace them. Hwang lost his place in new leadership and defected to the South in February 1997. Kang has already been replaced by Hong Song-nam. Kim Jong Il relied heavily on the old military leaders of his father's generation such as O Chin-u and Ch'oe Kwang, but he has already replaced these men with younger leaders, such as Marshal Cho Myong-nok and Vice-Marshal Kim Il-ch'ol.

4. Kim Jong Il, *On Some Problems of Education in the* Chuch'e *Idea: Talk to the Senior Officials of the Central Committee of the Workers' Party of Korea on July 15, 1986* (Pyongyang: Foreign Languages Publishing House, 1987).

5. There is ample evidence that Kim Jong Il was born in the Russian Maritime Province. His parents were not in Korea at the time of his birth, and since it was February of the year, any sort of travel from Paektusan to Khabarovsk would not have been possible. There is testimony from a woman named Yi Chae-dok, who claims that she nursed Kim Jong Il at Vyatsk because his mother was weak. *Chungang ilbo,* October 4, 1991.

6. For official North Korean accounts for Kim Jong Il, see, among others, Tak Jin, Kim Gang Il, and Pak Hong Je, *Great Leader Kim Jong Il,* vols. I and II (Tokyo: Sorinsha Publishers, 1984); and Choe In Su, *Kim Jong Il: The People's Leader,* vols. I and II (Pyongyang: Foreign Languages Publishing House, 1983 and 1985). For his writings, see *Kim Jong Il: Selected Works,* vols. I and II (Pyongyang: Foreign Languages Publishing House, 1992 and 1993).

7. For the text of the theses by Kim Il Sung, see *Theses on the Socialist Rural Question in Our Country* (Pyongyang: Foreign Languages Publishing House, 1964). The text of Kim Jong Il's graduation thesis is not available.

8. *Nodong sinmun,* June 19, 1994.

9. For details of the Poch'onbo raid and the trial and execution of these people, see *Gendaishi shiryo* (Tokyo: Hara shobo, 1967). For Kim Il Sung's account of the raid, see his memoir, *Segiwa toburo,* vol. 6 (Pyongyang: Choson nodongdang ch'ulp'ansa, 1995).

10. For the details of personnel and organizational changes within the party, see Dae-Sook Suh, *Korean Communism, 1945–1980: A Reference Guide to the Political System* (Honolulu: University of Hawaii Press, 1981).

11. Yi Song-un was a member of the KOC arrested after the Poch'onbo raid for assisting the guerrillas. He was tried and convicted but was not executed. He was later released and supposedly went to the Soviet Union to study law. When Yi returned to North Korea after the end of World War II, he was also identified as a member of the partisan group and served as one of Kim Il Sung's most notorious prosecutors, looking after the interests of the partisans in North Korea. Yi Song-un prosecuted Pak Hon-yong, Yi Sung-yop, Yi Kang-guk, and other members of the domestic group for treason after the Korean War. Members of the domestic group were convicted and executed.

12. *Choson nodongdang yoksa* [History of the Workers' Party of Korea] (Pyongyang: Choson nodongdang ch'ulp'ansa, 1991).

13. Election of Kim Jong Il to the Secretariat and the Political Committee was not reported in 1973 or in 1974. It was reported only when the work of his succes-

sion was completed in the 1980s. For official recognition of the election, see *Choson nodongdang yoksa*.

14. See detailed analysis on this point in a good study of Kim Jong Il by Yi Ch'an-haeng, *In'gan Kim Chong-il, Suryong Kim Chong-il: Kuui sidae wa pukhan sahoe* [Kim Jong Il as a Person and as the Supreme Leader: His Times and North Korean Society] (Seoul: Yollin sesang, 1994).

15. *Nodong sinmun*, April 25, 1974.

16. For the details of the Three-Revolution Team Movement, see Dae-Sook Suh, *Kim Il Sung: The North Korean Leader* (New York: Columbia University Press, 1988).

17. Kim Il Sung, *Kim Il Sung chojakchip*. 34 vols. (Pyongyang: Choson nodongdang ch'ulp'ansa, 1982–1994). There is an English version, Kim Il Sung, *Works*. 38 vols. (Pyongyang: Foreign Languages Publishing House, 1980–1993).

18. For the Sixth Party Congress and the election of officers of the party, see the report on the party congress in *Nodong sinmun*, October 14, 1980.

19. Yi Sung-gi was the foremost scientist in North Korea. He is credited with many scientific achievements, including the discovery of "vynalon" fabric and the creation of a laboratory for nuclear energy. He was not on the funeral committee because he was too old. He died on February 8, 1996, at the age of ninety-one. See *Nodong sinmun*, February 9, 1996. For detailed information on those political leaders who died after Kim Il Sung died in July 1994, see the list in Appendix 2.

2

Prospects for the North Korean Economy

Marcus Noland

North Korea exhibits the usual problems of centrally planned economies (CPEs) exacerbated by the *chuch'e* ideology of self-reliance and extreme centralization of power: There has been an overemphasis on heavy industry to the detriment of consumer goods and services; there has been overaccumulation and misallocation of capital; the infrastructure is in dire condition; enterprises operate using outdated technology, and the country is largely unable to acquire new technology from abroad; the suppression of international trade has contributed to foreign exchange shortages, which have inhibited the importation of even essential products such as cooking coal; shortages of power and parts have reduced capacity utilization; the bureaucratization of agriculture has contributed to falling production, and a famine of unknown magnitude may well be under way; regional development is unbalanced; and, as in many socialist CPEs, real living standards are reduced by environmental degradation, a massive military, and the diversion of resources into what Aidan Foster-Carter has described as "monumental edifices."[1]

North Korea was further hit by a series of negative macroeconomic shocks in the late 1980s and early 1990s, and because of its inability to increase significantly either exports or borrowing from abroad, it was forced to accept reduced domestic output and absorption. Most recently, it was hit by severe flooding and has accepted grain on a concessional basis from Japan, South Korea, China, and the broader international community through the UN's World Food Program. It is difficult to disentangle to what extent North Korea's current problems are due to secular decline and to what extent they reflect temporary difficulties brought on by natural disasters.

The Democratic People's Republic of Korea (DPRK) has begun to initiate some modest reforms that should not alter the fundamental centrally planned character of the economy, but the reforms to date are probably inadequate to address the task at hand. Thus, the regime faces the question of whether to accelerate and widen the reforms or to stand firm and try to ride out the current difficulties, risking collapse if the situation worsens.

In the longer run, Pyongyang may be forced to consider more wide-ranging reforms, and because of very different initial conditions, the Chinese or Vietnamese path of gradual reform does not appear to be a viable option. Fundamental economic reform would result in an enormous expansion of international trade and transformation of the composition of output. Whether such precipitous change would be politically sustainable is disputable, and systemic collapse cannot be ruled out.

Organization of the North Korean Economy

The North Korean economy is organized along lines similar to other CPEs.[2] Since North Korea's inception, property rights have resided primarily with the state, and resource allocation is largely carried out through the planning mechanism, not markets. The roles of money, prices, and other familiar institutional features of market economies are severely circumscribed. Output is measured on a material product basis, which is basically incompatible with the system of national accounts used in market economies.[3] The distinguishing feature of the North Korean case has been the extremes to which central planning has been taken.

A second, parallel military economy exists outside the central plan.[4] This parallel economy amounts to autarky-within-autarky: The military maintains a completely integrated economic system from farms and mines on up through facilities to manufacture uniforms and weapons, with separate administrative structures, including foreign trade firms. DKIH (Deutsch-Koreanische Industrie- und Handelskammer) estimates that half of the army is engaged in what elsewhere would be civilian economic activities.[5]

The parallel military economy has privileged access to technology and imports, and 95 percent of weaponry is produced domestically. Much of what is produced is exported, with annual arms exports at times exceeding $500 million during the 1980s; more recent estimates of net exports of weaponry are much lower (see Figure 2.1). Arms, including Scud missiles, have reportedly been exported to the Middle East in exchange for oil, which was then resold on the international market for hard currency.[6] There is reason to believe, however, that the division between the civilian and military parts of the economy has been eroding under the pressure of the current difficulties.[7]

Figure 2.1 North Korean Arms Trade (current U.S.$ millions)

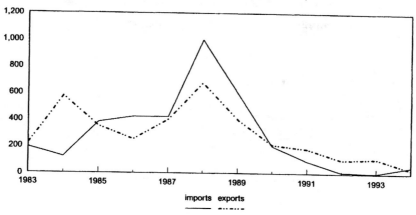

imports exports

Source: U.S. Arms Control and Disarmament Agency, *World Military Expenditures and Arms Transfers* (Washington, D.C.: U.S. Government Printing Office, 1995).

Statistical Indicators

Some socioeconomic data for North and South Korea are reported in Tables 2.1, 2.2, and 2.3. These data come from the national reporting authorities via the UN (the North Korean figures for 1992 are apparently a projection from a benchmark survey done in 1989). What is striking about Table 2.1 is how similar the figures are. South Korea appears to be further along in its demographic transition, as evidenced by the lower fertility and infant mortality statistics, but life expectancy, literacy, and urbanization appear comparable for the two countries.[8]

The overall impression is that North Korea is relatively well educated and urbanized, with a large military-industrial complex. In comparison to its Communist or former-Communist brethren, it is perhaps closer to

Table 2.1 Socioeconomic Indicators, 1992

	South Korea	North Korea
Life expectancy at birth (years)	70.4	70.7
Total fertility rate	1.7	2.4
Infant mortality rate (per 1,000 live births)	21	25
Adult literacy (percentage)	96.8	95.0
Urban population as percentage of total population	78.1	73.6

Source: UNDP, *Human Development Report 1994* (UNESCO, *Statistical Yearbook,* 1993).

Table 2.2   Educational Attainment Rates

Country, Year, Age	Graduates and Attendees of Post-Secondary Schools (percentage of adult population)
North Korea, 1987–1988 (16 yrs. and above)	13.7
South Korea, 1980 (15 yrs. and above)	9.2
Japan, 1980 (15 yrs. and above)	18.5
China, 1982 (15 yrs. and above)	0.9
Hong Kong, 1981 (15 yrs. and above)	6.6
United States, 1987 (16 yrs. and above)	36.0
East Germany, 1981 (15 yrs. and above)	14.9
Soviet Union, 1979 (16 yrs. and above)	9.4

Source: Eberstadt, *Korea Approaches Reunification,* Table 31.

Table 2.3   Distribution of Labor Force in Selected CPEs

Country	Sector		
	Agriculture	Industry	Other
USSR, 1987	19[a]	38[b]	43
Ukraine, 1990	20	40	40
Belarus, 1990	20	42	38
Romania, 1990	28[a]	38	34
Bulgaria, 1989	19[a]	47	34
North Korea, 1987	25[c]	57[b]	18
China, 1978	71	15	14
Vietnam, 1989	71	12	17

Sources: For USSR, North Korea, and Vietnam, see Ebertstadt, *Korea Approaches Reunification,* Table 6. For Romania and Bulgaria, see Simon Commander and Fabrizio Corricelli, *Unemployment, Restructuring, and the Labor Market in Eastern Europe and Russia* (Washington, D.C.: World Bank, 1995), Tables 5.1 and 6.11. For Ukraine and Belarus, see Barry P. Bosworth and Gur Ofer, *Reforming Planned Economies in an Integrating World Economy* (Washington, D.C.: Brookings Institution, 1995), Table 3-1. For China, see Jeffrey Sachs and Wing Thye Woo, "Statistical Factors in the Economic Reforms of China, Eastern Europe, and the Former Soviet Union," *Economic Policy* 18, pp. 101–145.
    Notes: a. Agriculture and forestry.
    b. Industry and construction.
    c. Farmers.

Eastern European countries like Romania or Bulgaria or some of the former republics of the Soviet Union than the more rural China or Vietnam (Tables 2.2 and 2.3).[9]

    Assessing the size of the North Korean economy or the level of per capita income is extremely difficult for several reasons. As indicated earlier, CPEs use a fundamentally different set of national accounting principles than market economies. From the standpoint of market economy accounting conventions, the material product approach double-counts some produced intermediate inputs and greatly undercounts the service sector, including housing services. It is difficult to move between the centrally planned accounting system and the market accounting system in the best of circumstances. This task is made virtually impossible by the overwhelming secrecy of the North Korean regime and the extreme paucity of statistical material emanating from the North. Even if one can calculate North Korean income in the domestic currency, one faces the very difficult task of estimating the shadow price of foreign exchange to convert measured income into a common international currency. Eui-Gak Hwang made a heroic effort along these lines, but in the end the results were not entirely persuasive.[10]

In response, researchers have attempted to estimate North Korean income indirectly through the method of physical indicators.[11] In this approach, a statistical relationship is established between income and various indicators for a sample of comparator countries. Then North Korean values of the development indicators are plugged into the statistical model to derive an estimate of North Korean income.

In Table 2.4, the fitted value for North Korea is reported along with the actual values for several other Asian countries and two CPEs. According to the econometric model, per capita income (in PPP [purchasing power parity]–adjusted—not market exchange rate—terms) in North Korea in 1990 was $2,284, similar to Indonesia, the Philippines, and Romania (in 1989) and about one-quarter that of South Korea.[12] Even with the relatively tight fit of the regression, the 90 percent forecast interval around this estimate (the values that would ensure that the true value has a 90 percent chance of being within this interval) is quite broad: from $1,339 to $3,897.[13]

Table 2.4 International Income and Capital Stock Comparisons

Country	GDP per Capita	Capital Stock per Worker	Capital-Output Ratio
South Korea	8,271	17,995	6.44
Bulgaria	7,529	n.a.	n.a.
Malaysia	5,997	n.a.	n.a.
Thailand	4,270	4,912	2.69
Romania	2,656	n.a.	n.a.
Indonesia	2,323	n.a.	n.a.
North Korea (regressions)	2,284	4,879	6.18
Philippines	2,112	3,698	4.39
China	1,536	n.a.	n.a.

Source: Penn World Tables Mark 5.6a. On-line database available from National Bureau of Economic Research, Cambridge, Mass.

Note: All figures for 1990, except Romania for 1989. GDP per capita is in current international dollars, capital stock per worker in 1985 international dollars. Capital-output ratio reflects adjustment for investment price-level change and the difference between total population and the economically active population. In the case of North Korea, the sample average was applied for the investment price change.

To facilitate comparison, estimates of the ratio of South Korean to North Korean per capita incomes (a common benchmark) are reported in Table 2.5, though even this normalization is not entirely adequate, since the non-PPP-adjusted figures exhibit spuriously high ratios. The estimates range from 5.40[14] to 2.49 from the same source using the official exchange rate to make the currency conversion.

Table 2.5   Ratio of South Korean to North Korean per Capita Income, 1990

Hwang[a]	5.40
National Unification Board	5.23
Chun	4.48
Jeong[b]	4.23
Noland	3.62
Hwang[c]	2.49

Notes: a. Converted to a common currency using the North Korean trade exchange rate.
b. 1989.
c. Converted to a common currency using the North Korean official exchange rate.

It should be emphasized that these estimates pertain to 1990, which may well have been the peak of North Korean per capita income. The relative disparity between North and South Korean income has widened considerably in the intervening period, and as of 1997, the ratio of South Korean to North Korean per capita incomes on a PPP basis is probably around 8:1 and growing.

The data discussed thus far pertain to the North Korean economy's level of development in comparison to other countries. A distinct issue is the time path of the North Korean economy. Figure 2.2 depicts several estimates of growth rates of the North Korean economy. There is a consensus that the economy suffered some severe shocks from 1989 on because of the withdrawal of Soviet assistance, bad harvests, and the collapse of the CIS (Commonwealth of Independent States) economies, which have been North Korea's largest trade partners. There does not appear to be a consensus as to the depth and persistence of this slowdown.

The most widely cited figures come from the Bank of Korea (BOK), which puts out the official South Korean estimates of North Korea's economy. These figures are apparently derived by taking classified data on physical output generated by South Korean intelligence agencies and then applying South Korean prices and value-added weights to indices of physical production. Because the original estimates of physical output are classified, there is little opportunity to check their plausibility. Nor is it obvious that South Korean prices and value-added weights are the most appropriate estimations. Moreover, the ultimate growth rate figure is reportedly subject to interagency bargaining within the South Korean government. Given these

Figure 2.2   Estimates of Real Growth Rates

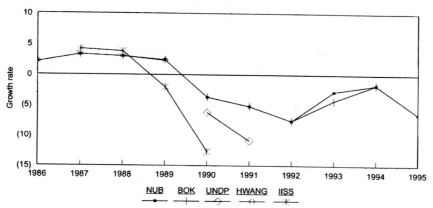

Sources: UNDP, *Human Development Reports* (New York: UNDP, 1994); Eui-Gak Hwang, *The Korean Economies* (Oxford: Clarendon Press, 1993).

Notes: NUB = National Unification Board; BOK = Bank of Korea; UNDP = UNDP, Human Development Programme; Hwang = Hwang, *The Korean Economies;* IISS = International Institute for Strategic Studies.

caveats, the BOK numbers are probably best regarded as coming with very large standard errors. For their part, the North Koreans report that industrial output increased by 5.6 percent annually during 1987–1993.[15]

Moreover, although the slowdown shown in Figure 2.2 looks quite grim, national income and personal welfare may diverge quite sharply. As has been the case in transitional economies such as Russia, the decline in national income probably overstates the decline in household welfare.[16] It is unlikely that services (such as housing services and education), which are undercounted in the material product accounting system and are not amenable to physical measurement (which forms the basis for the Figure 2.2 estimates), declined as much as manufactured output; people may not be operating very efficiently because of power shortages and a lack of spare parts, but they are still living in the same apartment and their children are still attending school. These considerations caution against interpreting the estimates displayed in Figure 2.2 as indices of hardship or political discontent.[17]

International Trade

North Korea is the world's most autarkic economy, with an international trade share (exports plus imports) of 12 percent of gross domestic product

(GDP), well below the 50–60 percent observed in South Korea, and a frac-
tion of the even larger share that North Korea would exhibit were it a "normal" country. The emphasis on self-reliance has been so great that North
Korea never joined its Communist brethren in the Council for Mutual
Economic Assistance, and its own central plans have been timed to frus-
trate the linkage of its central plan with those of the other planned
economies.[18]

Figure 2.3 displays the time path of aggregate imports and exports of
North Korea. The data show that imports have consistently exceeded
exports and that, after peaking in the late 1980s, trade has fallen substantially in the 1990s.[19]

Figure 2.3   North Korean International Trade (U.S.$ billions)

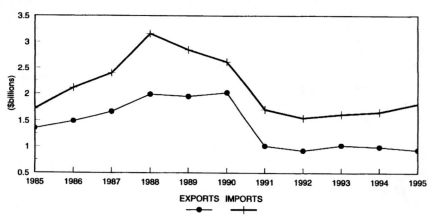

Source: "Direction of Trade Statistics," paper distributed by the International Monetary
Fund. See endnote 19 for details of computation.

Tables 2.6 and 2.7 disaggregate North Korean trade by commodity and
partner, respectively. The commodity and partner composition of North
Korean trade has varied significantly over time, largely in response to political factors. These data are subject to considerable uncertainty; the North
Korean government regards trade statistics as classified information and
has never published them. The figures reported here are based on partner
country reports to the General Agreement on Tariffs and Trade (GATT),
supplemented by data from the Korean Trade Promotion Corporation
(KOTRA) in the case of countries such as Iran that do not report the commodity structure of their trade with North Korea to the GATT.

Table 2.6   North Korean Trade by Largest Commodity Groups, 1992

Exports (U.S.$ thousands)	Share (percentage)	Industry
93,468	0.13	Other outer garments of textile fabrics
64,865	0.09	Universals, plates, and sheets of iron or steel
46,905	0.06	Gold, nonmonetary
43,828	0.06	Zinc and zinc alloys, unwrought
40,157	0.05	Crustaceans and mollusks, fresh, chilled, frozen, etc.
35,192	0.05	Anthracite, whether/not pulverized, not agglomerated
22,303	0.03	Suits, men's, of textile fabrics
22,111	0.03	Clay and other refractory minerals
22,110	0.03	Other fresh or chilled vegetables
20,852	0.03	Overcoats and other coats, men's
19,013	0.03	Iron ore and concentrates, not agglomerated
731,334	1.00	Total—all commodities

Imports (U.S.$ thousands)	Share (percentage)	Industry
139,820	0.12	Petrol, oils, and crude oils obtained from bituminous minerals
68,905	0.06	Maize (corn), unmilled
63,367	0.06	Fabrics, woven of continuous synthetic textiled materials
62,840	0.06	Anthracite, whether/not pulverized, not agglomerated
23,627	0.02	Fabrics, woven, containing 85% of wool/fine animal hair
22,135	0.02	Metal-cutting machine tools
19,382	0.02	Tractors fitted or not with power takeoffs, etc.
15,257	0.01	Passenger motor cars for transport of passengers and goods
14,772	0.01	Special transactions and commodities, not classified to kind
12.949	0.01	Meal and flour of wheat and flour of maslin
12,937	0.01	Knitted or crocheted fabrics
1,129,449	1.00	Total—all commodities

Source: "Statistics Canada, World Trade Database 1980–1992," Korea Foreign Trade Association, *Major Economic Indicators for North Korea* (Seoul: Korea Foreign Trade Association, 1993).

Note: Does not include trade with countries (such as Iran) that do not report the commodity composition of trade.

As shown in Table 2.6, North Korea's largest export sectors are apparel, iron and steel, and natural resource–based products such as zinc and crustaceans. North Korea's largest import sectors are petroleum, grain, textiles, and capital goods. What is not shown in this table are arms exports. As mentioned earlier, the domestic military economy has privileged access to technology and imports, 95 percent of weaponry is produced domestically, and much of what is produced is exported (see Figure 2.1).

Table 2.7   North Korea's Trade Partners, 1992

Country	Exports (U.S.$ thousands)	Share (percentage)
Japan	257,838	0.22
South Korea	178,166	0.15
China	155,417	0.13
Iran	115,000	0.10
Germany	87,098	0.08
Rest of world	362,838	0.32
Total	1,156,357	1.00

Country	Imports (U.S.$ thousands)	Share (percentage)
China	547,864	0.35
Russia	227,100	0.15
Japan	226,093	0.15
Iran	140,000	0.09
Hong Kong	107,730	0.07
Rest of world	306,244	0.19
Total	1,555,031	1.00

Source: "Statistics Canada, World Trade Database 1980–1992." Korea Foreign Trade Association, *Major Economic Indicators for North Korea* (Seoul: Korea Foreign Trade Association, 1993).

Note: Totals here do not equal those in Table 2.8 because of the inclusion of trade with countries (such as Iran) that do not report the commodity composition of trade.

The partner composition of North Korea's trade is reported in Table 2.7. Japan is North Korea's largest export destination, followed by South Korea, China, Iran, and Germany. Most of the trade between North and South Korea consists of apparel manufactured on consignment, which is transshipped through China. China supplies more than one-third of North Korea's imports, followed by Russia, Japan, Iran, and Hong Kong. The Hong Kong figure may reflect transshipping from South Korea, China, and Japan. In addition to this legal trade, smuggling occurs between North Korea and China.[20] In all probability, China's importance to North Korea's trade is greater than the statistics in Table 2.7 indicate. Noticeably absent is the United States, which effectively maintains an embargo against North Korea.

Historically, most of North Korea's international trade has been conducted on a barter basis, and although North Korea has been under pressure to pay cash for imports, it has been estimated that as much as two-thirds of North Korea's trade is still done on a barter basis.[21] Barter complicates analysis of North Korea's external position because trade prices cannot be observed, and it is thus difficult to determine North Korea's true terms of trade. According to the reported trade statistics displayed in Figure 2.3,

North Korea has been running a trade deficit on the order of half a billion dollars, adjusting for transportation costs. In the absence of nonrecorded exports, service exports, remittances, or other sources of revenue, this would have to be covered by external borrowing.[22]

Data on North Korea's accumulated foreign debt and its debt/export ratio are displayed in Figure 2.4. North Korea's debt is modest in absolute terms ($7.9 billion in 1993), and the vast majority of this figure ($6.2 billion) is long-term debt owed to former CPEs. Much of this debt is denominated in rubles, and it is questionable how much of any of this ruble-denominated debt will ever be repaid (some may be repaid in kind).[23] Some $649 million is long-term debt owed to Organization for Economic Cooperation and Development (OECD) countries, a figure that has been relatively constant, reflecting unwillingness on the part of Western banks, governments, and multilateral institutions to increase their long-term exposure in North Korea.[24] The remainder ($1 billion) consists of short-term loans that are generally rolled over. Given that in reality North Korea has defaulted on most of its long-term debt, its reservice payments are modest ($70 million) except for a spike in repayments during the period 1990–1991. Compared with other CPEs, North Korea's ratio of debt to exports (including the ruble-denominated debt) is quite high (770.6 percent), though the debt service to exports ratio is low (6.9 percent) because North Korea has essentially stopped paying its debt and no longer has access to long-term capital markets (see Table 2.8). What long-term capital inflows North Korea obtains apparently come from China.

Figure 2.4   North Korean Debt and Debt Service/Export Ratio

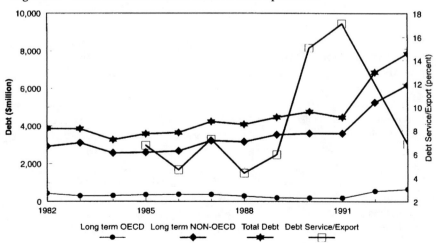

Source: Compiled by author.

Table 2.8   Debt-Export Ratio

Country	Debt/Export	Debt Service/Export
Bulgaria	207.7	18.2
Czechoslovakia	60.2	3.4
Hungary	162.7	13.2
Poland	259.4	25.4
Romania	70.1	2.5
North Korea	770.6	6.9

Source: William R. Cline, *International Debt Reexamined* (Washington, D.C.: Institute for International Economics, 1995).
Note: All figures 1992, except North Korea, 1993.

Remittances, however, are a major question mark. Published estimates range from $400 million to $2 billion, with most recent estimates tending toward the lower end of that range.[25] (If the latter figure is accepted, remittances would be twice North Korea's merchandise exports!) It is also thought that these remittances may vary considerably from year to year, depending on North Korean pressure on its Japanese supporters in Choch'ongnyon to raise funds for large political festivals or other events. In any case, these remittances might be important in financing North Korea's chronic trade deficits in light of the North's inability to make use of normal financing channels because of the debt defaults.

The size of these remittances can be estimated as a residual of the balance of payments under a series of assumptions. An accounting identity links remittances to the other trade aggregates

$$REM = (-TB) - (CAP + NRT)$$

that is, remittances (REM) are equal to the negative of the trade balance (TB) less net capital inflows (CAP) and whatever the balance is on non-recorded transactions (NRT), including nonrecorded trade and reporting errors and omission.

In the case of North Korea, some uncertainty surrounds each of these magnitudes. In the case of the trade balance, uncertainty exists because of the difficulties in constructing North Korea's partner country trade because of unreliable reporting by some partner countries, as previously noted. A second issue arises with respect to trade with other CPEs, since the terms of this trade may deviate significantly from market prices.[26] In response to these uncertainties, three estimates of the North Korean trade balance have been constructed for 1993, the most recent year that complete data are available (see Table 2.9). The first is based on the GATT trade data used to construct the previous tables, adjusted for known cases of misreporting (i.e., Mexico), and on the fact that imports are reported inclusive of transport costs and exports are not. Moreover, it is assumed that North

Table 2.9 Estimated Remittances, 1993 (U.S.$ millions)

Case	Trade Balance 1	Trade Balance 2	Trade Balance 3	Net Capital Inflow 1	Net Capital Inflow 2	Net Arms Sales 1	Net Arms Sales 2	Remittance
1	−498			933		30		−465
2	−498			933			0	−435
3	−498				5	30		463
4	−498				5		0	493
5		−638		933		30		−325
6		−638		933			0	−295
7		−638			5	30		603
8		−638			5		0	633
9			−91		5	30		56
10			−91		5		0	86
Memorandum item								
Mean								81
Median								71

Source: Compiled by author.
Key: Trade balance 1: Noland figures, adjusted for transportation costs.
Trade balance 2: KOTRA figures.
Trade balance 3: KOTRA figures, excluding trade with China and Russia.
Net capital inflow 1: Net capital inflow.
Net capital inflow 2: Net capital inflow from OECD countries.
Net arms sales 1: Arms sales, under assumption proceeds used to finance imports.
Net arms sales 2: Arms sales, under assumption proceeds accumulated as reserves.

Korea does not have any outstanding balances in services trade, where data are nonexistent. A second measure of the trade balance is from KOTRA data. A third expunges trade with CPEs, of which the overwhelming share is with China.

Capital flow data in Table 2.9 come from the OECD. The OECD reports the data in two breakdowns: transactions with OECD countries and transactions with non-OECD countries. Both are used here. The total flow concept would be appropriate if all North Korea's trade was hard currency–denominated and the capital inflows were also in hard currency form. The OECD-only formulation would be appropriate if trade with other CPEs was not denominated in hard currencies and was carried out on concessional or nonmarket terms. In this case, hard currency remittances would only be necessary to cover the hard currency deficit less hard currency net capital inflows. The situation in reality may well be somewhere between these two extremes, with some, though not all, trade with other CPEs effectively occurring on market terms.

With respect to nonrecorded trade, there is no reason to believe that either smuggling or recording errors or omissions are systematically biased toward a net deficit or surplus, and in any event, these cannot be observed. There is an estimate of $30 million of nonreported net arms exports in

1993. Again, treatment of this aggregate is problematic. It may well be that the $30 million reflects genuinely nonrecorded arms exports that are used to finance imports, and thus it should be subtracted from the balance-of-payments gap that remittances are necessary to fulfill. However, it is possible that this trade (allegedly undertaken with Middle Eastern countries that do in fact report trade with North Korea) is simply misreported in other commodity categories and does not represent a net addition to North Korea's balance-of-payments position. Another possibility is that this trade is beyond the control of the central planners, with some or all of it being accumulated as reserves against future contingencies by either the military or the party. If either the second or third hypothesis is correct, then some or all of the arms exports do not represent a genuine independent contribution to the financing gap and should not be used to calculate needed remittances. In response, two values of net arms exports are used in Table 2.9: $30 million as a nonrecorded addition to net exports, and 0 under the assumption that this trade is already being counted in other commodity categories or is being accumulated as reserves. Again, reality may lie somewhere between.

Ten possible combinations of these alternatives are listed in Table 2.9. The implicit remittances generated by these calculations exhibit an enormous range, from $633 million to –$465 million (in the latter case money would actually be flowing out of North Korea). The mean and median values across the ten alternatives are positive (implying capital inflow), though, with the mean value $81 million and the median $71 million. These figures are considerably lower than those that are often conjectured, and they suggest that the remittances may not be as critical as commonly thought.[27] Alternatively, if remittances are as high as usually reported, then either North Korea is running a surplus on its current account, accumulating foreign reserves, and exporting capital, or hundreds of millions of dollars in expenditures are unaccounted for.

Recent Reforms

North Korea has historically pursued an autarkic development strategy under the *chuch'e* ideology of Kim Il Sung. The 1970s push for military modernization left the country heavily indebted relative to its meager export earnings, and the 1975 default effectively cut it off from international capital markets. The economy suffered further negative shocks with the withdrawal of Soviet economic support in the mid-1980s and the collapse of the CIS economies, which had been North Korea's largest trade partners, in the early 1990s.[28] Although increased Chinese support has partly offset the loss of Soviet aid, China, too, has indicated that there are limits to how far it is willing to go to support the *chuch'e* economy, especially in light of the liberalizing economic reforms undertaken in China. By all appearances, North Korea is under significant balance-of-payments pressures, with deleterious implications for growth prospects.

In response to this building crisis, the North Korean regime has begun some tentative reform measures. In 1984, after visits to China by Kim Il Sung in 1982 and 1983, the North Korean government enacted a joint venture law, apparently modeled on China's (though this is denied by North Korea).[29] Large increases in inward foreign direct investment were not forthcoming, and in 1991, after another visit to China by Kim Il Sung, the government announced the creation of a special economic zone (SEZ) totaling 621 square kilometers in the area of Najin, Ch'ongjin, and Sonbong near the Tumen River delta in the extreme northeast of the country, which expanded in March 1993 to 742 square kilometers.[30] A spate of additional laws followed, establishing the legal framework for foreign firms operating in North Korea; on paper these conditions are better than those in the Chinese or Vietnamese SEZs.[31] Nevertheless, investments have remained relatively small. Choch'ongnyon accounts for 80 percent of investment, with the remainder coming mostly from firms based in South Korea and Germany. Most of the investment has been for processing on consignment; the North Koreans earn about 27 percent of the value of the exports.[32]

To the extent that SEZs can contribute to generating foreign exchange, they help relieve this pressure, but whether SEZs alone will be sufficient is another matter entirely. In most other countries that have made use of SEZs with the aim of importing technologies and establishing backward linkages with the rest of the economy, SEZs have been a failure. Little integration with the rest of the economy has occurred, and the SEZs have amounted to little more than export enclaves to exploit locally cheap labor.[33] Ironically, in the case of North Korea, the regime may have little interest in integrating the SEZs with the rest of the economy; indeed, it may prefer that they remain isolated enclaves. The question then becomes, will they be sufficient for even this limited purpose?

Skepticism seems warranted for at least two reasons. First, given the highly controlled nature of the rest of North Korean society, it would appear to be a difficult task to make the SEZ work. The successful operation of an SEZ requires freedom of movement and a culture of, if not efficiency, then at least noninterference. Everything in the broader North Korean society, where economics is subservient to politics, works against this. Second, North Korea is not alone. It must compete with China, Vietnam, and other countries throughout Asia and the world for business. High wages, poor infrastructure, and geographic isolation are all potential obstacles.[34]

Prospective Changes

At some point in the future, policymakers may conclude that the recent changes are inadequate to address the problems at hand and will have to confront the issue of whether and how to accelerate and deepen the economic reforms. A true reform strategy would have to include price reforms; introduction of the family responsibility system (or some other scheme) to debureaucratize agriculture; fundamental reforms of the planning mechanism, with the goal of encouraging greater reliance on market signals to inform the decisionmaking of economic agents and competition between domestic enterprises; and the development of functioning capital markets. This would not necessarily mean a movement toward private property; it might be possible to maintain forms of nonprivate ownership, such as the township and village enterprises in China. The critical requirement would be that enterprise managers respond to market signals.

If the regime were willing to undertake such reforms, it would face several alternatives with respect to its external relations (see Table 2.10). It could, for example, simply open in a nondiscriminatory fashion toward all foreigners, treating them equally in terms of trade and investment policy. This would be consistent with the precepts of the World Trade Organization (WTO) system.

Table 2.10   Alternative Reform Scenarios

Opening without reform
Opening with reform
 Nonpreferential opening
  Opening with restrictions on North-South integration (China-Taiwan model)
 Preferential North-South opening
  Free trade area (direct trade, no internal barriers)
  Customs union (common external barriers)
  Economic union (free movement of productive factors)
  Monetary union (common currency)
  Social union (common labor rules, social security systems, etc.)
  Political unification

Alternatively, North Korea could open preferentially—discriminating among foreigners on the basis of nationality. One variant would be to open to the rest of the world but to retain restrictions on trade and investment with South Korea similar to the restrictions that exist for trade and investment between Taiwan and China. This might be attractive if the regime were concerned about being, in effect, absorbed by the South.

It could also take the opposite tack—opening preferentially to the South.[35] Successively deeper forms of integration would include a free trade area (where goods would move freely within the Korean peninsula); a customs union (where North and South Korea would maintain a common set of trade policies toward the rest of the world); a common market or economic union (where productive factors as well as goods could flow freely); a monetary union (a common currency); a social union (common social insurance systems); and, finally, political union and the dissolution of North and South Korea as separate sovereign nations.[36]

South Korean government policy could accelerate or retard the process of integration. One can imagine greatly expanded trade and investment relations between North and South; it is much more difficult to imagine any South Korean government in the foreseeable future acceding to a free flow of productive factors that could involve the migration of millions of North Koreans to the South.

There are economic (and presumably domestic political) obstacles to reform. Successful gradual reform of a CPE requires resources to cushion adjustment in the heavy manufacturing sector. Propitious initial conditions may have benefited successful and relatively agrarian reformers such as China and Vietnam. First of all, in these countries the state-owned heavy industry sector was initially relatively small. Second, China and Vietnam were able to initiate reforms in the agricultural sector, where the price liberalization provoked rapid efficiency gains, freeing up low-productivity surplus agricultural labor to be absorbed by the emerging nonstate or semiprivate light manufacturing and service sectors. These new, expanding sectors were then taxed to provide state revenues to cushion the transition in the heavy industry sector.

The initial conditions of China and Vietnam are, however, irreproducible and such a path does not appear to be viable for more industrialized CPEs.[37] Piecemeal reforms have not been successful in industrialized CPEs facing economic crises; the more interdependent nature of industrial enterprises means that a whole host of reforms (e.g., macroeconomic stabilization; introduction of rational pricing; liberalization of international trade and introduction of a convertible currency; and tax, bankruptcy, and social safety net reforms) are a seamless web and must be instituted simultaneously for reform to be successful economically and sustainable politically. Even in China and Vietnam, adjustment in the old state-owned heavy industry sector has proved difficult.[38]

The question naturally arises, what would the North Korean economy look like if it were to undergo successful reform? There would be a reallocation of factors according to comparative advantage, and were reform accompanied by a reduction of political hostilities with the South, there could be a significant demobilization of the military and a release of productive factors for alternative uses. Based on the experience of other transitional economies, one would expect significant reorientation of international trade away from socialist allies and toward natural trading partners. One way to get a sense of how North Korea might look as a "normal" country is to use a standard "gravity" model of bilateral trade to simulate its post-reform trade pattern. The regression model, originally estimated by Jeffrey Frankel and Shang-Jin Wei, characterizes the volume of trade as a function of size, income level, proximity, and other factors.[39] North Korean values of these explanatory figures can then be substituted into the gravity model regression to generate North Korea's "natural" pattern of trade.

According to the results reported in Table 2.11, North Korea's natural trade partners would be South Korea, Japan, China, and the United States, in that order. South Korea and Japan alone would account for nearly two-thirds of North Korea's trade. Moreover, the share of international trade in national income would roughly quadruple (though the resource reallocation associated with such a large increase in trade would almost certainly boost income significantly as well). This gives some indication of the potentially dramatic scope for change in North Korea.

Table 2.11   Actual and "Natural" North Korean Trade Shares

Actual Trade Share	
China	26
Japan	18
Russia	11
Iran	9
Rest of world	36
North Korea: share of total trade in GDP	15
"Natural" Trade Share	
South Korea	35
Japan	30
China	13
United States	7
Rest of world	15
North Korea: share of total trade in GDP	71

Source: Compiled by author.
Note: Intra-Korean trade counted as international trade; GDP in current dollars from Bank of Korea.

North Korea's prospective comparative advantage can be analyzed using disaggregated trade and investment data for North Korea, South Korea, and Japan. Altogether 51 out of a possible 465 sectors meet the various statistical criteria for positive export prospects. North Korea's sectors of prospective comparative advantage would largely be in primary products sectors, where the North's natural resources convey a comparative advantage, and in light manufacturing industries, which are declining in

Japan and South Korea but could be competitive in lower-wage North Korea.[40]

This would mean an enormous change in the composition of North Korean output away from heavy and toward light industry, implying significant adjustments for many North Korean workers and enterprises. At the same time, the expanding industries would be labor intensive, which would appear to bode well for absorbing displaced labor (especially if military demobilization were to release a large number of workers for nonmilitary activities).

A recent, small computable general equilibrium model of the North Korean economy implies that North Korea is indeed an extraordinarily distorted economy. Real GDP increases by approximately one-quarter after liberalization, with most of the gain coming in the initial stages.[41] This is purely a static reallocation effect. Recent research indicates that the world is characterized by international technological spillovers. These are quite important in the case of developing countries, which benefit from technological developments abroad transmitted through international trade. In the case of North Korea, the parameters estimated by David Coe and his colleagues indicate that complete liberalization would result in a total factor productivity gain of approximately 20 percent.[42] This means that potential income gains for North Korea are enormous, on the order of 40–50 percent overall, with about half the gain coming from static reallocation of productive factors and half coming from trade-induced productivity increases. These, of course, are comparative static gains, and the economy would undoubtedly experience a decline in measured output during a transitional phase. Indeed, the obsolescence shock reduction in the value of the capital stock could be huge—on the order of 50 percent or more. Moreover, even if the North Korean economy were to expand by 50 percent, the income gap between the North and South would remain huge.

Conclusion

At first glance, it would not appear that North Korea is well positioned to undergo successful reform on either political or economic criteria. The political issue ultimately is an internal North Korean matter that does not seem susceptible to foreign influence. The economic issue is different, though. Reform in the North will require external support. This could come through a variety of channels.

The most obvious channel would be the Korean diaspora, including industrialists in South Korea, a factor not shared by other industrialized CPEs in their transition processes (with the exception of East Germany, which is a different matter altogether).[43] Successful implementation of the nuclear agreement would mean the provision of energy supplies and movement toward normalization of relations between the United States and North Korea.

Normalization of diplomatic relations between North Korea and Japan and the payment by Japan of postcolonial compensation would be yet another source of external support. The Japanese government paid the South Korean government $800 million in compensation for colonial and wartime activities at the time of normalization of diplomatic relations in 1965. The North Korean government expects similar compensation. Adjusting the South Korean payment for differences in population, accrued interest, changes in the price level, and appreciation of the yen since 1965, one obtains a figure of approximately $12 billion. Such a sum, properly deployed, could go a long way toward restoring North Korean creditworthiness and financing economic modernization.[44]

Under the right circumstances, multilateral development banks could also be tapped. The World Bank has mobilized $1.2 billion over three years for the two million residents of the Occupied Territories in the Middle East, or $200 per person per year. The Bank has indicated that this "emergency assistance program" is to "provide tangible benefits to the Palestinian population quickly, equitably, and efficiently" as a foundation for sustainable development and peace.[45] A program of similar magnitude scaled to the much larger Korean case could mean $4.4 billion annually. Under enlightened North Korean leadership, such capital inflows could go a long way to foster sustained development and peace on the Korean peninsula.

Notes

1. Aidan Foster-Carter, "North Korea After Kim Il-Sung: Controlled Collapse?" Research Report (London: Economist Intelligence Unit, 1994).

2. For overviews of the North Korean economy, see Joseph S. Chung, *The North Korean Economy* (Stanford: Hoover Institution Press, 1974); Deutsch-Koreanische Industrie- und Handelskammer (DKIH), *Nordkorea: Einblicke in Wirtschaft und Lebenweise* (Seoul: DKIH, 1991); Eui-Gak Hwang, *The Korean Economies* (Oxford: Clarendon Press, 1993); and Marcus Noland, "The North Korean Economy," *Joint U.S.-Korean Academic Studies,* vol. 6 (Washington, D.C.: Korea Economic Institute of America, 1996). The classic work on centrally planned economies is Janos Kornai, *The Socialist Economy* (Princeton: Princeton University Press, 1992).

3. The one significant piece of economic information that the DPRK government regularly publishes is its budget. Government expenditure accounts for around 60 percent of output; central government expenditures account for about 85 percent of this amount and local governments account for the remaining 15 percent. Approximately 60 percent of government expenditures go to economic development (this includes investment in plant and equipment of state enterprises), and about 12 percent goes to defense (although this may conceal much larger military expenditures in the economic development budget). These figures appear to be in line with those of other centrally planned economies. Central government revenue

comes primarily from the transactions revenue (the tax wedge planners insert between agents in the plan) and some minor taxes. Local revenue comes from taxes paid by local enterprises, some minor taxes, and subsidies from the central government. See Hwang, *Korean Economies.*

4. Its origins lie in a military modernization program adopted at the Fifth Plenum of the Fourth Central Committee of the Workers' Party of Korea in 1966 following the intensification of the Sino-Soviet split; see Bon-Hak Koo, *Political Economy of Self-Reliance,* Korean Unification Studies Series 14 (Seoul: Research Center for Peace and Unification in Korea, 1992); and Young Namkoong and Ho-Yeol Yoo, "North Korea's Economic System," in Tae Hwan Ok and Hong Yung Lee, eds., *Prospects for Change in North Korea* (Seoul: Research Institute for National Unification, 1994). This parallel economy is highly secretive, even internally. According to Nicholas Eberstadt, the State Planning Commission was reportedly deprived of access to information on it in the early 1970s, and meetings with outsiders are not held in the usual government ministries, but rather in unofficial locations such as hotels; see Eberstadt, "Reform, Muddling Through, or Collapse?" in Thomas H. Henriksen and Kyongsoo Lho, eds., *One Korea?* (Stanford, Calif.: Hoover Institution Press, 1994); see also DKIH, *Nordkorea.*

5. This would make the parallel military economy quite large; North Korea is the most militarized economy on earth, with 1.25 million men under arms, fully one-fifth of men of working age; see Nicholas Eberstadt, "Inter-Korean Economic Cooperation: Rapprochement Through Trade?" *Korea and World Affairs* 18, no. 4 (1994):642–661; Nicholas Eberstadt and Judith Bannister, "Divided Korea: Demographic and Socioeconomic Issues for Reunification," *Population and Development Review* 18, no. 3 (1994):505–531; and U.S. Arms Control and Disarmament Agency, *World Military Expenditures and Arms Transfers* (Washington, D.C.: Government Printing Office, 1995). Estimates of the military's share of output range from 20 percent to 40 percent and higher; see Noland, "North Korean Economy." Some of the discrepancies in these figures may be due to differences in definition—the defense budget versus military-controlled production, for example. A former professor at Kim Il Sung University estimated that, whereas the defense budget directly consumes only 15 to 25 percent of output, the military gets a share of all government spending programs and the true size of the parallel military economy is on the order of half of total output (Cho Myong-jae, interview with author, July 8, 1995). David Von Hippel and Peter Hayes compute that energy use for narrowly defined military purposes (as opposed to all activities undertaken by the North Korean military) accounts for only 5 percent of total energy consumed in North Korea; see Von Hippel and Hayes, "DPRK Energy Efficiency Scoping Study: Report on Work in Progress," paper presented at the Symposium on North Korea and Prospects for Korean Unification, University of California at San Diego, La Jolla, Calif., May 25–27, 1995.

6. See DKIH, *Nordkorea;* W. Robert Warne, "The Economics of Korean Unification," paper presented at the Third Annual International Convention of the Congress of Political Economists, Rio de Janeiro, January 8–12, 1992; *Economist,* May 28, 1994; and Doowon Lee, "Inter-Korean Economic Relation: Rivaled Past, Unbalanced Present, and Integrated Future," *Yonsei Economic Studies* 2, no. 1 (1995):131–160. The fact that the military maintains its own trading channels outside the central plan is potentially of enormous policy importance; to the extent that the proceeds from arms sales are going directly to the military, the military may have a purely pecuniary incentive to continue selling arms, even if other parts of the government would like to restrict sales for broader foreign policy reasons.

7. Tong Song-yong, interview with author, July 10, 1995; A. R. Michell, interview with author, July 11, 1995.

8. The question immediately arises: How reliable are these data? Fortunately, the North Korean demographic data have been subjected to intense analysis by Eberstadt and Bannister; see "Divided Korea." They conclude that the data appear to be reported as collected without invention, adjustments, or tampering and that quality is similar to that observed in developing countries (i.e., bad sampling methodologies, but no obvious falsification). Eberstadt and Bannister use demographic models to reconstruct the North Korean data and produce estimates not radically different from those reported by the North Koreans: for 1992, life expectancy of 69.5 years (versus the reported figure of 70.7), an infant mortality rate of 29.5 per thousand (versus 25), and a total fertility rate of 2.4 (equal to the reported figure).

With respect to literacy, it should be recalled that North Korea has maintained longer compulsory education than the South and has a younger age structure of the population, both of which would presumably contribute to high adult literacy. Moreover, as indicated in Table 2.2, reported rates of postsecondary education for North Korea are on par with those of East Germany and significantly higher than those for the Soviet Union, at least in the late 1970s. North Korea appears to have a relatively well educated population, and the reported proximate universal literacy may not be far off the mark.

The urbanization data may be subject to the greatest error, simply because the definition of an urban area does not appear to be well standardized either within North Korea or internationally. North Korea was probably more urbanized than South Korea at the time of partition, but the *chuch'e* requirement of virtual self-sufficiency in agriculture must have slowed the rate of urbanization, as apparently confirmed by Eberstadt; see *Korea Approaches Reunification* (Armonk, N.Y.: M. E. Sharpe, 1995). It appears that the data may overstate the relative urbanization of North Korea, though it is difficult to determine by how much.

9. For more on the North Korea–Romania comparison, see Marcus Noland, "Why North Korea Will Muddle Through," *Foreign Affairs* 76, no. 4 (July/August 1997):105–118.

10. Hwang, *Korean Economies.*

11. See, e.g., Hong-Tack Chun, "Estimating North Korea's GNP by Physical Indicators Approach" (in Korean), *Korea Development Review* 14, no. 1 (1992):167–225; Kap-Yeong Jeong, "Comparing the North Korean Level of Economic Development by Principal Components Analysis," in Young Sun Lee, ed., *North Korea's Reality and Unification* (in Korean) (Seoul: Center for East and West Studies, Yonsei University, 1993); and Noland, "North Korean Economy."

12. Converting local income figures into a common currency using market exchange rates systematically understates income in poor countries where the prices of internationally nontraded goods (like housing) are low. PPP-adjusted estimates correct for this bias.

13. Using a similar approach, Jeong estimates that North Korea's per capita annual income is $1,181, and Chun puts the figure at $1,273, but these figures are not directly comparable to those reported in Table 2.4. Neither Chun nor Jeong uses PPP-corrected data, and as a consequence both obtain downwardly biased estimates of North Korean (and other low-income country) incomes. Jeong, for example, estimates that per capita income in India is $52 and in the Philippines is $339 (less than one-third of his estimate for North Korea), whereas the estimates in Table 2.4 indicate that per capita income in these two countries is roughly the same. Chun does not report any international comparisons.

14. From Hwang, *Korean Economies,* using the North Korean trade exchange rate to convert to a common currency.

15. See Song Ryol Han, "Industrial Development in Korea," document distributed at the Symposium on North Korea and Prospects for Korean Unification, University of California at San Diego, La Jolla, Calif., May 25–27, 1995.

16. See Andrei Illarionov, Richard Layard, and Peter Orszag, "The Conditions of Life," in Anders Aslund, ed., *Economic Transformation in Russia* (London: Pinter, 1994).

17. However, recent visitors report that those leaving Pyongyang are searched for food—presumably to discourage the development of black markets in food-scarce regions.

18. See Hwang, *Korean Economies*.

19. There are enormous differences in the estimates of 1994 aggregate exports and imports generated by KOTRA, the National Unification Board, and the IMF. According to KOTRA and the National Unification Board, exports were $839 million and $810 million, respectively; according to the IMF, exports were $2.6 billion and imports were $2.2 billion (this would imply that North Korea was running a trade surplus).

The IMF data appear to have three possible problems. First, in the early 1990s, Mexico apparently began misclassifying its South and North Korean bilateral trade, raising imports from North Korea by over $600 million. Second, the IMF figures for Austria indicate an increase of more than $100 million in both exports and imports with North Korea between 1993 and 1994. This, too, may be a misclassification. Third, the IMF figures reveal an enormous increase in trade between China and North Korea. A growing share of North Korean trade consists of processing on consignment, much of which is transshipped through China. It may well be the case that these inflows and outflows are being double-counted by the Chinese, who do not use the same trade accounting procedures as the rest of the world. However, China and North Korea reportedly cracked down on smuggling in 1994, which might tend to both increase legal reported trade and reduce the true volume of trade inclusive of smuggling.

KOTRA and the National Unification Board apply an indirect adjustment to the underlying partner country data.

20. Observers estimate that the magnitude of this illegal trade is in the $100 millions; if so, this would account for an appreciable share of North Korea's total trade. However, in 1994 China and North Korea reportedly cracked down on smuggling.

21. Sang-Kyom Kim, "Opening North Korea's Economy," in Jang-Hee Yoo and Chang-Jae Lee, eds., *Northeast Asian Economic Cooperation,* Policy Studies 94-08 (Seoul: Korea Institute for International Economic Policy, 1994).

22. North Korea may obtain additional revenues from illicit activities such as drug trafficking and counterfeiting; see Foster-Carter, "North Korea After Kim Il-Sung."

23. As with nearly everything else concerning North Korea, these figures need to be interpreted carefully. The Soviet Union reportedly provided oil to the North Koreans at two-thirds of the world price. At the same time, North Korea was sending products to the Soviet Union, and it is not clear what the real terms of trade were. It could be that, while the Soviet Union was underpricing its oil, it was also extracting from the North Koreans imports at less than world prices, so the net magnitude of the subsidy is unknown. In 1990 Russia announced that it would no longer supply North Korea with subsidized oil (although there is disagreement about how quickly the Russians intended to put this into effect), and the North Koreans responded by suspending repayments. The volume of trade between North Korea and Russia has declined with the worsening of political relations and the implosion

of the Russian economy, though North Korea continues to supply (under an agreement that officially expired in 1993) 15,000–20,000 laborers to Russia to work in logging camps in the Russian Far East.

24. In reality, North Korea has defaulted on these debts and shows no indication of interest or willingness in making amends. When recently asked about the debt situation, Kim Mun-sang, chairman of the (North) Korean Committee for the Promotion of External Cooperation, replied: "It is a morally negative thing for business people to make bad rumors and big noises about a few pennies of debt in this country. If you lose this time, you may gain next time" (*Financial Times,* April 29, 1995). See Noland, "North Korean Economy," for further details.

25. These estimates have been made on the basis of everything from calculating the amount of currency Japanese residents visiting North Korea could take with them to estimates of profit margins in the pachinko industry in which Choch'ongnyon has a significant presence. If the money does come in significant part from the profits of the gaming industry, it may well have declined following the burst of the bubble economy in Japan. See Katsumi Sato, "Japan: Stop Funding KIS!" *Far Eastern Economic Review,* July 29, 1993; S.-K. Kim, "Opening North Korea's Economy"; Young Sun Lee, "The Current Status of the North Korean Economy and Prospects for Reform," *Osteuropa-Wirtschaft* 39, no. 2 (1994):135–145; *Nikkei Weekly,* May 23, 1994; and *Economist,* May 28, 1994. Nicholas Eberstadt, "Financial Transfers from Japan to North Korea: Estimating Unreported Flows," *Asian Survey,* May 1996:523–542. Also, Hwang Ui-gak (Eui-Gak Hwang), personal correspondence, March 10, 1995; Ko Tong-il (Dong-Il Koh), personal correspondence, March 13, 1995; Yon Ha-ch'ong (Ha-cheong Yeon), personal correspondence, March 20, 1995; conversations with Japanese government officials, April and May 1995; and Cho Myong-jae, interview with author, July 8, 1995.

26. See Noland, "North Korean Economy."

27. It should be noted that this calculation is for a single year, and there is reason to believe that the remittance flows may exhibit considerable time-series fluctuations.

28. It would be interesting to compare the responses of North Korea and Vietnam to the common shock of the withdrawal of Soviet aid and the collapse of the Soviet Union. My supposition is that the Vietnamese were far more effective in reforming their more agricultural economy and boosting exports to ease the balance-of-payments constraint, whereas, in the absence of greater export orientation, the North Koreans were forced to reduce the level of domestic activity. Unfortunately, the extreme uncertainty surrounding the North Korean balance-of-payments position (largely because of the issue of remittances) effectively precludes quantitative inquiry into the matter.

29. See, e.g., Koo, *Political Economy of Self-Reliance;* Sang-Kyom Kim, "North Korean Economy: Prospects for Opening and Inter-Korean Cooperation" (Seoul: Korea Institute for International Economic Policy, 1995, mimeo); and Sung Chull Kim, "Is North Korea Following the Chinese Model of Reform and Opening?" *East Asia Institute Reports* (East Asia Institute, Columbia University, New York, December 1994).

30. See, e.g., Hwang, *Korean Economies;* Ha-Cheong Yeon, "Practical Means to Improve Intra-Korean Trade and Economic Cooperation," KDI Working Paper 9301 (Seoul: Korean Development Institute, January 1993); and Jae-Jean Suh and Byoung-Lo P. Kim, "Prospects for Change in the Kim Jong-Il Regime," Policy Studies Report, series no. 2 (Seoul: Research Institute for National Reunification, December 1994).

31. See, e.g., Koo, *Political Economy of Self-Reliance;* Yeon, "Practical

Means"; Suh and Kim, "Prospects for Change"; L. Gordon Flake, "The DPRK External Economy," paper presented at the Sixth Annual Convention of the Congress of Political Economists [COPE], International, Seoul, January 5–10, 1995; S.-K. Kim, "North Korean Economy"; and Doowon Lee, "Assessing North Korean Economic Reform: Historical Trajectory, Opportunities and Constraints," *Pacific Focus* 8, no. 3 (1993):5–29.

32. See Young Sun Lee, "Economic Integration in the Korean Peninsula: Effects and Implications," paper presented at the Second Annual Korea-America 21st Century Committee Conference, Washington D.C., February 9–10, 1995.

33. Marcus Noland, *Pacific Basin Developing Countries: Prospects for the Future* (Washington, D.C.: Institute for International Economics, 1991).

34. See Noland, "North Korean Economy," for an analysis of these issues.

35. Some observers have noted that the tariff-free treatment of North Korean trade probably violates South Korea's WTO obligations, if any of its trade partners would be so churlish as to make a case of this. This issue might arise if significant numbers of firms entered the North Korean market as a backdoor to the South, though even in this eventuality a WTO case would seem unlikely.

36. For more on these types of schemata, see Hong-Tack Chun, "A Gradual Approach Toward North and South Korean Economic Integration," KDI Working Paper 9311 (Seoul: Korea Development Institute, November 1994); and Sang Man Lee, "A Study on Patterns of Economic Integration Between South and North Korea," *East Asian Review* 5, no. 3 (1993):91–113. For its part, North Korea has proposed a Confederal Republic of Koryo to be governed by a national assembly consisting of an equal number of representatives from North and South Korea. For details of this proposal, see Han Song Ryol and Tong U Choe, "Perspectives of Issues by the DPRK" (New York: DPRK Mission to the United Nations, 1995, mimeo).

37. See, e.g., James Riedel, "Vietnam: On the Trail of the Tigers," *World Economy* 16, no. 4 (1993):401–422; and Jeffrey Sachs and Wing Thye Woo, "Structural Factors in the Economic Reforms of China, Eastern Europe, and the Former Soviet Union," *Economic Policy* 18 (1994):101–145. For more on the relevance of China's reforms to the North Korean case, see Seung-yul Oh, "Economic Reform in North Korea: Is China's Reform Model Relevant to North Korea?" *Korean Journal of National Unification* 2 (1993):127–151.

38. See David Lipton and Jeffrey Sachs, "Creating a Market Economy in Eastern Europe: The Case of Poland," *Brookings Papers on Economic Activity,* no. 1 (1990):75–148; and Sachs and Woo, "Structural Factors." Ironically, North Korea's extreme centralization may prove advantageous in at least one regard. Whereas in other CPEs, many benefits—in particular, pensions and housing—are provided through the enterprise (and thus give workers an incentive to oppose enterprise reform), in North Korea these are provided directly by the state. As a consequence, North Korean workers may be more mobile and may oppose enterprise reform less than their counterparts in other CPEs in some future reform situation.

39. Jeffrey A. Frankel and Shang-Jin Wei, "Is a Yen Bloc Emerging?" *Joint U.S.-Korean Academic Studies* 5 (1995):145–175.

40. See Noland, "North Korean Economy," for details. The preceding analysis has been done partly on the basis of historical experience. It is possible that in the future, with the recent appreciation of the yen, industries of greater capital intensity (such as auto parts) could be candidates for relocation to North Korea. General Motors, for example, has expressed interest in constructing an auto parts plant in Najin-Sonbong (*Financial Times,* June 17, 1995).

41. This model also reports results for macroeconomic, sectoral output, and income distribution variables; see Marcus Noland, Sherman Robinson, and Monica Scatasta, "Modeling Economic Reform in North Korea," *Journal of Asian Economics* 8, no. 1 (Spring 1997):15–38.

42. David T. Coe, Elhanan Helpman, and Alexander W. Hoffmaister, "North-South R&D Spillovers," Discussion Paper 1133 (London: Centre for Economic Policy Research, February 1995).

43. For analysis of unification issues, see Eberstadt and Bannister, "Divided Korea"; Hwang, *Korean Economies;* S. M. Lee, "Patterns of Economic Integration"; Ha-Cheong Yeon, "Economic Consequences of German Unification and Its Policy Implications for Korea," KDI Working Paper 9303 (Seoul: Korea Development Institute, April 1993); Chun, "Gradual Approach"; Hy-Sang Lee, "Economic Factors in Korean Reunification," in Young Whan Kihl, ed., *Korea and the World* (Boulder, Colo.: Westview Press, 1994), pp. 189–215; Y. S. Lee, "Current Status," "Economic Integration," and "Economic Integration of the Korean Peninsula: A Scenario Approach to the Cost of Unification," in Sung Yeung Kwack, ed., *The Korean Economy at a Crossroad* (Westport, Conn.: Praeger, 1994); and Yang Lee and Joon-Hyung Kim, "Peace Building on the Korean Peninsula" (Washington, D.C.: United States Institute for Peace, December 1994).

44. The payments to South Korea took the form of $300 million in grants, $200 million in development assistance loans, and $300 million in commercial credits. The estimate of $12 billion assumes a 5 percent annual real rate of return since 1965 and a yen-dollar rate of 100. Obviously, with different assumptions, one could obtain different figures.

Japan's decision to consider granting official development assistance to the Palestine Liberation Organization was interpreted in some quarters as easing the way for Japan to provide aid to North Korea prior to the establishment of diplomatic relations; see *Financial Times,* June 6, 1995.

45. *Economist,* October 1, 1994.

PART 2

U.S.–North Korean Relations

3

U.S. Policy
Toward North Korea

Selig S. Harrison

On October 7, 1994, as negotiations on the U.S.–North Korean nuclear freeze agreement were nearing a climax, South Korean president Kim Young Sam told the publisher of the *New York Times* that the North Korean Communist regime was "on the verge of an economic and political crisis that could sweep it from power" and that U.S. concessions in the nuclear negotiations "might prolong its life."[1]

Predictions of a collapse in Pyongyang have subsequently become a standard refrain not only in Seoul but also in Washington. "Perhaps the worst feature of the freeze agreement," wrote former U.S. secretary of defense Caspar Weinberger, "is that we are now going to prop up North Korea, when it is closer to full collapse than at any other time in the past 40 years."[2] Bob Dole, then the U.S. Senate majority leader, based his opposition to the freeze on the Weinberger argument.[3] In April 1996, after a North Korean appeal for international food aid, General Gary E. Luck, the commander of U.S. and UN forces in South Korea, said in testimony before the U.S. House of Representatives that "the question is not will this country disintegrate, but rather how will it disintegrate, by implosion or explosion, and when."[4] Shortly thereafter, General John Shalikashvili, chairman of the Joint Chiefs of Staff, echoed Luck, declaring that "we are in a period where most who watch the area would say it's either going to implode or explode—we're just not sure when that is going to happen."[5]

The emerging debate over the future of U.S. policy in Korea hinges on two closely interlocked issues: (1) Is North Korea indeed on the verge of collapse? Or is it likely to survive and undergo an evolutionary transformation broadly similar to what is happening in China? (2) Would its collapse and absorption by South Korea be desirable? Or would U.S. interests be better served by a "soft landing"—a gradual process of unification through a loose confederation in which neither side is swallowed up by the other?

The recommendations that follow are based on the premise that the policies followed by the United States will have a decisive bearing on what happens in North Korea and that it is clearly in the United States' interest to promote a soft landing. In this view, the North Korean political system inherited from the late Kim Il Sung is not sustained by repression alone but is infused with a strong spirit of nationalism that did not exist in the fallen Communist systems of Eastern Europe.

This system is not likely to implode or explode in the foreseeable future. But in all likelihood it will erode over time if the United States, South Korea, and Japan remain wedded to obsolete Cold War policies that exacerbate the economic problems facing the North Korean regime since its loss of Soviet and Chinese aid. The key to its stability will be whether it can feed its people, and this, in turn, will depend on whether the international community provides food aid on a scale comparable to the levels provided in past humanitarian crises to other countries (for example, Ethiopia, India, Somalia, and Albania) without regard to their political systems. Protracted hunger could lead to incalculable consequences in Pyongyang, including massive refugee flows and civil strife that could spill over into a North-South military conflict involving the 37,000 U.S. troops stationed in the South. In the unlikely event of a complete political breakdown in Pyongyang, the costs of economic reconstruction in an absorption scenario would be colossal, greatly exceeding those in Germany.[6]

Despite the end of the Cold War, the United States continues to view its relations with North Korea as a subordinate aspect of a military alliance relationship with South Korea that arose in response to Soviet and Chinese military alliances with Pyongyang. Now the original rationale for the U.S. alliance with Seoul no longer exists. South Korea has much more significant economic links with Russia and China than the North does. Russia has nullified the operative clauses of its security treaty with Pyongyang, and China, while formally retaining its security commitment, has progressively diluted relations with Pyongyang in most spheres. Washington finds itself allied with one side in a civil war in which the other side is increasingly bereft of significant external support.

In addition to honoring its military obligations arising from the mutual security treaty with the Republic of Korea (ROK), the United States has felt compelled to seek South Korean approval for all of its behavior relating to North Korea. The United States has thus become a hostage to entrenched right-wing factions that continue to dominate policymaking in South Korea despite the end of military rule. The most extreme of these factions wants to promote a quick collapse and absorption of the North. A more widespread approach favors U.S. and ROK policies designed to debilitate North Korea gradually by maintaining economic sanctions and other forms of pressure, forcing it to unify with the South on South Korean terms without a sudden breakdown—the "contained collapse" scenario. Both approaches are fraught with risk, and both are opposed by South Korean advocates of a loose confederation, who would prevail, given U.S. support for their position.

The bottom line of these recommendations is that the United States can best promote a North-South accommodation by withdrawing its military presence in stages and that it should prepare the way for disengagement by seeking to replace the 1953 armistice with a new peacekeeping structure dedicated to defusing North-South tensions. U.S. forces should be a part of this structure. The United States should press Seoul as well as Pyongyang to negotiate the mutual redeployment and reduction of South and North Korean forces. Mutual force reductions would be one of the keys to the success of a soft landing policy, enabling the North to shift resources and labor from military to civilian purposes.

During a transition period of five or, at the most, ten years, the United States should be prepared to honor its security commitment to Seoul, retaining diminishing levels of ground, air, and sea forces in the South. However, the United States should serve notice that it will complete its disengagement and terminate the security treaty by the end of the designated transition period, irrespective of the degree to which tension has or has not been reduced, and that it will terminate its security treaty with Seoul if Beijing and Moscow take parallel steps to liquidate their military alliances with Pyongyang. Moreover, the United States should henceforth make clear that its alliance with the South is confined to the military sphere and that it will exercise its independent judgment in pursuing political, diplomatic, and economic interests in Pyongyang, recognizing that U.S. and South Korean interests will not always coincide.

The central goals of U.S. policy should be to sustain the nuclear freeze agreement; to move toward a nuclear-free Korea, including the removal of the U.S. nuclear umbrella as part of broader arms control agreements; to support a peaceful, orderly unification process; and to establish friendly relations with the people of Korea as a whole.

Economic Normalization: The Pivotal Issue

The removal of U.S. economic sanctions is a precondition for the overall liberalization of economic relations with the West and Japan that the North seeks as the key to solving its economic problems, especially its food shortage. It was primarily because the United States promised to remove these sanctions that Pyongyang decided to conclude the 1994 nuclear freeze agreement, known as the Agreed Framework. Article 2, Section 1, explicitly states that "within three months of the date of this document, both sides will reduce barriers to trade and investment, including restrictions on telecommunications services and financial transactions." This provision is unconditional and was not linked to performance on other issues. By contrast, Section 2 conditions the establishment of a liaison office on "the resolution of consular and other technical issues," and Section 3 makes upgrading relations from a liaison office to the ambassadorial level contingent on "progress on issues of concern to each side." But the commitment to reducing trade and investment barriers is unqualified, though it avoids specifying precisely how far and how fast the reduction should proceed.[7]

In formal and informal meetings with North Korean leaders in September 1995, on my fifth visit to Pyongyang, I found a much sharper emphasis on the sanctions issue than the official propaganda line projects; there is a feeling that the United States has cheated the North out of the most important benefits promised under the Agreed Framework. Pyongyang is not seriously threatening to break the agreement—yet—but the North Korean leaders I met[8] clearly felt that it was not working out. What they said, in effect, was: "We're living up to our side of the deal. We have frozen our nuclear program and this has been verified by International Atomic Energy Agency inspectors and by U.S. government experts. But you are not living up to your part of the deal. We've given up our nuclear independence, and we've done it for one reason, because we thought this would lead to friendly relations with the United States, particularly economic relations. But you have made only token reductions of trade and investment barriers."

An objective evaluation of the sanctions issue indicates that the North Korean grievance is justified. By July 1996, all that the United States had done to implement Article 2 was to lift sanctions on the exports of one commodity, magnesite, and to grant permission to American Telephone and Telegraph (AT&T) to open telephone and fax communications. The few U.S. companies that have gone to Pyongyang and shown interest in investing cannot get U.S. Treasury Department licenses. Despite the specific reference to liberalizing "financial transactions" in Article 2, $14 million in hard currency belonging to North Korean entities remained blocked in U.S. banks.

The Clinton administration defends its failure to carry out its pledge by pointing to the fact that Article 2 does not specify how much liberalization is required. In reality, when the Agreed Framework was concluded on October 24, 1994, the administration had intended to move decisively on the sanctions issue within the required three months by permitting the foreign subsidiaries of U.S. firms to deal with North Korea. This would have permitted General Motors and other firms with such subsidiaries to invest in the North. But the unexpected Republican sweep of Congress less than one month later aroused administration fears that the removal of sanctions would stir up opposition to the freeze agreement as a whole and endanger the congressional support needed to implement it.

In defending its position, the Clinton administration has frequently misrepresented what the agreement provides, seeking to give the impression that it conditions the removal of sanctions on North Korean concessions on other issues. For example, a U.S. State Department official responsible for economic relations with North Korea said incorrectly that "under the agreement, the United States has said that it would ease more sanctions on North Korea as progress is made on other areas of interest to us."[9] Similarly, the administration has pointed to its license to the Stanton Group to refurbish an oil refinery as a concession under Article 2. But the investment in question was in fact approved under Article 1, Section 2, as part of the replacement of nuclear facilities with nonnuclear facilities pledged in the agreement.

The continuation of sanctions imposed during a period of Cold War military tensions is increasingly anachronistic in the context of the North Korean effort to liberalize its foreign economic relations and to win international respectability. In the new Najin-Sonbong free trade and investment zone, foreign investors can establish fully foreign-owned enterprises, get a five-year tax holiday and a 14 percent tax rate, and enter the zone without visas. Urging an end to the sanctions policy in April 1996, Kim Chong-u, chairman of the Democratic People's Republic of Korea (DPRK) Committee for the Promotion of External Economic Cooperation, acknowledged that "the world market today has been unified into a single market, the capitalist market." To join this market, he said, Pyongyang has launched

> an across-the-board introduction of business forms and modes that currently prevail in the international market, including a wide range of equity and contractual joint ventures as well as wholly foreign-owned businesses. . . . Our main objective is the active introduction of the high technology and foreign capital investment so urgently needed by our national economy. In this regard, the State has taken a series of measures aimed at doing away with all phenomena giving rise to our poor credit rating and is prepared, among other things, to extend in-kind or cash guarantees.[10]

In addition to its sanctions policy, the United States has actively promoted the conversion of the Cold War export control regime, COCOM (Coordinating Committee on Export Controls), into a new multilateral grouping of thirty countries targeted at Iran, Iraq, Libya, and North Korea. The "Wassenaar Arrangement," named after the Dutch town where it was established in 1995, is designed to block the export of conventional weapons and dual-use technology to "rogue states." A more appropriate initiative, given the end of the superpower military rivalry, would have been a universal, nondiscriminatory regime addressed to the worldwide problem of burgeoning conventional arms sales. Such an approach would have attempted to curb arms sales to Seoul and Pyongyang alike. In any case, bilateral U.S. steps to liberalize economic sanctions would become meaningless if dual-use technology was defined rigidly in applying the Wassenaar Arrangement to North Korea.

The United States could properly seek to block exports to Pyongyang with a direct military application but should permit trade and investment that does not have a clear military utility. As a first priority, it should remove all restrictions on North Korean exports so that Pyongyang can begin to acquire the foreign exchange necessary to finance food imports.

Although a soft landing would serve U.S. interests, the United States and its allies cannot ensure this result. On the one hand, the United States should not subsidize North Korea, assuming the role of patron played during the Cold War by the Soviet Union and China. On the other hand, it should stop obstructing the North Korean effort to adapt to post–Cold War realities and should cooperate with Pyongyang economically for mutual benefit.

One of the most promising areas for such cooperation would be U.S. government encouragement for private sector development of the North's untapped gold, iron, manganese, zinc, lead, and other mineral resources, with payment for technological help in kind. The United States should not extend bilateral economic aid to North Korea but should encourage Japan to do so as a near neighbor with a much greater geopolitical stake in Korea. In normalizing relations with South Korea in 1965, Japan made a "reparations" or "economic cooperation" payment of $800 million. At the end of 1994, a comparable sum would have been $3.76 billion, based on the consumer price index at that time, but North Korean spokesmen have advanced arguments that seek to justify a payment by the Japanese of $5–$10 billion.[11]

Above all, the United States should support multilateral assistance to North Korea, starting with support for the United Nations Development Programme, until now the only foreign aid agency with permanent representation in Pyongyang. U.S. support would open the way for North Korean admission to the Asian Development Bank, the Asia Pacific Economic Cooperation (APEC), the World Bank, and other multilateral agencies.

Food Aid and Agricultural Reform

A U.S. policy designed to promote a soft landing would include urgent action to help alleviate North Korea's food shortage. The United States should acknowledge that the current crisis has resulted in large part from factors beyond North Korea's control and should actively help mobilize a short-term international humanitarian relief effort. The areas most severely damaged in the 1995 and 1996 floods were the breadbasket provinces in the south and west that produce most of North Korea's grain. Even before the floods struck, North Korean agriculture had been paralyzed by the loss of the Soviet oil that had fueled its tractors and fertilizer factories.

North Korea is a mountainous country with only 18 percent of its land arable. It has thus faced food scarcity since its inception. Despite ambitious irrigation, reclamation, and mechanization programs that have brought impressive increases in food production, Pyongyang has relied on significant food imports, especially concessional imports from China. Beginning in 1989, China toughened its terms but continued to be a reliable source of food grains, shipping 600,000 tons of corn in 1994. Then, in 1995, rising domestic demand led Beijing to decide not to export grain, and it cut off grain shipments to North Korea abruptly, leaving Pyongyang in the lurch just when the floods struck. In April 1996, China extended 120,000 tons of emergency food grains aid and signed a five-year agreement with Pyongyang to provide 500,000 tons of grain annually, half of it as a grant and half at concessional prices. But this agreement was expected to leave an annual gap of 1.5 million tons in the years immediately ahead.

In response to the food shortage, Kim Jong Il is making announced and unannounced changes in agricultural policy similar to those adopted by China and Vietnam in the early stages of their movement toward market reforms. The most important announced change is an increase in production incentives. Until now, farmers in government-controlled cooperative farms have been organized in work teams made up of as many as twenty-five members. Since payment is made by the state to the team as a group, laggards and those who work hard benefit equally from increases in output. Under the new system, work teams will consist of eight members, which will put pressure on the laggards to produce. Each team will be permitted to keep up to 30 percent of what it harvests, the amount retained dependent on the extent to which it meets or exceeds production targets.

What makes this modest reform significant is that it goes together with an unannounced decision by some local authorities to permit private markets where work teams can sell or barter their surplus and individual farmers can sell or barter food grown on their household plots. This change is clearly being made with the approval of Kim Jong Il but without any formal doctrinal justification that would upset the party old guard.

In selected experimental areas, such as Hoeryong in North Hamgyong, the government has also introduced contract farming. Individuals or families may enter into fifteen-year agreements to lease land under which they must sell a fixed amount of food to the state but can dispose of the rest in private markets. When contract farming was introduced in China, the state quota was gradually whittled down under pressure from farmers. For more than a decade land contracts have been bought and sold in China without government interference.

The United States should not seek to condition food aid or the relaxation of sanctions on specific economic reform measures. Surrendering to direct foreign pressure would only weaken Kim Jong Il's position and complicate the process of reform. However, if it were to help mobilize international food aid, the United States should make clear that it will contribute to the UN effort only for the next two or three years as a short-term response to a humanitarian crisis, thus applying indirect pressure for reform.

Replacing the Armistice

Apart from economic sanctions and food aid, the central challenge facing U.S. policymakers in Korea is how to replace the forty-three-year-old armistice with more stable arrangements that will ensure peace on the peninsula. This challenge was recognized when the United States and South Korea made a joint proposal for a four-power peace conference (the United States, South Korea, North Korea, and China) on April 16, 1996.

North Korea responded predictably that the United States would have to honor Article 2 of the Agreed Framework as an initial precondition for its participation. Moreover, the fact that the United States made the proposal in concert with the South underlined North Korean anxieties that a four-power meeting would be used mainly to step up U.S. and ROK pressure on the North for a bilateral North-South peace treaty. Given the fact that the South did not join in signing the armistice with the UN Command, China, and North Korea, it would be unrealistic to push the idea of peacekeeping arrangements or an eventual peace treaty limited to the North and South. The United States made its alliance with South Korea in 1953 precisely because South Korean president Syngman Rhee would not sign the armistice. Rhee wanted the United States to march North with him to unify the peninsula militarily. U.S. president Dwight Eisenhower reluctantly decided that the United States had to buy Rhee off with the mutual security treaty and large-scale aid. The South still refused to sign, as a matter of principle, but agreed not to interfere with the armistice.[12] Against this background, the United States was not justified in installing a South Korean general as chairman of the Military Armistice Commission in 1993, and the North's decision to withdraw from the commission was not surprising.

The United States properly resisted earlier North Korean demands for a bilateral peace treaty excluding South Korea. But it is not enough for Washington and Seoul to say that peace in Korea is a matter strictly between North and South and that peace can be stabilized by simply concluding a bilateral North-South treaty and honoring the North-South agreements concluded in December 1991. Although the 1991 accords should be carried out, they should be accompanied by broader arrangements involving the United States. The path to peace and reunification does not lie exclusively in a bilateral U.S.-DPRK peace treaty or bilateral North-South agreements but in a trilateral pattern of negotiations in which the United States joins in shaping and implementing what the North has variously called a "new peace mechanism," "new peace system," and "new peace arrangements."

The North Korean foreign ministry stated on May 12, 1995, the armistice system defines the bilateral relations between the DPRK and the United States as those of hostile parties and is thus incompatible with the normalization of relations envisaged in the nuclear freeze agreement. Given the U.S. forces present in the South, the U.S. mutual security treaty with Seoul, and U.S. operational control over South Korean forces in the event of a war, Pyongyang correctly points out that it would be unrealistic to exclude the United States from new peace arrangements. What the North has not accepted so far is that it would be equally unrealistic to exclude the South from such arrangements. In the May 1995 statement, Pyongyang showed a degree of flexibility by referring only to "a new peace mechanism" and avoiding any mention of a bilateral treaty with Washington. But the statement reaffirmed that "the replacement of the armistice system with a peace mechanism should be resolved between the DPRK and the United States."

In my September 1995 visit to Pyongyang, I asked for an authoritative presentation of precisely what North Korea meant by a "new peace mechanism." Foreign ministry officials emphasized that the conclusion of a formal peace treaty could wait, pointing to the fact that Japan does not have a peace treaty with Russia. But they added that replacing the armistice and the UN Command with new arrangements suited to the friendly relations envisaged in the nuclear freeze agreement was a precondition for diplomatic relations.

I spent four hours with Lieutenant General Yi Ch'an-bok, the representative of the Korean People's Army at Panmunjom. He made a significant proposal for a two-track peacekeeping structure that would alter the role of the United States in Korea. First, the U.S. and North Korean armed forces would set up what might be called a "Mutual Security Commission" that would consist solely of military officers and would not have government representation. Immediately following the establishment of the commission, the North Korea–South Korea Joint Military Commission negotiated in 1992 would begin to operate in parallel with the DPRK-U.S. commission. When I suggested that the two bodies should be established simultaneously, the idea was brushed aside, but a key North Korean spokesman subsequently agreed in Washington that this would be possible.[13]

The functional role of both commissions would be to prevent incidents in the Demilitarized Zone (DMZ) that could threaten the peace and to develop arms control and confidence-building arrangements. At present, the United States is nominally in Korea to defend the South against possible North Korean aggression. The idea of a strictly U.S.-DPRK entity as part of the new structure would be to broaden the U.S. role. The United States would become a stabilizer and balancer for the peninsula as a whole, helping to prevent any threat to the peace. First Deputy Foreign Minister Kang Sok-chu told me that "the armistice was concluded between two hostile parties. By contrast, the United States and the DPRK will conclude the new peace mechanism to guarantee the security of the peninsula as a whole. The new mechanism [would] help to prevent any threat to the peace, whether from the South against the North, or the North against the South."

General Yi said explicitly that the North would not object to the presence of U.S. forces in Korea if the armistice and the UN Command were replaced:

> The Americans think that if they join in establishing the new peace mechanism that we will raise the question of withdrawing troops from the Korean peninsula. But it's clear from the Asian strategy of the United States that the U.S. army will not pull out tomorrow. It will take a long time. Accordingly, we will set up a new peace mechanism on the basis of a mutual understanding that U.S. forces will continue to be stationed in Korea indefinitely.[14]

Off the record, one of the key officials I met said that "Korea is surrounded by big powers—Russia, China and Japan. We must think of the impact of the withdrawal of U.S. troops on the balance of power in the region." Another said that "if U.S. troops pull out of Korea, Japan will rearm immediately."

I went to Pyongyang with some of my own specific proposals about how the armistice could be replaced. My message was that I did not think the United States would terminate the UN Command as the basis for the U.S. presence unless tensions at the thirty-eighth parallel were first reduced. I proposed a mutual pullback of offensive forces or, at the very least, significant reductions in offensive forces. I also emphasized that the North-South Joint Military Commission would have to go into effect simultaneously with the proposed U.S.-DPRK commission and that the two bodies should be closely coordinated within one overall trilateral structure. The North-South commission should properly handle all military issues involving only the two Koreas, because the United States could not speak for South Korea. General Yi's answer was that the North is willing to negotiate a compromise on the modalities of a new structure and to consider arms control measures. But these issues should be discussed between North Korean and U.S. generals, he said, and the United States has refused to hold such discussions.

After the capture of a U.S. helicopter pilot over North Korean territory in February 1995, the United States and North Korea did initiate contacts at the DMZ. Fourteen meetings were held at the level of colonel until South Korean protests led to their suspension in September 1995, shortly before a crucial meeting at which plans for contacts at the level of general were to be finalized. The South Korean position was that discussions on the replacement of the armistice should not be held between the United States and North Korea. Instead, Seoul argued, the South and the North should decide what role, if any, the United States, China, and other powers should play in future peacekeeping.

To counter North Korean pressures for direct talks with the United States on replacing the armistice, South Korea began to float trial balloons in June 1995, suggesting a four-power peace conference to include China. President Kim Young Sam was expected to make a formal proposal for such a conference when he visited Washington the following month. However, faced with an uncertain U.S. response and domestic controversy over the proposal in the South, Kim shelved the idea until the United States agreed to join in advancing it in April 1996.

Pyongyang is likely to resist Chinese participation in any future peace-keeping machinery for two reasons: first, because it fears that its giant near neighbor will become a dominant influence in Korea and wants to offset Chinese power with a U.S. presence; second, because it believes Seoul's support for Chinese involvement is designed to neutralize the type of U.S. role sought by General Yi. Whether or not a Chinese role proves to be negotiable, U.S. participation in peacekeeping arrangements for a transition period, including U.S. forces, would serve U.S. interests, provided that it is accompanied in practice by a meaningful role for the North Korea–South Korea Joint Military Commission.

The United States should work for a compromise that combines some elements of General Yi's proposal for a two-track structure with a trilateral coordinating body that would prevent the North from using the new structure to drive a wedge between the United States and the South. At the same time, the United States should make clear that U.S. forces will remain in Korea no longer than five or, at the most, ten years, while the North and South negotiate on mutual force redeployments and reductions.

In his book *Tripwire,* which calls for a phased withdrawal of U.S. forces from South Korea and the termination of the security treaty within four years, Doug Bandow does not envisage a role for the United States in reducing tension in Korea.[15] By contrast, my approach rests on the premise that the United States would be uniquely situated to play a mediating role in Korea if it adopted a more balanced posture in dealing with Seoul and Pyongyang. For this reason I support a continued U.S. presence for five to ten more years if and only if the armistice is replaced with new peacekeeping arrangements. Nevertheless, I agree with the arguments advanced by Bandow for a U.S. withdrawal and share his view that a definite cutoff date is necessary. With respect to termination of the security treaty, however, I believe that this should be conditioned on parallel Russian and Chinese action.

A fundamental factor Bandow recognizes only obliquely is that the economic subsidy represented by U.S. forces and U.S. bases, and in earlier years by numerous forms of aid, has enabled the South to have a maximum of security with a minimum of sacrifice. Although the direct cost of stationing U.S. forces in the South is only $3 billion per year, as Bandow notes, creating and sustaining the relevant units cost substantially more—at least an additional $10.5–$12.7 billion. Moreover, to measure the full extent of the cost it is necessary to take into account the expense of maintaining all U.S. military units in the Pacific earmarked for a Korean conflict, which would add another $16 billion or more to the total.

The South's upper- and middle-income minority, in particular, has acquired a vested interest in the status quo. As long as the South has the U.S. military presence as an economic cushion, it is under no compulsion to explore the mutual force reductions long sought by the North. Opponents of disengagement have argued that the South would react to a U.S. withdrawal by accelerating its defense buildup and that its accompanying anxieties would foreclose meaningful dialogue with the North. But this line of analysis is not borne out by the South's approach to North-South dialogue in recent years. Far from exploring mutual force reductions, the South has been moving in the opposite direction, expanding its defense budgets and its military-industrial complex.

The United States should do what it can to set in motion a process of tension reduction before completing its disengagement. But it should be prepared for failure and should stick to its disengagement timetable come what may. In the final analysis, an open-ended presence is more likely to result in continued tension than a departure preceded by ample notice and a serious mediation effort. Only in the absence of U.S. forces would Seoul have to face up to post–Cold War realities, choosing between the sacrifices required to match the level of defense strength now provided by the United States and an accommodation with the North based on a loose confederation and the coexistence of differing systems.

Arms Control and Peacekeeping

The replacement of the armistice with new peacekeeping machinery would require the termination of a UN Command role in Korea based on the adversarial relationship between the North and the United States that existed at the end of the Korean War. But the UN Security Council would be likely to condition the dissolution of the UN Command on progress toward reducing the tensions that led to UN intervention in the first place.

A significant proposal for combining conventional arms control and confidence-building measures with the replacement of the armistice has been advanced by James Goodby, a distinguished senior U.S. diplomat, and U.S. Air Force colonel William Drennan, who formerly served in South Korea. Goodby and Drennan suggest "a restructuring of conventional force postures" by North and South "based on the principles of 'non-offensive defense,' a concept in which both sides relinquish the capability to conduct deep-penetration attacks into the opponent's territory." Among the specific steps they propose are greater transparency in order to reduce the danger of war through miscalculation; "constraints on deployments near the Demilitarized Zone," including thinning out North Korean forces; reductions in North and South Korean manpower; reductions in the levels and types of equipment; changes in deployment patterns, and parallel reductions in U.S. forces and equipment in Korea. "Mechanisms established to oversee and monitor these arrangements," write Goodby and Drennan, "might replace or revise the institutional arrangements set up by the 1953 armistice agreement."[16]

What makes these cautiously worded proposals potentially important is that they resemble in some respects the 1989 North Korean arms control plan, in which U.S. forces would pull back from the DMZ and eventually leave Korea in stages linked to mutual North-South force reductions. But Goodby and Drennan speak only of reductions in U.S. forces, not their redeployment or their departure from Korea. North Korea is not likely to consider pulling back its own offensively deployed forces from the DMZ unless both the United States and the South also do so.

In May 1992, I made a third visit to North Korea, accompanied by General Edward C. Meyer, former U.S. Army chief of staff. We presented arms control proposals similar to the Goodby-Drennan proposals to Lieutenant General Kwon Chong-yong, deputy chief of staff of the North Korean army. He responded immediately that South Korean and U.S. superiority in airpower placed the North at a military disadvantage and made it necessary to maintain forward-deployed ground forces to offset the South's ability to "leap-frog over our defenses far into our territory." Significantly, Goodby and Drennan open the door slightly to limitations on the role of U.S. aircraft, suggesting that an agreement on dangerous military activities might affect U.S. air and naval forces operating in the vicinity of the Korean peninsula.

Many observers believe that mutual suspicions and the strength of entrenched vested interests make arms control proposals unrealistic. In both North and South, they point out, the armed forces and related industries dependent on military contracts bitterly oppose force reductions. But my own view is that the North is eager to channel funds and labor used for military purposes into consumer goods production and that its armed forces would accede to force reductions.

The arms control proposals made by Pyongyang in 1987, 1988, and 1990 were progressively more explicit, centering on force reductions in three stages over a three- or four-year period, accompanied by a phased withdrawal of U.S. conventional and nuclear forces. By the end of the first stage, the armed forces of North and South would each be cut by 30,000. The United States would pull back its ground forces and its nuclear weapons during the first stage to a line running between Pusan and Chinhae (35 degrees, 30 minutes north latitude). By the end of the second stage, North and South force reductions would reach a level of 200,000 and U.S. ground forces and nuclear weapons would be completely out of Korean territory. By the end of the final stage, with force levels down to 100,000, U.S. air and naval forces would also be gone.

Until the prime ministers of North and South began their series of meetings in Seoul in September 1990, the South had never directly acknowledged the existence of the North's offers. Thus, it was a breakthrough when Premier Kang Yong-hun offered to consider "the withdrawal of forward-deployed offensive arms and troops to the rear area and the reduction of offensive arms and troops to prevent surprise attack and a recurrence of war" coupled with arms and force reductions based on the principles of parity, with "the superior side reducing its arms and troops to the level of the inferior side."[17]

By accepting the principle of reductions, Kang opened the way for a meaningful arms control dialogue. He refused, however, to put reductions on the negotiating agenda, declaring that this issue should "be pursued only after political and military confidence-building have been realized." Kang's insistence on the principle of parity contrasted with the North's concept of equal reductions, reflecting the South's belief that the North is the "superior side," with more than one million men under arms, compared with its own figure of 650,000. The North, for its part, claims that its armed forces number 450,000. Thus, the first step in any force reduction process should be an attempt to agree on the facts concerning the military balance.

Together with exploratory discussions on force reductions, negotiations could be initiated on proposals for an "offensive weapon–free zone" on both sides of the DMZ. Tanks, mechanized infantry, armored troop carriers, multiple rocket launchers, and self-propelled artillery would be barred completely from this zone, and the number of infantry divisions would be subject to agreed limits. In one of the earliest of these proposals, Yim Tong-won, coordinator of the North-South dialogue during the Roh Tae Woo regime, proposed a 62-mile zone, emphasizing that equipment is easier to quantify—and verify—than personnel.[18]

Comparing the arms control approaches of the North and South, James Goodby, who played a key role in East-West negotiations on conventional force reductions in Europe, concluded that "the similarities in positions are greater than one might expect" at this stage of the North-South dialogue.[19]

For example, although the North has not formally proposed mutual redeployments, its spokespeople, when pressed on the issue at Washington seminars in 1989, 1991, and 1996, have agreed that pullbacks would be a legitimate arms control agenda item.[20]

Is Seoul ready for serious movement toward force reductions? Entrenched vested interests in the South, centered in the armed forces and a politically powerful military-industrial complex, have so far resisted a positive response to the North's force reduction proposals. There is also a military-industrial complex in the North, allied with hard-liners in the ruling Workers' Party, and force reductions are not popular with this faction either. In the case of the North, however, economic factors have made such reductions imperative and have tipped the scales in the intraparty debate. By contrast, because the South spends so much less of its gross national product (GNP) on defense, the pressures for reductions are not as great as in the North. The South's rapid economic growth has enabled successive regimes to avoid increasing the proportion of GNP allocated to defense while steadily raising the actual level of defense expenditures.

Getting a process of conventional force reductions and redeployment started is the key to replacing the armistice; however, nuclear arms control is an inseparable element of a tension reduction strategy in Korea. The South's fear of a surprise attack by the North's forward-deployed conventional forces underlies its desire for U.S. nuclear protection. Conversely, the nuclear dimension of U.S.-ROK strategy has prompted the North to deploy its forces so far forward and to resist a firm commitment to comprehensive nuclear inspections in the 1994 freeze agreement. Both Washington and Seoul should recognize that equity is the key to settling the nuclear issue. If they expect the North to surrender its nuclear option, they must be prepared to give up the concept of nuclear deterrence as the basis for the South's defense. In this concept, the United States threatens the first use of nuclear weapons if the North attacks the South with its conventional forces.

At present, while removing its nuclear weapons from the South, the United States continues to deploy nuclear missiles in its Pacific submarine fleet and has not ruled out their use in any new Korean conflict. Nor has the reintroduction of nuclear weapons in the South been ruled out. For this reason, Pyongyang has repeatedly called not only for the removal of U.S. nuclear weapons from the peninsula but also for lifting the U.S. nuclear umbrella either unilaterally or as part of a multilateral agreement on a nuclear-free zone. The United States is, in effect, saying to the North, "You give up your nuclear option, but we will keep ours in order to make our security commitment to the South credible." It will be difficult to resolve the issue of "special inspections" and to determine how much plutonium the North accumulated prior to the 1994 freeze unless the United States gives up its nuclear-first-use strategy in Korea. This would still leave the United States with a nuclear second-strike capability that could be used against the North if it develops nuclear weapons secretly and seeks to use them.

It was significant that in its June 11, 1993, joint statement with the North, the United States accepted the "principle" of "assurances against the threat and use of force, including nuclear weapons." Similarly, in Article 3 of the 1994 Agreed Framework, the United States pledged to "provide formal assurances to the DPRK against the threat or use of nuclear weapons by the U.S." By July 1996, the United States had taken no action to fulfill these pledges, which could be translated into a unilateral U.S. no-first-use declaration, a unilateral no-use declaration, or U.S. sponsorship of a multilateral agreement not to use or deploy nuclear weapons in Korea.

Rejecting the North's demand for a no-use pledge, Washington has thus far refused to go beyond a 1978 declaration that it would not use nuclear weapons against any non-nuclear weapons state party to the Treaty on the Non-Proliferation of Nuclear Weapons, "except in the case of an attack on the U.S. or its allies, by such a state allied to a nuclear weapons state." Since the United States is allied to the South and Pyongyang is allied to two nuclear weapons states, the U.S. stand has meant, in effect, that the United States is reserving the right to use nuclear weapons in Korea.

Whereas the Russian security commitment to Pyongyang has become ambiguous, the 1961 Treaty of Friendship, Cooperation and Mutual Assistance between Beijing and Pyongyang remains in effect, with Article 2 stipulating that "the two signatory nations guarantee to adopt all necessary measures to oppose any country that might attack either nation." Thus, a unilateral U.S. no-use pledge would leave South Korea dangerously exposed. By the same token, a multilateral nuclear-free-zone agreement would be desirable for the United States and South Korea if it could be used to make the North's nuclear program fully transparent. In such an agreement, the United States, Russia, China, Japan, and North and South Korea would pledge not to use or to deploy nuclear weapons on the Korean peninsula.

The removal of the nuclear umbrella from the South would have to be preceded or accompanied by the redeployment of the North's forward-deployed forces as part of mutual pullback and redeployment arrangements. But meaningful progress is not likely on either the conventional or the nuclear front in the absence of an overarching North-South understanding relating to unification and the broad political and economic settlement between the United States and North Korea envisaged in the 1994 Agreed Framework.

Confederation or Absorption?

U.S. policy concerning how Korea should be unified has been deliberately vague. Until U.S. president George Bush addressed the National Assembly in Seoul on February 27, 1989, the United States had remained completely silent on the subject of unification, prompting charges that it favored continued division. To counter these accusations, Bush declared that "the American people share your goal of peaceful unification on terms acceptable to the Korean people."[21] However, this formulation avoided the operative policy issue. Does the United States favor unification on terms acceptable to the North as well as the South through some form of confederation based on the coexistence of differing systems? Or does it favor unification on terms favorable to the South through the destabilization and eventual absorption of the Pyongyang regime?

During the Roh Tae Woo period, South Korea was moving cautiously toward the concept of a loose confederation based on the coexistence of differing systems, departing from earlier policies designed to freeze the status quo.[22] President Kim Young Sam initially indicated his intention to continue moving in the direction of a loose confederation; however, since July 1993, he has shifted to a more cautious and ambiguous policy, emphasizing that democracy, economic freedom, and unification must go together.[23] Kim's three-stage unification policy makes no mention of a confederal structure, diluting Roh's explicit concept of a confederal structure as the vehicle for increased contacts.[24]

Taken together with the Clinton administration's focus on converting authoritarian states to market democracies, Kim Young Sam's approach has reinforced the North's suspicions that the South is bent on absorption. This is the principal obstacle prohibiting meaningful North-South dialogue. A successful U.S. effort to promote a reduction of North-South tensions, a nuclear-free Korea, and stable relations between North Korea and its neighbors would require a balanced unification policy based on the coexistence of differing systems.

Deputy Prime Minister and Foreign Minister Kim Yong-nam told me during my 1995 visit that U.S. support for a confederation is "the key" to winning North Korean trust in U.S. intentions. Revealing a reversal of previous policy, he volunteered that U.S. forces would not have to be removed as a precondition for a confederation, a position consistent with the assurances offered by General Yi and other leaders that the North does not seek the withdrawal of these forces.

As originally defined in a series of pronouncements during the 1960s and 1970s, the North's confederation proposals envisaged a tightly integrated structure. The confederal government would have a combined army and a standing committee that would supervise the two regional regimes. Since this would be a transitional stage on the road to full unification, the people would decide when, whether, and how to change the structure. Predictably, Seoul rejected this idea, contending that Pyongyang would merely use such a system to subvert the South. During the past decade, however, the North has adopted a more realistic position. When I objected to the North's proposal as unrealistic during my 1987 visit, Hwang Chang-yop, secretary of the International Department of the Workers' Party, replied, "You will find us very flexible if we are all going in the same direction, toward confederation, rather than toward legitimizing two Koreas."

In the North's changing approach to unification, Hwang explained, confederation is no longer a transitional phase but the "final stage" of unification; integration of the two differing social and economic systems is not envisaged. In principle, a combined army would be a long-term objective, but "if we can improve relations between the two Koreas, then having two armies would be acceptable, especially if their size can be reduced."

The late Kim Il Sung repeatedly emphasized in formal pronouncements that the North's terms for a confederation were negotiable.[25] During a visit to Washington in June 1991, former vice–foreign minister Han Si-hae made the most explicit North Korean statement to date elaborating what Pyongyang had in mind. "We envisage a loose confederal state," he said, in which "all ongoing entities in North and South would be kept intact as they are for the time being. Both would have independent military affairs and diplomatic relations, and the confederal state would be limited to a coordinating function." On the critical doctrinal issue of when full unification would be achieved, he volunteered that this would come "when the confederal government has the full power of diplomacy and defense." Even then, however, the North and South would continue to have independent economic and cultural relations with foreign countries.

Repeating several times that the North had "no intention or capability at all to communize South Korea," he offered a new rationale in support of this position. "It would be strategically unfavorable for our side to change the southern capitalist system into a communist system," he argued, because "we want to improve our relations with many countries that have large investments in the South, especially the United States and Japan."[26]

The North's proposal for a "Confederal Republic of Koryo" envisaged confederal bodies composed of an equal number of representatives of the two sides, notwithstanding the fact that the South's population (45.3 million in 1995) is almost twice that of the North (23.9 million). By contrast, successive South Korean governments have advocated free elections in North and South to choose the legislature of a unified Korea. Thus, it was a significant departure when President Roh advanced his proposal for a "Korean Commonwealth" or a "Korean National Community" on September 11, 1989. The new plan explicitly accepted the principle of equal representation in a projected transitional twenty-member Council of Ministers, hundred-member Council of Representatives, and Joint Secretariat to be located within the DMZ:

> The council of ministers would be co-chaired by the prime ministers of the North and the South and would comprise around ten minister-level officials from each side. Under the council standing committees could be created to deal with humanitarian, political, diplomatic, economic, mili-

tary, social, and cultural affairs. The council of ministers of the North and the South would discuss and adjust all pending North-South issues and national problems and would ensure their implementation.

To support the activities of the council of ministers and the council of representatives, to implement decisions, and to handle other administrative affairs, the North and the South would establish a joint secretariat and dispatch resident liaison missions to Seoul and Pyongyang. The institutions and facilities of the merger of the North and the South, including the joint secretariat, would be established in a peace zone to be created within the Demilitarized Zone. . . .

The North-South council of representatives will be composed of around 100 North-South parliamentarians, with equal numbers representing each side. It will draft a unified constitution, prepare methods and concrete procedures to realize reunification, and advise the North-South council of ministers at its request.

Still, this plan continued to envisage the eventual integration of the two Korean states as a democratic republic following elections, and the new republic was to have a bicameral legislature in which the lower house would be based on population.[27]

Roh's plan differed radically from the North's proposal, which assumes the indefinite coexistence of two differing systems. Nevertheless, DPRK foreign minister Kim Yong-nam made a conciliatory response to the South Korean president on September 28, 1989. Although still convinced that a confederal republic was the "best way" to achieve reunification, "with a view to getting reconciled with each other, respecting and making concessions to each other," Kim said, "we are ready to have open-hearted, sincere discussions over other reunification proposals and magnanimously accept any proposal if it is helpful to unification."[28]

Opposition leader Kim Dae Jung's cautiously advanced alternative approach to confederation, unlike the Korean Commonwealth proposal, accepts without qualification the cardinal principle of the North's proposal: equal representation of the two sides. More important, it assumes that the two confederating units would indefinitely retain their present political and economic systems. At the same time, Kim's "confederation of Korean republics" would differ fundamentally from Pyongyang's single confederal republic because North and South would begin what is envisaged as a protracted confederating process, possibly over a period of decades, without surrendering any of their sovereignty. On August 15, 1987, addressing the Council for the Promotion of Democracy in Seoul, Kim declared:

As a first stage, we should recognize the North Korean communist regime as a communist regime which is an independent government and [they should] firmly recognize the Republic of Korea as a democratic government which is an independent government. Then both sides, for the sake of peaceful coexistence, should dispatch their representatives to make a confederal system with very weak powers. . . .

The confederal republic proposed by Kim Il Sung in North Korea seeks to create, in a single stroke, a genuine single state in the form of a federation like the United States or Canada. But this is utterly impossible. I oppose this. What I have spoken of is a confederation of republics— even the name is the opposite. We must move forward on the road toward building, atop two independent republics, a confederal system having limited authority and functions.[29]

One of these functions, he said in a 1973 speech, would be to "seek to adopt a joint diplomacy."

What I envisage is a loose federal system linking the North and South under the flag of One Korea. Each side would be free to conduct in its own way its own foreign policy, military affairs and domestic politics but would seek to adopt a joint diplomacy toward all countries of the world. This would be the first stage in a gradual movement toward full reunification.[30]

In 1993, Kim added an important modification, stating: "Perhaps up to a decade after beginning this confederation, both Koreas would build a national consensus toward establishment of a multi-party and open market system. We would then enter into the second stage of the unification process." In this second stage, "one federal government of two local autonomous governments would be formed, with foreign affairs and defense controlled by the federal government."[31]

In contrast to the explicit character of the Roh and Kim Dae Jung proposals, President Kim Young Sam has kept his options open, outlining his approach to unification in broad-brush terms with few specifics. His three-stage plan would "move from the initial step of reconciliation and cooperation," he declared, "to the next phase of Korean commonwealth and to a final stage of a unified nation of one people and one state." Whereas Roh's plan provided in detail for a Council of Ministers, Council of Representatives, and a Joint Secretariat, all constituted on a basis of equality, Kim's plan, as enunciated by former deputy prime minister and unification minister Han Wan-sang, did not envisage a confederal structure. During this phase, Han said in his major speech on the subject that

a National Community Charter will be promulgated to govern the North-South relations. At this point inter-Korean relations will be regularized to some extent and some North-South organizations launched. Between the two governmental authorities, cabinet-level meetings, legislative conferences and summit meetings will be institutionalized. And at the civilian level, North and South will seek to enlarge the room of integration and enhance homogeneity through expanding trade and exchange visits.[32]

Han insisted that President Kim Young Sam's plan was "not fundamentally different" from that of his predecessor. But by dropping the concept of a confederation, it was indeed a different and much less ambitious plan. Han's concept of the second stage is reminiscent of the limited plan for more systematic exchanges and consultation envisaged when the abortive North-South Coordinating Committee was established in 1972.

Explaining why Kim Young Sam had decided to water down Roh's plan, Han argued that it was necessary to achieve a "national consensus" by "accommodating the conservative and the critical voices" in the right and left in the South before unification could be effectively pursued. He called for "bold steps to dissolve not only the Cold War between North and South but also the Cold War establishment within both systems. . . . Both North and South should launch an ideological reform from above to dismantle the Cold War structure."

U.S. support for a unification policy in which neither side swallows up the other would decisively tip the balance in the South, strengthening leaders who seek to "dismantle the Cold War structure" left over from three decades of military rule. Conversely, by remaining silent on this critical issue, the United States helps the advocates of unification-by-absorption and progressively undermines the possibility of a soft landing.

Notes

1. James Sterngold, "South Korean President Lashes Out at U.S.," *New York Times,* October 8, 1994, p. 3.

2. Caspar W. Weinberger, "The Appeasement of North Korea," *Forbes Magazine,* November 21, 1994, p. 35.

3. Federal News Service, January 21, 1994, remarks before the winter meeting of the Republican National Committee in Washington, D.C.

4. Testimony before the U.S. House Committee on National Security, March 28, 1996.

5. General Shalikashvili made this statement at a luncheon with editors of the *Washington Post,* April 1, 1996.

6. Marc Fisher, "Germany Groans Under the Huge Cost of Unification," *Washington Post,* July 2, 1991, p. 4. See also "Seoul Estimates Unification Cost," *New York Times,* January 31, 1993, p. 6.

7. "Agreed Framework Between the United States of America and the Democratic People's Republic of Korea," *Arms Control Reporter,* January 1995.

8. For example, Deputy Prime Minister and Foreign Minister Kim Yongnam; First Deputy Foreign Minister Kang Sok-chu; and Lieutenant General Yi Ch'an-bok, the North Korean representative at Panmunjom.

9. Stephanie Eshelman, "Problems and Prospects for North Korea–U.S. Trade and Economic Relations," paper presented at a conference sponsored by the Gaston Sigur Center for East Asian Studies, George Washington University, April 22, 1996, p. 5.

10. Kim Chong-u, "Some Issues of North Korea's External Economic Policy,"

paper prepared for "Korea: Prospects for Economic Development," a conference sponsored by the Gaston Sigur Center, George Washington University, April 22, 1996, pp. 3, 4, 6.

11. In addressing a Carnegie Endowments for International Peace seminar in Washington, D.C., on May 1, 1996, Yi Chong-hyok, vice-chairman of the Korea Asia-Pacific Peace Committee, said that "nothing less than $10 billion" would be equitable.

12. See Dulles Oral History Project, Princeton University Library, transcripts of interviews with Paek Tu-jin, pp. 11, 15; Son Won-il, pp. 14–15; and Chung Il-kwon, p. 35.

13. Yi, Carnegie Endowment seminar.

14. Interviews with General Yi Ch'an-bok, September 28, 1995, and officials of the UN Command in Seoul, October 1, 1995.

15. Doug Bandow, *Tripwire: Korea and U.S. Policy in a Changed World* (Washington, D.C.: Cato Institute, 1996).

16. James Goodby and William Drennan, "Koreapolitik," *Strategic Forum* (National Defense University), May 1995.

17. "Gist of the Opening Statement by Kang Yong-hun, Prime Minister of the Republic of Korea, at the First South-North High-level Meeting on September 5, 1990," Embassy of the Republic of Korea, Washington, D.C., September 8, 1990.

18. Yim Tong-won, "Conditions for Arms Control Between South and North Korea," *Choson ilbo,* October 10, 1989, p. 6.

19. James Goodby, "Confidence and Security-Building in the Korean Peninsula," in Eric H. Arnett, ed., *Science and International Security* (Princeton: Princeton University Press, 1990), p. 183.

20. Kim Chong-su, deputy director of the Institute for International Relations, later appointed deputy permanent representative of the DPRK to the UN, at the Carnegie Endowment for International Peace, Washington, D.C., May 30, 1989; Ambassador Han Si-hae, former permanent representative, at the Carnegie Endowment for International Peace, Washington, D.C., June 5, 1991; and Yi Chong-hyok, vice-chairman, Korea Asia-Pacific Peace Committee, Washington, D.C., May 1, 1996.

21. *Public Papers of the Presidents: George Bush,* vol. 1, p. 148.

22. Park Chung Hee's unification policies are discussed in detail in Selig S. Harrison, *The Widening Gulf: Asian Nationalism and American Policy* (New York: Free Press, 1978), esp. pp. 217–224.

23. Kim Ch'ang-bi, *Choson ilbo,* July 7, 1993, p. 3.

24. The three-stage unification policy is spelled out most completely in "The Kim Young Sam Government's Unification Policy: Basic Structure and Its Three Pillars," keynote address by Deputy Prime Minister and Minister of National Unification Han Wan-sang at the Ninth U.S. Forum on the Problems of the Korean Peninsula, Arlington, Virginia, July 16, 1993.

25. Committee for the Peaceful Reunification of the Fatherland, "Milestone Showing the Way for Achieving Korea's Unification in the 1990s," *Information Bulletin,* no. 99 (February 1991):6.

26. This statement was made in a tape-recorded address at a dinner in Han Si-hae's honor at a symposium sponsored by the Carnegie Endowment for International Peace over which I presided, Washington, D.C., June 5, 1991.

27. "Address by President Roh Tae Woo at the Opening Session of the 147th ROK National Assembly, Seoul, 11 September 1989," Appendix E, *Dialogue with North Korea* (Carnegie Endowment for International Peace: Washington, D.C., 1990), pp. 61–63.

28. Korean Central News Agency, September 28, 1989. Kim expressed similar sentiments in an interview with the author in New York, October 3, 1991.

29. "The Path to Unification," text released by the Council for the Promotion of Democracy, August 15, 1987, p. 3.

30. Foreign Correspondents Club of Japan, Tokyo, March 12, 1973.

31. Kim Dae Jung, "Avenues to Korean Stability?" *Washington Times,* October 7, 1993, p. 10.

32. "Kim Young Sam Government's Unification Policy," p. 8.

4

North Korean Policy Toward the United States

B. C. Koh

Despite the veil of secrecy surrounding its policymaking processes, North Korea's policy outputs are by no means invisible. By their very nature, in fact, its foreign policy outputs are strikingly transparent. One can therefore essay an assessment of North Korean foreign policy by measuring its manifest outputs against the yardstick of Pyongyang's goals and interests. The latter, however, are not necessarily obvious. To put it differently, the manifest—that is, officially stated—goals can be either incomplete or misleading; they need to be supplemented or even modified by latent goals—those that have not been revealed or acknowledged.

Although this necessarily injects a speculative component into analysis of North Korean foreign policy, two factors help keep such an endeavor from degenerating into an idle exercise. First, notwithstanding its highly idiosyncratic nature, the North Korean political system shares with other systems certain irreducible needs, such as the need for survival, that allow the observer to make reasonable inferences about its interests. Second, the disparity between North Korea's manifest and latent goals appears to be much smaller than might be assumed. Construed in their proper context, the manifest goals may go a long way toward explaining Pyongyang's international behavior.

Since 1990 North Korea has suffered a series of setbacks in foreign policy, the most noteworthy of which are (1) the establishment of diplomatic relations between the Soviet Union (now Russia) and South Korea in September 1990, (2) Pyongyang's reversal of its UN policy in May 1991, which paved the way for the simultaneous admission of the two Korean states to the UN four months later, and (3) the establishment of diplomatic relations between China and South Korea in August 1992.

Of these three events, the only one over which Pyongyang had some control was the reversal of its UN policy. Had it not changed its position, however, the Democratic People's Republic of Korea (DPRK) would have suffered a far more serious setback than a humiliating reversal of its long-standing opposition to separate membership by the two Korean states in the world organization. The Republic of Korea (ROK) would have become a full-fledged UN member alone, which would have upset the hard-won symmetry in the status of the two Korean states at the UN, and the DPRK would have remained an observer, a distinctly second-class citizen lacking the power to offset the ROK's vote on issues impinging on Pyongyang's interests. In a strict sense, then, North Korea's reversal of its UN policy helped protect and even enhance its national interests; the reversal was therefore not a real setback but an act of pragmatic adaptation to a changing environment.

As far as the other two events are concerned, there was probably nothing Pyongyang could have done to forestall their occurrence. The decisions by Moscow and Beijing to normalize their relations with Seoul owed to a multitude of circumstances, encompassing the surge of pragmatism in the former Soviet Union and China, their economic interests, and Seoul's growing economic power and energetic pursuit of its *nordpolitik*. All of these factors were plainly beyond Pyongyang's control.

It is against this backdrop that the DPRK's policy toward the United States—a policy that seems to be the brightest star in the constellation of North Korean policy, both domestic and foreign—must be assessed. In terms of the results obtained thus far, it can be rated as one of the most successful policies the DPRK has ever pursued. Although this assessment is predicated on the premise that the Geneva accord of October 21, 1994, will not fall apart, even its premature termination would leave intact some of Pyongyang's gains, most of which are symbolic. However, with the signing of a supply agreement for the light-water reactors (LWRs) between the DPRK and the Korean Peninsula Energy Development Organization (KEDO) on December 15, 1995, the Geneva accord is well on its way toward implementation. The efficacy of North Korean policy owes to a conjunction of circumstances, among the most noteworthy of which are North Korea's own nuclear program, particularly its calculated opacity; the emergence of nuclear nonproliferation as a top policy goal in Washington; and the policies and behaviors of the ROK, Japan, China, and the International Atomic Energy Agency (IAEA).

I begin my inquiry by delineating the position of the United States in North Korea's strategic calculus. I underscore the apparent change from negative to positive in Pyongyang's perception of the United States. I then turn to North Korea's tactical behavior, identifying and explaining its salient aspects. Finally, I venture an impressionistic assessment of North Korean policy, using its own goals and interests as the principal yardstick.

The United States in North Korea's Strategic Calculus

From the early 1950s to the late 1980s, North Korea viewed the United States as the principal barrier to the reunification of the Korean peninsula on Pyongyang's terms. All of the strategies and operational directions Pyongyang followed or devised in quest of reunification thus featured the removal of U.S. military presence from the South as a fundamental requirement or goal. Ironically, however, it was North Korea's own strategy of war, embodied in its invasion of the South in 1950, that brought U.S. troops back to the Korean peninsula, from which they had withdrawn a year earlier.

The strategy of revolution Pyongyang embraced in the 1960s sought to increase the pressure, both in the South and in the world arena, for the withdrawal of U.S. troops and weapons from the South. The strategy of confederation, which Pyongyang unveiled in 1980, also called for the dismantling of all military alliances and the removal of all foreign troops from Korean soil. Since around 1990, however, there has been a notable change in strategy. Although it continues to see the U.S. military presence in the South as an impediment to reunification, Pyongyang may have concluded that the United States can play a positive role by helping to bolster Pyongyang's security, broadly defined to encompass not only security in a military sense but also the survival of the regime.

Security in a narrow sense, of course, implies either deterrence against external military threats or the capability to deal with them; a measurable diminution of external threats is an important factor in the equation as well. The negative security guarantee Pyongyang sought from Washington during high-level talks in the early 1990s, reflects this consideration. In the U.S.-DPRK joint statement of June 11, 1993, North Korea seemed to place a high value on the explicit endorsement of "principles of . . . assurances against the threat and use of force, including nuclear weapons; peace and security in a nuclear-free Korean peninsula . . . mutual respect for each other's sovereignty and noninterference in each other's internal affairs; and support for the peaceful reunification of Korea."[1]

The initiation of U.S.-DPRK high-level talks in and of itself was perceived by Pyongyang as a significant achievement, for in its view the talks simultaneously elevated North Korea to a coequal status with the United States and relegated South Korea to a disgruntled spectator of a high-stakes negotiating game. Even though close consultations between the United States and South Korea enabled the latter to play a much greater role than was immediately apparent, what mattered most to the North was that it had undermined the self-esteem and, it hoped, even the legitimacy of its archrival in the South. The tangible economic benefits that would accrue to Pyongyang from a deal with Washington would, moreover, go a long way toward rejuvenating the sagging North Korean economy. All this would help strengthen the ability of North Korea to safeguard its unique political system.

The transformation of the United States from a threat to an asset in North Korea's strategic calculus may have been triggered by a series of major developments, both internal and external. Internally, economic stagnation, aggravated by the collapse of socialism in the Soviet Union and Eastern Europe, must have compelled Pyongyang's leadership to reassess its priorities. The attempt to legitimate political succession under way in the North, moreover, made it imperative that economic conditions improve markedly. Externally, the stunning success of Seoul's *nordpolitik,* coupled with its growing power, called into question the wisdom of clinging to the goal of hegemonic reunification. Although North Korea initiated its nuclear program before some key events occurred, it nonetheless realized the program's value as a bargaining tool vis-à-vis the United States.

North Korea's Tactical Behavior

The most salient feature of North Korea's tactical behavior is brinkmanship, which seems to have played a key part in its policy toward the United States. Brinkmanship, as practiced by Pyongyang, consists of at least three steps: Precipitate a crisis; leave the door open for negotiation; and once negotiation gets under way, do not yield until the last minute.

The DPRK government's statement on March 12, 1993, illustrates the first two of these components. The statement, which unveiled Pyongyang's decision to withdraw from the Treaty on the Non-Proliferation of Nuclear Weapons (NPT), precipitated a crisis. Given the NPT's requirement for a three-month notice before withdrawal, however, there was still time to defuse the crisis by persuading Pyongyang to change its mind. Most important, Pyongyang conspicuously left open the possibility that its decision might be reversed. After characterizing its decision as an "unavoidable measure" to "safeguard the country's supreme interests," the DPRK government stated that "our principled stand will not change until the United States ceases its nuclear threat against us and the Secretariat of the International Atomic Energy Agency restores the principles of independence and impartiality [in its relations with the DPRK]."[2]

North Korea resorted to the tactic of precipitating a crisis again in May 1994 when the chances of resuming U.S.-DPRK high-level talks appeared slim. North Korea's removal of all eight thousand spent fuel rods from the 5-MW experimental reactor in Yongbyon not only undercut the ability of the IAEA to ascertain North Korea's past nuclear activity but also increased the danger that North Korea might try to extract enough plutonium to make four or five atomic bombs. Pyongyang, in other words, had succeeded in raising the stakes of the game, leaving Washington little choice but to shift its priority from the past to the present. When the Clinton administration accepted Kim Il Sung's offer in June 1994 to freeze his government's nuclear program in exchange for the resumption of the high-level talks and assistance in replacing the North's graphite-moderated reactors with light-water reactors, Pyongyang could justifiably feel that it had scored a tactical victory—for it was clearly Washington that had blinked.

Pyongyang's brinkmanship in negotiations is well known. In the third round of the U.S.-DPRK high-level talks, North Korea tried hard to exclude provisions on the inter-Korean dialogue in the Agreed Framework until the last minute, relenting only after it became clear that no deal would be possible without them.[3] In this case the North's brinkmanship served only to delay an agreement, but another aspect of North Korea's tactical behavior became manifest in that episode: By inserting an escape clause in agreed statements or texts, one can keep options open.

For example, the Agreed Framework, signed on October 21, 1994, in Geneva, has the following provision: "The DPRK will engage in North-South dialogue, as this Agreed Framework will help create an atmosphere that promotes such a dialogue."[4] The Korean-language text of the same provision published by Pyongyang, however, conveys a different meaning. When retranslated into English literally, the provision reads: "Following the creation of an atmosphere that promotes dialogue, the DPRK will engage in North-South dialogue."[5] Although the shared understanding of both sides is that the English text of the Agreed Framework will be controlling, not its Korean-language translation, in practice the latter will serve as the basis for Pyongyang's implementation of the framework. It is, in fact, precisely the Korean-language translation (the DPRK version) that Pyongyang subsequently invoked to justify its refusal to resume dialogue with Seoul, repeatedly prodding Seoul to take certain measures to create an atmosphere conducive to dialogue.

The measures Pyongyang has specified have included (1) an apology by ROK president Kim Young Sam for cracking down on the South Korean citizens who tried to express their condolences to the North on the death of DPRK president Kim Il Sung in July 1994; (2) the repeal of the national security law that, inter alia, defines North Korea as an "anti-state organization" and imposes harsh penalties on anyone who has any kind of dealings with it without official permission; and (3) the return of three former North Korean soldiers who have served long prison terms in the South for participating in antigovernment guerrilla campaigns and for refusing to renounce communism after serving their original sentences; the South Korean authorities have prevented the soldiers from repatriating themselves to the North.[6] Although Pyongyang has signaled that the fulfillment of just one of these conditions by Seoul would suffice,[7] it has actually set aside all its rhetoric and putative conditions to engage in a limited dialogue with Seoul when necessity dictated—that is, when Pyongyang sought Seoul's assistance in dealing with a severe shortage of rice. "Vice-ministerial-level" negotiations between the North and the South in Beijing in June 1995 produced an agreement under which Seoul would provide 150,000 tons of rice to Pyongyang free of charge.[8]

Returning to the Geneva accord, one should not rule out the possibility that the manifest distortion of the provision's meaning in the North Korean text may bespeak not a deliberate tactic but a bona fide difference in interpretation; however, this incident is not the only example of its kind. The last sentence of the DPRK-U.S. joint statement of June 11, 1993, reads: "In this respect, the Government of the Democratic People's Republic of Korea has decided unilaterally to suspend as long as it considers necessary the effectuation of its withdrawal from the Treaty on the Non-Proliferation of Nuclear Weapons."[9] In the Korean-language text published by North Korea, however, the word "temporary" (*imsi*) modifies the word "withdrawal"; in other words, North Korea underscores that it reserves the right to change its mind any time.[10]

North Korea does in fact change its mind and make new demands after reaching an understanding or concluding an agreement, which appears to be an important part of its tactical repertoire. Pyongyang's refusal to accept South Korean–model LWRs is a case in point. Pyongyang did eventually accept the South Korean model, but without publicly acknowledging that it was doing so—another case of Pyongyang's brinkmanship. This and other aspects of North Korea's tactical behavior can be explained in terms of *chuch'e sasang,* the reigning ideology of the DPRK.

Chuch'e's apotheosis of independence (*chaju*), sovereignty (*chugwon*), and the dignity of the nation (*minjogui chonom*) spawns a mindset that tends not only to equate concessions with a temporary tactical retreat but also to encourage efforts to regain lost ground. Moreover, having boasted endlessly that its own system is superior to South Korea's, Pyongyang would find it intolerable to allow Seoul to display technological sophistication and engineering prowess in its own backyard.

The fluidity of Pyongyang's political dynamics may also play a part in its tactical behavior. The military has increased its influence in North Korea under Kim Jong Il, which may help explain the hardening of Pyongyang's posture on the reactor issue and in inter-Korean relations. Pyongyang's handling of an incident in which one U.S. helicopter crew member was killed and another captured also suggests the enhanced role of the Korean People's Army in decisionmaking. If the DPRK foreign ministry had its way, Chief Warrant Officer Bobby Hall would probably not have been held in captivity for thirteen days. Pyongyang's attempt to extract an apology from Washington for spying and to "hold direct bilateral military talks that could lead to a peace treaty between the two countries" failed.[11]

The U.S.-DPRK talks on issues related to the recovery and return of the remains of U.S. servicemen killed in the Korean War, held in Honolulu on January 11–14, 1996, helped bolster the view that North Korea's military and foreign ministries have differing tactical orientations and priorities. Opposition by "two senior military officers in the seven-man North Korean delegation" to a U.S. proposal for "a joint mission to recover the remains" of U.S. soldiers in the North reportedly caused the talks to break down. North Korean foreign ministry officials in the delegation were reported to have "favor[ed] some agreement."[12] According to the South Korean press, the North reiterated its erstwhile position that the issues raised by the United States should be resolved in the context of the settlement of a larger issue—namely, the conclusion of a bilateral peace treaty that would replace the armistice agreement, which the North has tried to nullify and, in a de facto sense, may have succeeded in doing. The North failed to attain a key goal in the talks: persuading the United States to pay $4 million as reimbursement for the expenses the DPRK had allegedly incurred in the recovery and return of 162 sets of remains between 1993 and 1994.[13]

The manner in which a compromise was reached on the reactor model issue is instructive. While accepting in substance both the South Korean model and South Korea's central role in the project, North Korea took pains to accentuate the leadership role of the United States. Had the United States not agreed to the omission of any reference to South Korea in the joint press statement, issued on June 13, 1995, in Kuala Lumpur, North Korea might not have withdrawn its opposition to the South Korean model. The North, according to the joint press statement, was to receive "two pressurized light water reactors with two coolant loops and a generating capacity of approximately 1,000 MW(e) each. The reactor model, selected by KEDO, will be the advanced version of U.S. origin, design, and technology currently under production."[14]

The joint press statement also states that, although KEDO will select the prime contractor for the reactor project, its "program coordinator," who will supervise the overall implementation of the project, will be a U.S. firm. The two sides have reaffirmed the continuing validity of the letter of assurance written by U.S. president Bill Clinton on October 20, 1994, and addressed to "His Excellency Kim Jong Il, Supreme Leader of the DPRK." In the letter, Clinton pledged to "use the full powers of my office to facilitate arrangements for the financing and construction of a light water nuclear power reactor project within the DPRK . . . subject to the approval of the U.S. Congress." The joint press statement further notes that KEDO is "under U.S. leadership," that "the U.S. will serve as the principal point of contact with the DPRK for the LWR project," and that "U.S. citizens will lead delegations and teams of KEDO as required to fulfill this role."[15]

By thus underscoring the U.S. role in the management of KEDO and the LWR project alike, the Kuala Lumpur agreement helped create the impression that South Korea's role in the project would be subordinate, not central. At a news conference held in Kuala Lumpur on June 13, 1995, Kim Kye-gwan, a deputy foreign minister who led the North Korean team in the negotiations, asserted that the agreement reflected "our consistent position," including the refusal to recognize the South Korean–model LWRs. The reference in the joint press statement to the "advanced version of U.S.-origin, design and technology," he said, meant that, in Pyongyang's view, the United States had concurred. Kim was careful not to mention any role South Korea was expected to play in the project, stressing that the United States would take "complete responsibility" for the provision of the reactors to the North.[16]

A spokesperson for the DPRK foreign ministry reiterated these points in a statement issued in Pyongyang two days later. He claimed that it was the United States, not North Korea, that had blinked in Kuala Lumpur; in his words, "fortunately, at the final stage of the talks the U.S. side expressed understanding of our consistent stand and accepted it and at last the final agreement could be reached." The reference to the "advanced version of U.S.-origin, design and technology" in the joint press statement, according to the spokesperson, "practically shows that 'South Korean model' reactors do not exist and cannot be the object of argument." He added that the joint press statement "reaffirmed that the United States alone is the principal partner of the DPRK in the LWR project."[17]

Such rhetoric, however, is far removed from the reality. On the same day the joint U.S.-DPRK press statement was issued, the executive board of KEDO, consisting of representatives from the United States, South Korea, and Japan, met in Seoul and passed a resolution reconfirming South Korea's central role in the LWR project. The executive board "determine[d] that, as stipulated in Article II(a) of the Agreement [on the establishment of KEDO], the LWR project in North Korea will consist of two reactors of the Korean standard nuclear plant model with a capacity of approximately 1,000 MW(e) each, and that Ulchin 3 and 4 will be the reference plants specified in the prime contract." The executive board further "determine[d] that KEDO will select a qualified firm from the Republic of Korea as a prime contractor, which will carry out the LWR project, including design, manufacture, construction, and management."[18] What is more, President Clinton sent a letter to President Kim Young Sam on the same day reaffirming the foregoing. Clinton stressed that a U.S. firm would serve as a "subcontractor" to the South Korean firm chosen as the prime contractor.[19]

What the Kuala Lumpur agreement demonstrated was Pyongyang's capacity for pragmatic adaptation. The joint press statement represented a carefully crafted diplomatic compromise in which substantive concessions by Pyongyang were glossed over by the insertion of phrases calculated to create an illusion of U.S. preeminence in the reactor project. It is possible, of course, that providing the bulk of the financing for the project as well as the actual reactors to be installed might not necessarily make South Korea the dominant player; the United States may continue to play the leading role, as it has done thus far.

Most of Pyongyang's tactical repertoire was on display during the two rounds of negotiations culminating in the signing of the first KEDO-DPRK agreement in New York on December 15, 1995. According to Seoul's version of the negotiations, the North not only resorted to brinkmanship but also tried to use "salami tactics"—the practice of "repeatedly demand[ing] additional concessions through an incomplete agreement." KEDO responded by "consistently maintain[ing] the principle of package resolution while allowing no room for North Korea to break up the talks with KEDO in favor of bilateral negotiations with the United States."[20] Even though the North showed pragmatism by not "disputing the use of the South Korean standard model [LWRs] or South Korea's central role [in the LWR project]," "until the last moment, [it] tenaciously demanded [an] additional supply of [power] transfer and distribution facilities, a nuclear fuel fabrication plant, improvement of harbor facilities, etc., as well as compensation for [its] investment [in] graphite moderated plants."[21]

In the end, however, the North accepted KEDO's terms regarding the scope of supply. The North would thus get only those items that would be essential to the construction and operation of the LWR plants, such as roads for use in construction in the site area, industrial water lodges related to construction, cooling water intake and displacement facilities, barge yards, water-pumping facilities including submerged dikes, and simulated training yards.[22]

Regarding repayment terms, the initial positions of the two sides were poles apart: Whereas KEDO proposed repayment in fifteen years without any grace period, the North wanted repayment in thirty years with a ten-year grace period.[23] The final compromise stipulated a three-year grace period followed by repayment of the principal in seventeen years with no interest payments. The North's repayment will begin three years "after completion of each LWR plant" in equal, semiannual installments. The North "may pay KEDO in cash, cash equivalents or through the transfer of goods."[24]

In short, Pyongyang ended up making more concessions than KEDO. The flood of 1995, reportedly one of the worst in recent history, seems to have aggravated the North Korean economy, which had been in the doldrums for many years. Pyongyang's stake in the LWR project therefore increased. It was, for example, in no position to forgo 150,000 tons of heavy oil that continues to be supplied every year free of charge—until the first reactor becomes operational—as long as the reactor project is on track. A further relaxation of trade restrictions by the United States and the exchange of liaison offices, moreover, hinged on progress being made in implementing the reactor project. Last but not least, these developments would help improve the prospects for a resumption of DPRK-Japan negotiations on diplomatic normalization, which if successfully concluded would ensure the infusion of a large amount of Japanese funds into the North.

The December 1995 KEDO-DPRK agreement was also notable because it was negotiated with ROK participation. South Korea, along with Japan, was a full-fledged participant in the negotiations, on a par with the United States. Legally, however, Pyongyang's negotiating partner was KEDO, not the United States, South Korea, or Japan. Pyongyang's policy of avoiding official dialogue with Seoul, therefore, was but marginally undercut. That policy, however, was jettisoned in April 1997, when North Korea participated in a series of talks with both South Korea and the United States on a proposal for four-party peace talks made jointly by Presidents Bill Clinton and Kim Young Sam. In April 1996, at the end of their summit meeting on Cheju Island, at the southern tip of the Korean peninsula, the two leaders suggested that the two Koreas, the United States, and China hold talks to discuss the replacement of the armistice agreement with a peace treaty and related issues. Although the North neither rejected nor accepted the proposal, it made clear that it preferred a bilateral peace treaty between itself and the United States.

Then, in September 1996, a serious incident erupted that threatened to upset Pyongyang's plan to improve its relations with Washington as a means of enhancing its security. A North Korean submarine with twenty-six crew members and commandos on board ran aground in South Korean territorial waters near Kangnung, on the east coast. The North Korean infiltrators—eleven of whom had died, apparently at the hands of their comrades—triggered a massive manhunt involving 60,000 South Korean troops for over six weeks. Although all but two North Korean infiltrators were killed (one was captured and another remained at large), South Korea suffered heavy casualties: Thirteen soldiers and policemen and four civilians were killed, some by friendly fire, and over a dozen soldiers were wounded.[25]

South Korea called on North Korea to apologize for the provocative act and persuaded the United States and Japan to delay the dispatch of a KEDO site survey team to North Korea. North Korea claimed that the submarine had developed mechanical problems during a routine training exercise and demanded the South return both the vessel and the remains of the dead crew, as well as the lone captured commando. Pyongyang also threatened to stop implementation of the Geneva accords altogether. Because North Korea, bedeviled by severe shortages of food, hard currency, and energy, could not afford to give up the 500,000 tons of heavy oil it was getting from KEDO annually as part of the Geneva accord, it entered into negotiations with the United States on resolving the impasse. In the end, the North agreed to a carefully worded statement of regret: On December 29, 1996, the DPRK foreign ministry issued a statement expressing "deep regret for the submarine incident . . . that caused the tragic loss of life." The

DPRK also pledged to "make efforts to ensure that such an incident will not recur . . . [and to] work with others for durable peace and stability on the Korean peninsula."[26]

This set the stage for a "three-party briefing" on the four-party talks proposal. After some false starts—North Korea requested a last-minute postponement on two occasions—the briefing finally occurred on March 5, 1997, in New York. The hope that agreement would be reached on the four-party talks, however, was dashed in subsequent meetings in New York, in April 1997, when the North balked at making a firm commitment. Pyongyang was reported to be demanding a number of preconditions for the acceptance of the proposal, such as the guarantee of substantial food aid by both the United States and South Korea, diplomatic normalization between the DPRK and the United States, and a lifting of economic sanctions by the United States.[27]

Although the United States had already pledged $25 million in food assistance to the North and South Korea had pledged $16 million, both through the UN World Food Program (WFP), in the weeks preceding the start of talks in New York, North Korea wanted more. According to North Korea's own statements, as well as estimates by South Korea and international relief organizations, North Korea would need 2.3 million metric tons of grain from outside sources to feed its 23 million people in 1997.[28]

Meanwhile, the implementation of the Geneva accords appeared to be on track. As of April 1997, the DPRK and KEDO had signed five of the fourteen protocols needed for the LWR project. KEDO teams, consisting predominantly of South Koreans, had made eight visits to Sinp'o, in the South Hamgyong province, the site of the LWR project. Ground breaking for the construction of basic facilities—such as access roads, dormitories for workers, and offices—took place in August 1997. The initial work, for which four South Korean firms will spend 2 billion won (about $22 million), was expected to be completed by the end of the year, thus paving the way for the main LWR project.[29]

An Assessment

As noted earlier, the overall record of the DPRK's policy toward the United States can be rated as a success. To gauge the dimension of North Korea's success, one must use Pyongyang's own goals, both manifest and latent, as the measuring rod. Pyongyang's goals may be divided into two broad categories: negative and positive. Inducing Washington to remove what Pyongyang sees as threats to its security, persuading Washington to jettison "hostile policy" toward the DPRK, and using direct bilateral dialogue to undercut Seoul fall under the first category. The second category is more inclusive, subsuming as it does such a wide array of goals as securing from

Washington an explicit commitment to respect the DPRK's sovereignty and independence, continuing direct bilateral dialogue, establishing full diplomatic relations, obtaining economic assistance, developing economic exchanges, and opening channels for military dialogue and exchanges.

It is plain that Pyongyang has attained many of these goals already, even though the outcome remains tentative and reversible in most areas. Pyongyang's interim track record is somewhat stronger in the negative column than in the positive one. The United States has gone a long way toward allaying the DPRK's sense of insecurity with three documents: the U.S.-DPRK joint statement of June 11, 1993; the agreed statement of August 11, 1994, between the DPRK and the United States; and the Agreed Framework of October 21, 1994, between the DPRK and the United States, establishing that the United States would refrain from "the threat and use of force, including nuclear weapons." The removal of all U.S. tactical nuclear weapons from the South in 1991, which actually went beyond the Bush administration's initial plan, is an important factor in the equation. Pyongyang, however, has publicly questioned the veracity of former ROK president Roh Tae Woo's claim that as of December 18, 1991, no nuclear weapons existed in the South.[30]

The conduct of the high-level talks, the visits by diplomats to each other's capital, and the phased removal of "barriers to trade and investment, including restrictions on telecommunications services and financial transactions" pursuant to the October 1994 Geneva accord—all of these point to the end or at least the suspension of hostile relations between the United States and the DPRK. In early 1996 there were further signs that Washington-Pyongyang relations were improving, notably Washington's decision in February to contribute $2 million for relief of North Korea's flood victims through the WFP, Pyongyang's prompt expression of appreciation for that gesture, and Washington's decision in March to lift restrictions on humanitarian aid to Pyongyang. The United States contributed $6 million more to the WFP later in the year, and as noted earlier, it has pledged $25 million in the first few months of 1997. Pyongyang's goal of persuading Washington to jettison hostile policy is well on its way toward full realization.[31]

Pyongyang has clearly scored points in its pursuit of the goal of undercutting Seoul. Although the DPRK has not really undercut the legitimacy of the ROK, it has nonetheless succeeded in undermining the Kim Young Sam government's image at home. Seoul's total exclusion from the U.S.-DPRK high-level talks was criticized in the South by politicians, both from the ruling and opposing parties, editorial writers, students, and ordinary citizens. The unprecedented open criticism of the Clinton administration by Kim Young Sam indicates that such feelings were shared at the highest level of the ROK government. On October 7, 1994, Kim told James Sterngold of the *New York Times* that the administration did not really understand the North Koreans and was displaying "an overeagerness to compromise." Kim "expressed deep doubts about whether the North Koreans could be trusted to live up to any agreements and whether the American negotiators understood that possibility."[32]

Signs of discord surfaced again in January 1996, when the Kim Young Sam government reportedly decided to convey to the Clinton administration "strong concerns" (*kangnyokhan uryo*) about the United States' eagerness to provide food aid to the North and to improve relations with the DPRK. A high-ranking ROK official was reported to have complained that "prior consultations" were being replaced by "notifications of *faits accompli*" by the United States with increasing frequency.[33] Although Seoul struck a markedly harder line toward Pyongyang in the wake of the submarine incident of September 1996 than did Washington, the two allies managed to forge a consensus, which helped produce the statement of regret from Pyongyang in December of that year. By early 1997, when negotiations for four-party talks got under way, the U.S.-ROK ties appeared to have solidified measurably.

Turning to Pyongyang's goals in the positive column, one sees a mixed record: Some goals have been attained, but other, more important goals remain to be realized. The U.S.-DPRK joint statement of June 11, 1993, contains a commitment by both sides to the principles of "mutual respect for each other's sovereignty, . . . noninterference in each other's internal affairs, and support for the peaceful reunification of Korea." The statement also mentions the two governments' agreement "to continue dialogue on an equal and unprejudiced basis." Pyongyang's high appraisal of this development is evident not only in First Deputy Foreign Minister Kang Sok-chu's remarks following the conclusion of the first round of high-level talks but also in Kim Il Sung's reference to the joint statement in his New Year's message for 1994, which proved to be his last, and in his interviews with the foreign press.[34]

Kang, who served as the DPRK's chief negotiator in the high-level talks, characterized them as "historic," pointing out that the joint statement was the first of its kind. He later stated that the adoption of the joint statement "put an end to 40-odd years of hostile relations between [North] Korea and the U.S., provided a basis for [removing] the root cause of the nuclear problem, and would contribute not only to . . . the denuclearization of the Korean peninsula but also to the peace and security of the world." He particularly welcomed the opportunity to continue high-level dialogue with the United States.[35]

The Agreed Framework of October 21, 1994, envisages the opening of liaison offices in each other's capital as a first step toward the eventual establishment of full diplomatic relations. As for economic benefits, the North initially received 50,000 metric tons of heavy oil from the United States and now receives 500,000 metric tons annually. Trade and investment by U.S.-based firms may soon follow; telephone links were opened in April 1995. Military dialogue and exchanges have not occurred, and the probability of their realization seems exceedingly low. Nor is Pyongyang likely to make any headway in its campaign to substitute a U.S.-DPRK peace treaty for the armistice agreement, which Pyongyang has abrogated de facto. The DPRK's decision to participate in talks with Seoul and Washington on the four-party peace talks proposal in early 1997 shows that Pyongyang has actually abandoned its campaign altogether.

On balance, then, Pyongyang has managed to attain a significant proportion of its U.S. policy goals. Most of what it has gained thus far, however, can be characterized as not only symbolic but also temporary; it could easily be erased should the Geneva accord unravel. Logic and common sense would lead one to predict that, given the huge stakes, Pyongyang would not allow its hard-won gains, particularly the opportunity to reap more tangible benefits in the months and years ahead, to evaporate. The KEDO-DPRK agreement of December 15, 1995, and the smooth implementation of the Geneva accord in the subsequent months serve to bolster this line of reasoning.

Pyongyang's track record cautions us, however, against applying the rational actor model to its behavior. Not only is the logic used in Pyongyang colored by its *chuch'e*-based values and perceptions, but decisionmaking in post–Kim Il Sung North Korea is subject to additional constraints emanating from the dynamics of political transition. Policymakers in Washington, Seoul, and Tokyo, therefore, are faced with the herculean task of simultaneously empathizing with Pyongyang's predicament and fashioning a solution that optimizes the interests of all concerned.

Notes

1. *South-North Dialogue in Korea,* no. 58 (October 1993):73–74.
2. *Nodong sinmun,* March 13, 1993, p. 1.
3. Young C. Kim, "Beicho kankei wa do shinten suruka" [How Will U.S.– North Korea Relations Develop?], *Sekai* (April 1995):155.
4. *South-North Dialogue in Korea,* no. 61 (December 1994):29.
5. *T'ong'il sinbo,* October 29, 1994, p. 1. The "agreed framework" is translated as *kibon habuimun,* which literally means "basic agreement."
6. The three—Kim In-so, Ham Se-hwan, and Kim Yong-t'ae—belong to the same category of people to which Yi In-mo belongs. Yi, however, was allowed to return to the North in March 1993 as one of the first acts of reconciliation toward the North by the newly inaugurated Kim Young Sam government. Pyongyang's failure to reciprocate Seoul's goodwill gesture was one of the factors that led to the ouster of Han Wan-sang as the deputy prime minister and minister of unification. Han, the principal architect of Yi's release, had been a vocal proponent of a conciliatory policy toward the North. On the three "long-term prisoners," see Kim Kwon-hwi, "Nam Choson tangguk un pijonhyang changgisudurul konghwaguk pukban-buro songhwan haeya handa" [The South Korean Authorities Must Repatriate to the

Northern Part of Our Republic the Long-term Prisoners Who Have Refused to Renounce Communism], *T'ong'il sinbo,* December 17, 1994, p. 4.

7. Han Song-yol, a minister-counselor at the DPRK Permanent Mission to the United Nations, said at a symposium held at the University of California at San Diego in May 1995 that fulfilling one of the three conditions would pave the way for the resumption of North-South dialogue.

8. Even though the rice negotiations held in Beijing June 17–21, 1995, were labeled "vice-ministerial-level," only the South sent a real vice-minister—Yi Sok-chae, the vice-minister of finance and economy. Yi's negotiating partner from the North was Chon Kum-ch'ol, an adviser to the Committee for the Promotion of External Economic Cooperation. This appeared to be part of Pyongyang's tactic of trying to dilute or undercut the appearance of government-level negotiations.

9. *South-North Dialogue in Korea,* no. 58 (October 1993):74.

10. *Nodong sinmun,* June 13, 1993, p. 1.

11. *New York Times,* December 30, 1994, pp. A1 and A7.

12. Ibid., January 15, 1996.

13. *Han'guk ilbo,* July 25, 1995.

14. *Korean Report,* no. 299 (June 1995):2. This is a monthly publication of the International Affairs Bureau of the General Standing Committee, Choch'ongnyon, the Federation of Korean Residents in Japan, a front organization for North Korea.

15. For the text of the Clinton letter, see *Korea Report,* no. 291 (October 1994):5.

16. *T'ong'il sinbo,* June 17, 1995, p. 4.

17. *Korea Report,* no. 299 (June 1995):4.

18. For the text of the resolution, see *U.S.-Korea Review,* no. 3 (May/June 1995):9. For a press release by KEDO on the executive board meeting, see *Nambuk taehwa,* no. 62 (December 1994–June 1995):63–64.

19. *Nambuk taehwa,* no. 62 (December 1994–June 1995):61–62.

20. *South-North Dialogue in Korea,* no. 63 (January 1996):92.

21. Ibid., p. 93.

22. Ibid., pp. 93–95.

23. *Han'guk ilbo,* December 14, 1995.

24. *South-North Dialogue in Korea,* no. 63 (January 1996):99–100.

25. B. C. Koh, "South Korea in 1996: Internal Strains and External Challenges," *Asian Survey* 37, no. 1 (January 1997):6–7.

26. Ibid., p. 8. Emblematic of the importance the United States attached to the resolution of the submarine incident are President Clinton's statement on the same day the North issued its statement of regret and the special briefing by high-ranking U.S. government officials on the statement the following day.

27. *Tong-a ilbo,* April 26, 1997.

28. On April 7, 1997, the UN launched its third annual appeal for urgent humanitarian assistance to the DPRK with the aim of raising $126.2 million. This amount is three times last year's target, which failed to be met. See UN Press Release, IHA/628, April 7, 1997, New York.

29. *Korea Herald,* January 9 and April 15, 1997; *Tong-a ilbo,* April 25, 1997.

30. For Pyongyang's insistence that U.S. nuclear weapons had not been withdrawn from the South, see the DPRK government's statement of March 12, 1993, announcing its intention to withdraw from the NPT in *Nodong sinmun,* March 13, 1993, p. 1. U.S. president George Bush inferentially confirmed Roh's statement on nuclear weapons in Seoul in January1992 when he said that he "would not argue" with it, even though the United States continued to adhere to a "neither-confirm-nor-deny" policy; see "North Korea, Nuclear Proliferation, and U.S. Policy: Collective Engagement in a New Era," statement of Arnold Kanter, undersecretary

of state for political affairs, before the Senate Foreign Relations Committee, Subcommittee on East Asian and Pacific Affairs, February 6, 1992, p. 4.

31. For an elaboration of U.S. goals vis-à-vis the DPRK, see "U.S. Policy Toward the Korean Peninsula," an address by Winston Lord, the assistant secretary of state for East Asian and Pacific affairs, to the Korea/United States 21st Century Council, Washington, D.C., February 8, 1996; and "U.S. Policy Toward North Korea," testimony of Mark Minton, director of the Office of Korean Affairs, before the Senate Foreign Relations Committee, Subcommittee on East Asian and Pacific Affairs, Washington, D.C., September 12, 1996.

32. *New York Times,* October 8, 1994. Saying that North Korea was on the verge of collapse, Kim "explained that compromise might just prolong the life of the North Korean government and would send the wrong signal to the North's leaders. . . . Time is on our side." Kim added: "There is no reason why we have to hasten ourselves. It is North Korea that is restless." He also "expressed bitterness over the Clinton administration's failure to raise the issue of human rights with Pyongyang, and its treatment of the government as a suitable dialogue partner rather than a ruthless and deeply isolated dictatorship." One may ask how Kim Young Sam would explain his own pursuit of dialogue with the deceased North Korean leader Kim Il Sung, going so far as to conclude an agreement to hold summit talks in Pyongyang in 1994. The talks would undoubtedly have materialized had it not been for the sudden death of Kim Il Sung a few weeks before their scheduled dates.

33. *Han'guk ilbo,* January 8, 1996, p. 1.

34. For Kim Il Sung's references to the joint U.S.-DPRK statement, see *Nodong sinmun,* January 1, 1994; *Washington Times,* April 19, 1994; "Answers of President Kim Il Sung to Questions Put by Director General of Prensa Latina News Agency of Cuba," *People's Korea,* May 28, 1994, p. 2.

35. *Nodong sinmun,* June 13 and 19, 1993.

5

North Korea:
From Containment
to Engagement

C. Kenneth Quinones

Exhausted and uncertain, the delegation of North Korean foreign ministry officials led by Vice-Minister Kang Sok-chu paused at the arrival gate. They had just arrived at Kennedy Airport aboard a Northwest flight from Bangkok in the early afternoon of May 31, 1993. Kang recognized me from our meeting in Pyongyang six months earlier, yet he refused to step into the airport terminal from the arrival gate. Then I realized that the two men flanking me were U.S. Customs officials carrying loaded pistols. Kang was obviously very suspicious of them and of my intentions. But once he had accepted my assurances of safe passage, he and his delegation followed me down several empty corridors into the noisy, chaotic processing area for people newly arrived from abroad. Only after all the members of the delegation had been quickly processed through customs and reunited with their baggage did they relax and engage me in chitchat as we rode together toward Manhattan.

The delegation had come to New York to engage in the first U.S.–North Korean negotiations since the Korean War. The decision to do so had been traumatic for foreign policy makers, not just in Washington but in Seoul, Tokyo, Moscow, and Beijing. In many capitals, particularly Washington and Seoul, some were concerned that the United States appeared to be rewarding Pyongyang's threat to withdraw from the Treaty on the Non-Proliferation of Nuclear Weapons (NPT) by ending more than four decades of diplomatic estrangement with high-level talks. Critics feared that this "abrupt relaxation" by Washington might encourage other nations to make similar threats in the hope of gaining easy concessions from the United States. Actually, however, these fears ignored the fact that both Washington and Seoul had been pursuing a policy of gradually expanding diplomatic and commercial contact with Pyongyang. The U.S.–North Korean nuclear talks that began in June 1993 in New York, eventually producing the Agreed Framework in Geneva in October 1994, were actually a continuation of a trend in U.S. foreign policy that had begun as early as 1988.

Old Goals, New Methods

U.S. foreign policy toward the Korean peninsula during the past decade has continued to undergo a profound, glacial shift from containment to engagement of Communist North Korea, the Democratic People's Republic of Korea (DPRK). The shift predates by several years the nuclear proliferation problem on the Korean peninsula that captured world attention in 1993 and 1994. The decision to hold the so-called nuclear talks was neither a hasty nor a shortsighted adjustment in U.S. policy. Rather, it was a consequence of changes in U.S. foreign policy brought about by the ever-changing reality at home and abroad.

Movement toward engagement and away from containment began in East Asia long before its recent application to U.S. dealings with Pyongyang. The process has altered the methods for pursuing U.S. goals throughout East Asia but has had little impact on those goals. In East Asia, the United States remains committed to preserving peace and political stability, fostering the region's economic dynamism, and encouraging representative government. What began as "Vietnamization" toward the end of the Vietnam War became a withdrawal of the once formidable U.S. military presence throughout Southeast Asia, including Thailand and the Philippines. The U.S. bilateral security treaty system remains in place, but each of the United States' allies, particularly South Korea, Japan, the Philippines, and Thailand, has assumed far more responsibility for its own defense.

Gone also is the United States' once extensive foreign assistance program. Instead of promoting economic development, Washington has turned to negotiating economic cooperation and free trade and to promoting regional economic associations. Along the way, the United States has increased its reliance on diplomatic and commercial engagement and inducement to assert its will while lowering its military profile. The consequences of this approach are most astonishing in U.S. dealings with China. In fifteen short years, China has gone from being one of the United States' most hostile nuclear rivals to one of its largest trading partners. Trade in weapons has replaced a once extensive economic sanctions regime.

Obstacle to Engagement

The extension of engagement to the Korean peninsula was slow in coming. There the United States has had to move with great caution. Division of the peninsula into two mutually hostile halves greatly complicates any attempt to alter the U.S. approach to either half. The legacy of deeply rooted mistrust brought about by the Korean War weighs heavily on the minds of all involved. Even the slightest shift in the U.S. stance toward the peninsula triggers anxieties in both its halves. South Korea's political leadership, responsible to a population that still harbors vivid memories of sudden war in 1950, works to preserve a firm U.S. commitment to the defense of the Republic of Korea (ROK). By definition, they are understandably much more inclined to resist than condone any change in the U.S. approach to Pyongyang. At the same time, North Korea's paranoia and hostility have convinced many in the U.S. foreign policy community that the methods of engagement might be misread in Pyongyang as a flagging of U.S. resolve to defend South Korea.

Further compounding the situation has been the potential for the collision of superpower interests on the Korean peninsula. Nowhere else in the world do the interests of the world's mightiest nations bump against one another to such a degree. Until 1990, the Soviet Union and China competed for North Korea's allegiance while proclaiming a resolve to defend it from foreign attack. Japan kept a weary eye on the peninsula's stability as it successfully pursued first normalization and then extensive commercial engagement with South Korea. But of the four superpowers, only the United States maintained a military force on the peninsula. Despite the potential risk of instability, the superpowers preferred the arrangement because it preserved stability at relatively minimal costs to each concerned power. Changing the arrangement posed the possibility of what all wished to avoid: increasing the risk of instability on the Korean peninsula.

The Modest Initiative of 1988

Change did come: In 1988 the United States proposed a "modest initiative" that added a benign element to its continuing military presence on the Korean peninsula and maintenance of comprehensive economic sanctions against the DPRK. Washington's first steps toward engaging the North appeared to be unilateral, but they were actually taken in conjunction with South Korean president Roh Tae Woo's declaration of July 7, 1988, a new effort by Seoul to reopen dialogue with Pyongyang.

After his election to the ROK presidency in December 1987, Roh Tae Woo launched his policy of *nordpolitik*.[1] His long-term aim was to reduce tension on the peninsula by defusing the North's hostility with a resumption of North-South dialogue. This was to be accompanied by a program of inducements designed to draw the DPRK out of isolation and into the international community.[2] Seoul's shorter-term objective was to hold a peaceful

Olympiad in Seoul in 1988, one not threatened by terrorism from the North. Washington shared these goals.

Washington's modest initiative of 1988 was designed to reinforce Seoul's efforts. Instead of continuing the traditional reliance on sticks to deter misconduct by Pyongyang, a few carrots were extended as potential rewards for good conduct. Washington indicated a willingness to suspend its campaign to isolate the DPRK from the rest of the world. For the first time, the United States also held out the possibility of eventual normalization of bilateral relations with Pyongyang. Both were significant steps away from the forty-year effort of Washington and Seoul to isolate Pyongyang diplomatically and commercially from the free world.

But first, North Korea had to convince the United States through its international conduct that it merited expanded access to the United States and the free world. It was urged to adopt a more humanitarian posture in its dealings with other nations, beginning with a reopening of dialogue with South Korea to resolve differences. Pyongyang was called on to make a public and unrestricted renunciation of the use of terrorism as a means to promote its objectives.

Twice in the previous five years North Korean terrorists had committed outrageous acts against their fellow countrymen in South Korea. In October 1983, North Korean terrorists sought to assassinate the president of South Korea, Chun Doo Hwan, by exploding a bomb in Rangoon at a site he was scheduled to visit. He arrived late and escaped the blast, but many members of his cabinet were killed. Then, in September 1987, two North Korean terrorists placed a bomb on a Korean Air (formerly Korean Airlines) flight from the Middle East to Bangkok. All 167 people aboard died when the plane exploded over the Bay of Thailand. The modest initiative was announced less than one year later.

As further evidence of humanitarian sensitivity toward the people of the United States, Pyongyang was called on to facilitate the return of the remains of more than 8,200 servicemen still listed as missing in action. Despite Pyongyang's promises to do so at the end of the Korean conflict, it had done nothing in this regard since 1954. As a gesture of its humanitarian concern for the people of North Korea, the U.S. government committed itself to allowing, on a case-by-case basis, the export of "basic human needs" to North Korea by U.S. companies. These exports could include food, medicine, clothing, and educational materials. The step was significant because it was the first time since 1950 that the U.S. government had relaxed its multilayered economic sanctions against the DPRK regime. The modest initiative also promised the issuance of U.S. visas to North Koreans seeking to visit the United States in connection with social, educational, and athletic exchanges. U.S. citizens were told that they could travel to the DPRK without restriction from their government.

Finally, the United States extended the offer of opening in Beijing a formal channel for diplomatic contact between U.S. and North Korean diplomats. The "Beijing channel" enabled both sides to exchange views in private, rather than communicate through the news media or rely on intermediaries, as had been the case for several decades. But the arrangement was strictly regulated from the beginning to ensure that the encounters were nothing more than an exchange of formal notes. When Washington had something to say, the Office of Korean Affairs at the Department of State drafted a text and circulated it for interagency clearance. The process took at least twenty-four hours and resulted in numerous changes to the text. Once approved by the National Security Council, the text was cabled to Beijing with specific instructions on the date and time of delivery. The political counselor at the U.S. embassy in Beijing would arrange to meet his DPRK counterpart on neutral territory, the International Club, two blocks from the embassy. After a brief exchange of greetings, the text of the message was read and a copy delivered. Questions to clarify meaning were permitted, but the verbal exchange had to be limited to the text being passed, nothing else. The absence of any flexibility in the "Beijing channel" ruled out the possibility of actual negotiations.

Nevertheless, the opening of the Beijing channel was a significant step toward engagement. It facilitated the exchange of "substantive" diplomatic communication. Until then, contact between U.S. and DPRK diplomats had been limited to so-called smile diplomacy. Authorized in 1984, "smile diplomacy" meant that U.S. diplomats could respond with polite small talk to approaches by DPRK diplomats at social functions hosted by a third party. No other contact was permitted, a situation hardly conducive to bridging decades of distrust.

Antecedents for Engagement

President Roh's and Washington's efforts at engagement were a continuation of a process that had begun in 1983. President Chun Doo Hwan had used his position as a powerful general to assume the presidency in 1980 and to launch a new republic in 1981. Eager to affirm the legitimacy of his administration and at the same time confirm to the world that South Korea would be a major new player in international affairs, President Chun aimed to have Seoul host the 1988 Olympics. Toward this end, he launched his version of *nordpolitik* early in 1983. A successful Olympiad required broad international participation by nations from both the "free world" and "Communist bloc," as nations were then categorized. Chun shelved South Korea's traditional avoidance of involvement with Communist nations and set out to engage as many North Korean allies as possible. Using the inducement of commercial ties, athletic competition, and cultural exchange, South Korea launched an extensive program of engaging the Communist bloc.[3]

The first success of this innovative endeavor was Seoul's hosting of the 1983 meeting of the Inter-Parliamentary Union (IPU). The effort was far from painless for South Koreans, as evidenced by the experience of national assemblyman and retired general Kwon Chong-dal. Kwon chaired South Korea's IPU organizing committee; his counterpart in the IPU secretariat was a Soviet parliamentarian. In mid-September 1983, Kwon overcame feelings of rage and met his Soviet counterpart, the first Soviet official to visit South Korea since the Korean War. Two weeks prior to their meeting, Kwon's daughter had been returning home from study in the United States. Tragically, she was a passenger aboard Korean Airlines flight 007, which a Soviet fighter destroyed on the night of September 1 after the airliner had strayed into Soviet air space. Kwon's composure was indicative of that of his countrymen at the time, and he helped initiate a process of engagement between Seoul and Moscow that a decade later culminated in diplomatic normalization between the two former enemies.

Between 1983 and 1988, Seoul's eagerness to engage Communist nations proved to be a diplomatic coup vis-à-vis Pyongyang. While Pyongyang remained diplomatically isolated in its self-imposed cocoon, Seoul's diplomats, traders, and athletes roamed the globe visiting every nation in the world, free and otherwise. Ultimately, Seoul's broad-based policy of engagement brought the world to the Seoul Olympiad of 1988.

Engagement Questioned

Pyongyang's initial response to the modest initiative was predictably hesitant and distrustful. North Korea's leader, Kim Il Sung, demanded more evidence of U.S. sincerity. He insisted that the United States end its alleged nuclear threat to his nation. As a show of earnestness in this regard, he demanded the discontinuation of Team Spirit, which he had long claimed was a nuclear war exercise.[4] Ironically, Team Spirit was a conventional U.S.-ROK defensive exercise initiated during the Carter administration to demonstrate the ability of the United States to redeploy its forces quickly to the Korean peninsula in anticipation of their permanent relocation back to the United States, which was then being planned. To Kim, though, Team Spirit symbolized the hostility of the United States toward the DPRK, and the subordination of Seoul to Washington.[5]

In Washington, the advocates of engagement were hard-pressed to broaden support for their position given Pyongyang's ambivalent reaction. In 1990, the remains of a few Korean War military personnel were returned to a U.S. congressman at Panmunjom. The gesture was appreciated, but it fell far short of establishing acceptable procedures for the return of the remains of the eighty-two hundred service personnel still listed as missing in action. The following year, North Korea began importing wheat and corn from the United States as provided for in the modest initiative, and a trickle of official DPRK visitors began to arrive in the United States, but there was no renunciation of terrorism. Rather than reacting constructively to the opportunities extended to the North, Kim Il Sung seemed intent only on maximizing his gains without relinquishing anything substantial.

More worrisome than terrorism was the increasing evidence that North Korea was intent on creating an indigenous nuclear weapons capability. Soviet-trained North Korean nuclear engineers had successfully built and in 1985 began to operate a 5-MW reactor at the Yongbyon Nuclear Research Center sixty miles north of Pyongyang. By 1990, there was mounting evidence that North Korea had also built a facility at Yongbyon to reprocess spent uranium fuel into weapons-grade plutonium.[6] Simultaneously, the North was building and exporting Scud ballistic missiles to the Middle East. Profits from these exports apparently financed the development of longer-range missiles. A marriage of such missiles to nuclear warheads could eventually give North Korea the ability to threaten not only Seoul but even Tokyo and Osaka.

Just as the Soviet nuclear threat seemed to be waning, Washington, Seoul, and Tokyo faced the possibility of a new regional nuclear power, North Korea. This threat divided the Washington foreign policy community. One group, sometimes labeled hard-liners, advocated the reassertion of containment and the discontinuation of engagement. They believed that Pyongyang's nuclear ambitions could be deterred only with a highly visible show of force and, if ultimately necessary, "taking out" Yongbyon with an aerial attack.[7] Their antithesis, the so-called moderates, countered that this stance could become a self-fulfilling prophecy in that it would back North Korea into a corner and unavoidably lead to war. Moderates argued that it would be less dangerous if Pyongyang could be induced to forgo its isolation and nuclear ambition in exchange for the respectability, legitimacy, and numerous other benefits of membership in the international community.

The immediate consequence of the policy debate was a carrot-and-stick approach to the North Korean nuclear problem. Containment (the stick) and engagement (the carrot) would be pursued simultaneously. First, North Korea had to be convinced that any assault on the South would be foolhardy. The Nunn-Warner Plan (named for its sponsors in the U.S. Senate) to phase out the presence of U.S. ground forces on the peninsula before the year 2000 was suspended. Impressive and highly visible qualitative improvements were made to the equipment used by U.S. Forces Korea and the ROK military. Team Spirit was expanded and the number of participants increased significantly. The massive Abrams main battle tank and

Cobra helicopter gunship were added to the already substantial U.S. arsenal in South Korea. A coproduction agreement enabled South Korea to begin assembling an advanced version of the F-16 fighter-bomber. The ROK navy added submarines to its fleet, and the U.S. Navy replaced the aging aircraft carrier USS *Midway* with the much larger, modern USS *Independence.*

At the same time, both Seoul and Washington held open the door for Pyongyang to reopen dialogue and join the international community. For reasons still unclear, Pyongyang finally began to take advantage of these opportunities in 1991. Possibly the demise of the Soviet Union and China's toying with capitalism had a profound effect on thinking in North Korea. Whatever the reasons, Pyongyang moved in 1991 to avoid further isolation by reopening dialogue with Seoul and joining the UN.

In spite of these promising steps, North Korea still had to be persuaded to forgo its nuclear ambition. Pyongyang had signed the NPT in 1985 as part of a package deal in which the Soviet Union promised North Korea four light-water nuclear power plants financed by a long-term "soft" loan. Moscow, hampered by a lack of funds, proved unable to carry out the project, and the entire deal fell through in 1988.

Nevertheless, Pyongyang remained obligated by its signing of the NPT to work out a nuclear safeguards agreement with the International Atomic Energy Agency (IAEA).[8] Article 3, paragraph 1, of the treaty requires "non-nuclear" signatories, as North Korea claimed to be, to "accept safeguards, as set forth in an agreement to be negotiated and concluded with the International Atomic Energy Agency. . . . The safeguards required by this article shall be applied to all source or special fissionable material in all peaceful nuclear activities within the territory of such State." Article 3, paragraph 4, requires that "non-nuclear-weapon states party to the treaty" initiate negotiation of a safeguards agreement with the IAEA within 180 days of having signed the NPT. The safeguards agreement is to be enforced within eighteen months of a state's having joined the NPT.

Pyongyang had done neither by 1991, and concern about its nuclear program continued to mount. For the next four years, this concern defined one of Washington's foreign policy priorities: to bring Pyongyang's nuclear activities under IAEA safeguards and deter any North Korean effort to acquire a nuclear weapons capability. The clear preference was to use diplomacy to achieve this goal. Reliance on the key element of containment, military might, put the people of South Korea at too high a risk of war. Additionally, in 1991 the United States was preoccupied with the collapse of the Soviet empire and Iraq's aggression in the Persian Gulf. Ironically, and some would say fortunately, these concerns made engagement on the Korean peninsula the preferred option for resolving the Korean nuclear issue.

Nuclear Initiatives of the United States and South Korea

In the fall of 1992 the situation on the Korean peninsula—apparently triggered by a U.S. initiative—took an abrupt turn for the better. In an address to the nation on September 27, 1991, President George Bush said: "Last year, I canceled US plans to modernize our ground-launched theater nuclear weapons. . . . I am, therefore, directing the United States to eliminate its entire worldwide inventory of ground-launched short-range—that is theater—nuclear weapons. We will bring home and destroy all our nuclear artillery shells and short-range ballistic missile warheads."[9] President Bush clearly had the Soviet Union in mind when making the speech, but his directive had global ramifications. Pyongyang professed disbelief but quietly sought confirmation.

President Roh Tae Woo soon followed in November with an equally profound statement, titled "Declaration of Non-Nuclear Korean Peninsula Peace Initiatives." His aim was clear: to "initiate the resolution of the nuclear issues on the Korean Peninsula." He pledged that the Republic of Korea would "not manufacture, possess, store, deploy or use nuclear weapons." He also promised that Seoul would "submit to comprehensive international inspection of all nuclear-related activities and materials on its territory in compliance with the NPT and with the nuclear safeguards agreement" it had concluded with the IAEA. Furthermore, Seoul would not "possess nuclear fuel reprocessing and enrichment facilities."[10]

These inducements severely tested the assumptions of those who advocated engagement. If North Korea could be influenced to alter its behavior and foreign policy priorities without reliance on coercive methods, now was the time to see some results. Otherwise, the advocates of containment and the use of coercion would have their chance.

Engagement paid off, with unexpected dividends. First came the North-South Agreement on Reconciliation, Non-aggression and Exchanges and Cooperation. Signed on December 13, 1991, the agreement called for joint efforts to achieve "peaceful unification" and mutual respect. Article 5 provided that "both parties shall endeavor together to transform the present armistice regime into a firm state of peace between the South and the North and shall abide by the present Military Armistice Agreement [of July 27, 1953] until such time as such a state of peace has taken hold." In Article 9, both parties promised not to use armed force against each other.

Alas, this important document did not address the nuclear issue. This would require one more inducement, a declaration that South Korea was free of nuclear weapons. President Roh made just such a declaration on December 18, 1991. In a statement titled "A Special Announcement on a Nuclear-free Korean Peninsula,"[11] President Roh reaffirmed his November pledge that South Korea would not manufacture, possess, store, deploy, or use nuclear weapons. He went on to propose "in consultation with the U.S. Government," the conducting of simultaneous nuclear inspections of facilities in the South, including U.S. military bases. Roh then punctuated this with the stunning public declaration that "there do not exist any nuclear weapons whatsoever in the Republic of Korea."

Working in tandem, Washington and Seoul clearly had Pyongyang on the defensive, and they were turning up the pressure diplomatically by extending one inducement after another. President Bush took full advantage of his January 1992 visit to Seoul to support President Roh's efforts and to press for resolution of the nuclear issue. In his January 6 address to the Korean National Assembly in Seoul, President Bush confirmed his order that tactical nuclear weapons be withdrawn around the world. He also affirmed Roh's declaration of December 18, 1991. In both his speech and a press conference later the same day, he reiterated the need for North Korea to bring its nuclear program under IAEA-supervised safeguards procedures and inspections. As an inducement to do so, he said, "If North Korea fulfills its obligation and takes steps to implement the inspection agreements, then President Roh and I are prepared to forego the Team Spirit exercise of this year."[12]

In an unprecedented move, the U.S. State Department's undersecretary for political affairs, Arnold Kantor, invited ranking officials from the DPRK to New York for a one-day meeting in late January 1992. Kim Yong-sun, secretary for international affairs of the Workers' Party of Korea, accompanied by a small delegation, met at the U.S. Mission to the UN. The meeting's purpose, as defined by the U.S. side, was to ensure that the highest levels of the DPRK government fully understood the U.S. government's policy toward North Korea and the potential benefits of the 1988 modest initiative and compliance with international nuclear safeguards norms. The North's representatives responded in kind by explaining their perspective on the situation. There were no negotiations, and no agreements were attempted during the brief exchange, but the precedent had been set for both sides' policymakers to engage in political discussions.

Pyongyang Responds

These magnanimous steps clearly placed the ball in North Korea's court. Pyongyang's response was swift and constructive. Two weeks after President Bush had addressed the National Assembly in Seoul, the prime ministers of North and South Korea on January 20 signed the Joint Declaration on the Denuclearization of the Korean Peninsula. Engagement and inducement, not containment and coercion, had achieved what only a few months earlier had proved impossible.

Through the first half of 1992, the United States was able to sit back and watch with wonderment the relatively rapid progress joint North-South commissions made on detailed provisions for the implementation of the reconciliation and nonaggression accord. The joint nuclear control commission focused on formulating a bilateral nuclear inspection regime, a process that made little progress.

The IAEA, however, did work out a safeguards agreement with Pyongyang. During the summer of 1992, it was able to conduct several inspections of North Korea's nuclear facilities at Yongbyon. The inspections aimed at verifying the accuracy of the amount of plutonium North Korea had declared was in its possession. Some members of the U.S. and South Korean governments believed that North Korea might have more plutonium than it was willing to admit. Preliminary evidence suggested the possibility that the declared amount indeed might be inaccurate.

Equally worrisome were the North's efforts in August 1992 to conceal what was suspected of being a nuclear waste storage site. Access to the site and analysis of its contents might have enabled the IAEA to determine more accurately how much plutonium North Korea had produced. North Korea's repeated, adamant denial of IAEA access to the site shattered the fragile trust that had been built up during the first half of 1992.

The Korea Central News Agency in Pyongyang announced on March 12, 1993 (the evening of March 11 in Washington), that North Korea would withdraw from the NPT system. The news was stunning and a bit frightening. The treaty's mandatory ninety-day advance notice had been served. Article 10 of the NPT, the so-called withdrawal clause, reads:

> Each Party shall in exercising its national sovereignty have the right to withdraw from the Treaty if it decides that extraordinary events, related to the subject matter of this Treaty, have jeopardized the supreme interests of its country. It shall give notice of such withdrawal to all other Parties to the Treaty and to the UN Security Council three months in advance. Such notice shall include a statement of extraordinary events it regards as having jeopardized its supreme interests.

Could the intended withdrawal lead to hostilities on the Korean peninsula? The possibility could not be dismissed. Could the situation escalate to nuclear war in Northeast Asia? Again, this was a distinct possibility. What would be the global impact on the NPT? The questions were endless, the answers unknown at the time.

Initial U.S. Reaction

March 12 at the Office of Korean Affairs was frantic. First there was press guidance to be drafted and cleared—a three- to four-hour process that involved eight to twelve offices in the Departments of State and Defense, plus the National Security Council. The guidance read in part: "We join the international community in deploring this announcement by the DPRK that it intends to withdraw from the Nuclear Non-proliferation Treaty (NPT). This contradicts its commitment under both the NPT and its joint declaration on the denuclearization of the Korean Peninsula not to possess or develop nuclear weapons."[13]

Deadlines and format—not national interests or theoretical models of international relations—drive foreign policy decisions. Draft it, clear it, edit it, and format it: This is the vocabulary of policy formulation at its most fundamental level. All drafts that touched on the North Korean nuclear issue had to be cleared with a myriad of offices: the Bureaus of Political Affairs, International Security and Technical Affairs, Political and Military Affairs, Public Affairs, East Asian and Pacific Affairs and the Offices of Korean Affairs, Chinese Affairs, Japanese Affairs, and UN Political Affairs in the Bureau of International Organizations. The concerns of the National Security Council's advisers for Nuclear Non-Proliferation and East Asian Affairs had to be heeded. At the Pentagon, the Department of Defense's director for international security affairs in the Office of the Secretary of Defense and advisers to the Joint Chiefs of Staff had valid reasons to be involved in the process of deciding how best to deal with North Korea.

U.S. interests were broadly outlined as maintaining peace and prosperity on a nuclear-free Korean peninsula. The NPT had to be preserved and strengthened. Not only did North Korea have to be persuaded not to pull out of the NPT, it had to be made to fulfill its nuclear safeguards commitments under that treaty. All the while, war had to be avoided while South Korea's security was ensured.

Within a few days of North Korea's announcement, the United States had reached a decision: to preserve global nonproliferation and the NPT while preserving peace on the Korean peninsula through diplomacy. Hostilities there were to be avoided if at all possible.

Bilateral and Multilateral Diplomacy

Diplomacy, both directly with U.S. allies and through international organizations and regional groups, was to be pursued simultaneously.[14] Washington, Seoul, and Tokyo all wanted a peaceful, nuclear-free Korean peninsula; they differed only on the matter of priorities. Seoul, understandably, wanted peace above all. War would have risked millions of casualties, especially in its sprawling capital just thirty miles, or two minutes by ballistic missile, south of the Demilitarized Zone (DMZ). Tokyo felt less threatened but was intensely concerned that it could be drawn into a war. U.S. bases in Japan's home islands surely would be priority targets for the

North Korean missiles in the event of war. Washington was concerned about the region, but from a global perspective. Preservation of peace was crucial, clearly preferred, and the policy priority, with the accent on preservation of global nonproliferation. With amazing ease, Seoul, Tokyo, and Washington began to coordinate their policies toward North Korea. Pyongyang had accomplished the seemingly impossible—long-term cooperation and coordination between Seoul and Tokyo.

The immediate goal was to convince North Korea that pulling out of the NPT would only isolate it from all the potential benefits of becoming a respected member of the international community and that continuing its efforts to develop a nuclear capability would sacrifice its access to all it needed to achieve international respectability and regain its economic vitality. The aim was to induce, not coerce, Pyongyang into remaining in the NPT and forgoing a nuclear capability. This necessitated engaging the DPRK, not reinforcing its diplomatic and economic isolation. Inducement required drawing the country out of its self-imposed isolation. Granted, North Korea had little to offer in return, other than the potential of building its own nuclear capability. Fortunately, each member of the trilateral coalition in Northeast Asia had something to offer and thus also to deny an uncooperative North Korea.[15]

Seoul held out the promise of economic revitalization for Pyongyang, an enticing inducement in the summer of 1992. When North Korea's prominent advocate of economic reform, Kim Tal-hyon, visited Seoul in July 1992, President Roh Tae Woo had welcomed him with the promise of economic cooperation if the two sides could conclude a bilateral nuclear inspection regime. But in March 1993, Seoul made clear that the North's withdrawal from the NPT would preclude economic cooperation and access to South Korea's impressive stocks of investment capital and technology.

Tokyo stepped forward to remind Pyongyang that dropping out of the NPT would cost it Japan's offer of diplomatic normalization and compensation for past colonization. In the late 1960s, South Korea had received the substantial sum of $800 million from Japan in grants and loans as compensation. Effective investment of these funds, combined with access to Japan's technology, helped establish South Korea as a major producer of steel, electronic goods, and ships. North Korea's aging and technologically retarded infrastructure would benefit enormously from an infusion of Japanese capital and technology.

Washington highlighted its own impressive package of inducements. North Korea was reminded that diplomatic normalization with the United States and its allies, membership in the Asian Development Bank and World Bank, and the phasing out of U.S. economic sanctions hinged on North Korea's conduct.[16] Withdrawal from the NPT would gain Pyongyang nothing more than intensified isolation, diplomatically and economically, and the disdain of the international community.

At no time did the United States or its allies threaten war against North Korea as a potential consequence of leaving the NPT. Doing so would have been counterproductive. North Korea repeatedly proclaimed its sovereign right to back out of the NPT, as provided for in the treaty, and avowed its determination to defend itself.[17] No nation contested North Korea's right in this regard. Nor did the Clinton administration or its close allies advocate punishing North Korea. When testifying to the U.S. Congress on March 25, 1993, Secretary of State Warren Christopher alluded to the possibility of sanctions against Pyongyang, but his allusion was in the context of a possible future option, not a point of policy.[18]

Vienna, the headquarters for the IAEA, quickly became the center of activity. The international community perceived North Korea's unilateral effort to leave the NPT as threatening efforts to deter the spread of nuclear weapons through voluntary restraint and the IAEA's global inspection system, which aimed to ensure compliance with the norms for nuclear activity set forth in the treaty.

North Korea's decision was greeted with global disdain. Within three weeks of the announcement, 140 nations, without any prodding from the United States, unilaterally and through regional associations denounced Pyongyang's intended withdrawal. At Russia's request, the depository nations of the NPT (Russia, the United Kingdom, France, and the United States) jointly chastised North Korea.[19] The European Union soon followed with its own statement. North Korea's decision was a diplomatic disaster.

On March 18, 1993, the IAEA Board of Governors approved a resolution that reaffirmed the February 25 resolution passed by the membership of the IAEA. The March resolution urged North Korea to comply with its obligations under the NPT and urged Pyongyang to engage IAEA director general Hans Blix in diplomatic consultations to resolve differences over access to the suspected nuclear waste disposal sites near Yongbyon. The March 18 resolution essentially ignored North Korea's March 12 withdrawal announcement and avoided any threatening language.[20] During these tense, uncertain days, the so-called Beijing channel was frequently relied on to reassure Pyongyang that U.S. intentions were not hostile and to ensure that Pyongyang had an accurate understanding of U.S. policy.[21]

North Korea stood firm, defending its intransigence in terms of sovereignty. It accused the IAEA of unfairly singling it out for unprecedented special inspections of the two suspect nuclear waste storage sites, in spite of the fact that the nuclear safeguards agreement Pyongyang had signed the previous year provided for such inspections. To further justify its denial of IAEA access to these sites, Pyongyang proclaimed them to be within a military region.

When the IAEA Board of Governors met in Vienna on April 1, there was no recourse but to escalate the crisis, particularly in light of the fact that the IAEA had given North Korea several months to resolve the issue of access to the suspected nuclear waste sites through quiet diplomacy. The board approved a resolution that found North Korea in noncompliance with its safeguards agreement and again urged it to allow IAEA inspections of the two suspect waste sites. As required by Article 12 (c) of the IAEA statute, and by Article 19 of the safeguards agreement between the IAEA and North Korea, the resolution directed that North Korea's noncompliance be reported to the UN Security Council and General Assembly. Indicative of world opinion, the resolution passed with twenty-eight countries voting for the resolution, two against (China and Libya), and four abstaining (India, Pakistan, Syria, and Vietnam).[22]

The UN

The IAEA Board of Governors' resolution of April 1 shifted the focus of activity to the UN Security Council. Most members agreed that they should pass a statement supportive of the IAEA and at the same time urge North Korea to cooperate. But first, key members of the Security Council jointly issued the following statement on April 1 to highlight their concern and regret over the DPRK's decision:

> We express regret and concern at the announcement by the DPRK of its intention to withdraw from the Treaty on the Non-Proliferation of Nuclear Weapons (NPT). Since the NPT is an essential element of international peace and security, DPRK withdrawal from the NPT would constitute a serious threat to regional and international stability. We question whether the DPRK's stated reasons for withdrawing from the Treaty constitute extraordinary events relating to the subject matter of the Treaty. In this regard, we recall that nuclear related security assurances have been provided to the DPRK as a non-nuclear weapon state party to the NPT. Remaining a party to the Treaty and complying fully with its terms would be in the DPRK's interests. It would help to reassure the international community about the nature of the DPRK's desire for positive international relations, including peaceful nuclear cooperation. Moreover, DPRK withdrawal from the NPT would jeopardize stability on the Korean peninsula, which has improved in recent years, and undermine efforts to implement the North-South Joint Declaration on the Denuclearization of the Korean Peninsula. We urge the DPRK to retract its announcement and to comply fully with its Treaty commitments and its safeguards obligations, which remain in force. In this respect, we strongly support the efforts of the International Atomic Energy Agency to implement its safeguards agreement with the DPRK. The three governments call upon all NPT parties to associate themselves with this statement and to urge the DPRK to reconsider its position and to fulfill its commitments under the Treaty.[23]

China held the trump card on the UN Security Council. So far, it had repeatedly called for a Korean peninsula free of nuclear weapons and urged resolution of the crisis through diplomacy. But Beijing's vote against the

IAEA Board of Governors' resolution suggested to some that it was inclined to support Pyongyang's position. Repeated demarches to Beijing to align itself publicly with the international community were politely received but appeared to fall short of their objective.

The ambiguity of China's position combined with the decisiveness of its veto on the Security Council required caution before any resolution on the North Korean nuclear issue was put up for a vote. China had never cast a veto, but this was very slim assurance that it would not in a vote on a resolution concerning its close ally Pyongyang. First, China had to be convinced that all diplomatic options had been exhausted. At the same time, any coercive measures were to be avoided, lest China be alienated. Meanwhile, great effort was expended to assure China that it was being consulted to the same extent as the other key members of the Council. Any messages exchanged between Washington and Pyongyang were also made known to China.

A gentle, public reminder was sent to China via the State Department's press guidance on April 1, which read in part:

> It is the International Community, the IAEA, and the UN Security Council to determine the best course for dealing with North Korea's non-compliance with its safeguards responsibilities and decision to withdraw from the non-proliferation treaty. China plays a key role in this issue as a permanent member of the UN Security Council. It is important that China carry out its international responsibilities on this issue of great concern.[24]

The time was fast approaching for decisive action. Several months of diplomatic effort by the IAEA, resolutions by its Board of Governors, a global outcry from the international community, and quiet diplomacy by Washington, Seoul, and Tokyo working with Beijing had yet to bring North Korea into compliance with its safeguards obligations or to persuade it to remain in the NPT. North Korea had been condemned but not coerced.

Consistent with Secretary of State Christopher's "deliberate and sequential steps," and mindful of China's possible veto, the Security Council moved with deliberate caution. The day after IAEA director general Blix had briefed the Security Council on his efforts concerning North Korea's noncompliance, the Council president, with the support of all key members including China, issued a statement supportive of the IAEA and its efforts. He also stated that the members of the Security Council welcomed all efforts to resolve the situation.

Hoping to head off the need to escalate the UN-centered effort to a Security Council resolution, the State Department's press guidance on April 14 calmly hinted at a profound future prospect:

> We have said that we are prepared to play our part in that process. We have thus not ruled out a U.S. meeting with North Korea if it could help

resolve the situation. But as we have consistently said, this is an issue between North Korea and the international community, and our task is to support the efforts of the appropriate international bodies.[25]

Emotions were on a roller coaster, and everyone was quickly becoming exhausted from the stress of long, intense hours at posts along the DMZ and in offices in the major world capitals. None knew what might happen on the Korean peninsula. The complexity of the situation increased the possibility of a serious misunderstanding that could quickly escalate into a serious confrontation. Pyongyang's declaration of a state of "semi-war alert" did not help matters, but no extraordinary mobilization measures were apparent. Rumors of unusual troop movements on the Sino-Korean border near Sinuiju were stilled when it was learned that there had been sporadic domestic unrest in that North Korean city, possibly prompted by a shortage of food. The closure of Pyongyang's international airport on April 23 scared some, mostly people in Seoul, but had been done to expedite the return of longtime Pyongyang resident Prince Sihanouk to his homeland in Cambodia. On Sunday, May 2, a North Korean machine gunner fired two bullets southward across the DMZ. Fortunately, there were no injuries and the fire was not returned.[26]

The U.S. and DPRK political counselors met for the thirty-second and thirty-third times in Beijing on May 5 and 10, but these meetings were not successful. On May 6, North Korea heightened the tension when it informed the IAEA of its intention to refuel its 5-MW reactor in the near future. Doing so without the IAEA present would be a serious breach of its safeguards commitments and would make available to Pyongyang tons of uranium that could yield weapons-grade plutonium.

With China and Pakistan abstaining, the Security Council passed Resolution 825 on May 11. After summarizing an impressive list of documents supported by the international community, including Russia and China, the resolution urged Pyongyang to reconsider its decision to leave the NPT and to honor its nuclear safeguards obligations, and it called on the director general of the IAEA to continue his efforts. Finally, the Council urged "all member states to encourage the DPRK to respond positively to this resolution, and encourage[d] them to facilitate a solution."[27]

A few days later, DPRK ambassador Ho Chong informed the Department of State that his government was willing to engage the U.S. government in negotiations concerning the nuclear issue. This opening of the so-called New York channel and the arrival of the DPRK delegation in New York for the first round of nuclear talks led to a sustained policy of engagement between the United States and North Korea. Ultimately, the pursuit of engagement yielded the Agreed Framework of October 1994 and a process of gradual confidence building aimed at the eventual normalization of bilateral relations.

Conclusion

The decision by the United States to engage North Korea in nuclear talks beginning in June 1993 was not made hastily or out of the fear that North Korea might become a regional nuclear power. It was a consequence of a policy of engaging Communist societies that can be traced directly to South Korea's efforts in the early 1980s to ensure its successful hosting of the 1988 Olympics. In support of Seoul's efforts, Washington launched its own limited brand of engagement with the modest initiative of 1988. President Bush, following his South Korean counterpart's lead, facilitated the admission of both Koreas into the UN. This teamwork continued into 1992 with the global withdrawal of U.S. tactical nuclear weapons announced by President Bush and by President Roh's proclamation that South Korea was free of nuclear weapons.

Until September 1992, Seoul clearly led the effort to reorient the basic U.S.-ROK approach to Pyongyang from containment to engagement. The winter of 1992–1993 tested both nations' commitment to engagement, but given the options available by the spring, both continued to support engagement. Then Washington assumed the lead prior to the signing of the Agreed Framework, causing Seoul some discomfort.

North Korea's initial response to engagement was hesitant and uneven—understandable given its isolation from the international community and deep mistrust of Washington and Seoul. After two decades of dealing off and on with Seoul, the events of 1992–1993 appear to have convinced Pyongyang that the diplomacy of engagement better served its needs than its long tradition of confrontational diplomacy and saber rattling. At the same time, however, Pyongyang has demonstrated a clear preference since the fall of 1992 to deal with the United States and Japan.

Given all parties' preference for engagement, Seoul's interests would seem to be best served by striving to regain the diplomatic initiative it so ably demonstrated in dealing with the Communist bloc in the 1980s and with North Korea in the early 1990s. Otherwise, it could quickly estrange itself from the impressive progress made in recent years to ensure peace and prosperity on a nuclear-free Korean peninsula. South Korea's leadership role in the Korean Peninsula Energy Development Organization and the construction of the light-water reactors in North Korea augur well for Seoul continuing to play a constructive role in the process. Reopening dialogue with the North by striving to reactivate the North-South joint commissions on economic, military, social, and nuclear affairs would surely win it global praise and could restore progress to the North-South dialogue.

Notes

1. Roh Tae Woo, "Three Points Principles of Unification, August 15, 1989," *Korea and World Affairs* (Fall 1989):576–579.

2. Winston Lord, Assistant Secretary for East Asian and Pacific Affairs, "Address to the Korea-US 21st Century Council," Washington, D.C., February 8, 1996.

3. *White Paper on South-North Dialogue in Korea* (Seoul: National Unification Board, 1988), pp. 175–217.

4. Ibid., p. 216.

5. Kim Il Sung, "1988 New Year's Address," *Foreign Broadcast Information Service, East Asia* (*FBIS, EAS*), January 4, 1988, p. 10.

6. For one of the most balanced and thorough general discussions of this issue, see U.S. Institute of Peace, "North Korea's Nuclear Program: Challenge and Opportunity for American Policy," Spring 1994.

7. John H. Cushman, *Military Options in Korea's Enigma* (Berkeley: Nautilus Institute, 1994).

8. For a critical discussion of the more important agreements involving the North Korean nuclear issue before the conclusion of the 1994 Agreed Framework, see Larry Niksch, *North Korean Nuclear Controversy: Defining Treaties, Agreements, and Terms* (Washington, D.C.: Library of Congress, Congressional Research Service, September 16, 1994).

9. *U.S. Department of State Dispatch* 2, no. 39 (1992):1–4.

10. Roh Tae Woo, "Declaration of Non-nuclear Korean Peninsula Peace Initiatives," Seoul, November 1991.

11. *FBIS, EAS,* December 18, 1991.

12. George Bush, "The US and Korea, Entering a New World," and "US–South Korean Relations" (excerpts from a news conference, Seoul, January 6, 1992), *U.S. Department of State Dispatch,* January 13, 1992, pp. 23–26.

13. State Department Press Briefing, March 12, 1992.

14. Statement, Office of the Spokesman, Department of State, March 15, 1993; also Secretary Christopher's Testimony to the House Foreign Affairs Committee, March 25, 1993; and Secretary Christopher's Testimony to the Senate Foreign Relations Committee, March 30, 1993.

15. State Department Press Briefing, March 19 and 24, and April 2, 1993.

16. State Department Staff, "Restrictions on Relations with North Korea," unclassified information memorandum, October 27, 1993.

17. State Department Press Briefing, April 7, 1993.

18. Department of State, Secretary Christopher's Testimony to Congressman Livingston, March 26, 1993.

19. State Department Press Briefing, March 17 and 18, 1993.

20. Ibid., March 19, 1993.

21. Ibid., March 17 and 19, 1993.

22. Ibid., April 1, 1993.

23. Ibid., April 2, 1993.

24. Ibid., April 1, 1993.

25. Ibid., April 14, 1993.

26. Ibid., April 30 and May 3, 1993.

27. Ibid., May 12, 1993.

PART 3

Nuclear and Security Issues

6

Nuclear Issues Between the United States and North Korea

Doug Bandow

The Cold War on the Korean peninsula, always dangerous, grew vastly more complicated during the late 1980s and early 1990s. For forty years the threat of war between the Koreas, though serious, had been limited. Neither of the Koreas possessed nuclear weapons; although Washington had stationed tactical warheads in the South, Pyongyang's nuclear-armed allies seemed unlikely to risk a nuclear confrontation with the United States.

But then North Korea appeared intent on acquiring a nuclear capability. The issue quickly surged to the fore of regional politics. Amid the threat of war came negotiations and an apparent settlement—providing for allied construction of two light-water reactors to replace Pyongyang's older, graphite facilities in return for a halt in a weapons program North Korea said did not exist. The crisis is "defused," in the words of Robert Manning of the Progressive Policy Institute, but not resolved.[1] Hardly a month goes by without a reminder that North Korea remains, if no longer quite an outlaw regime, still a highly bizarre and unpredictable one. Even the best case for the years ahead probably involves a continuing stream of obstructions, prevarications, and ultimatums from a government that believes international diplomacy is like dealing at a Middle East bazaar. Nevertheless, the United States has so far succeeded in buying what it most wanted: a cessation in the North's nuclear program. And there is no better option than to stay engaged and bargain even if the North again resorts to brinkmanship.

But the United States should not merely sit back and react to North Korean actions. To the contrary, Washington needs to look beyond the issue of nuclear proliferation and develop a policy to draw North Korea further out of isolation and into the sort of international cultural, economic, and political relationships that characterize most nations. Increasing Pyongyang's stake in regional peace and prosperity would encourage the North not only to fulfill the nuclear agreement but also to pursue genuine détente with its neighbors.

The North Korean Nuclear Program

North Korea began its nuclear effort in the mid-1950s and joined the International Atomic Energy Agency (IAEA) in 1974, giving it access to technical assistance for the peaceful use of nuclear energy. Over the years Pyongyang constructed a 5-MW and a 50-MW reactor and began building a 200-MW reactor. For all of the furor generated by the nuclear issue, we actually know very little about the North's activities. In 1989 satellite photos first revealed what appeared to be a nuclear reprocessing plant. The Democratic People's Republic of Korea (DPRK) program is centered at Yongbyon, sixty miles north of Pyongyang, but with some facilities, including a reactor and reprocessing plant, located elsewhere.[2] North Korea could have additional, secret operations. Defense analyst Joseph Bermudez has warned, "The problem is that you can't tell what's inside the buildings and what's underground."[3]

Naturally, the North denies the existence of any program. And experts have disagreed for years about the imminence of any weapon. Some analysts believe that North Korea may already possess one; most assume that it is at least a couple of years away from creating a deliverable bomb. Indeed, all we really know is that, based on its 1989 nuclear refueling, Pyongyang possesses sufficient plutonium to make one or possibly two weapons if it has the capability and will to do so.

The most fearsome aspect of Pyongyang's program is its construction of a 200-MW reactor. Once operational, it could generate enough fuel to make seven to ten bombs annually. This would allow the North to create either an expansive arsenal or an export product for would-be nuclear weapons powers.

International Soap Opera

The North's behavior has only fed concern about its intentions.[4] Although the DPRK signed the Treaty on the Non-Proliferation of Nuclear Weapons (NPT) in 1985, it took seven years to accept a safeguards agreement, a process that normally takes about eighteen months.[5] Since then the issue has taken on all of the attributes of an international soap opera, with the North acting like the bride who accepts a marriage proposal one day, only to act like the woman scorned the next.

For years the DPRK program received little attention. Then, in 1989, the Central Intelligence Agency (CIA) came to believe that the North had, for the first time, unloaded weapons-grade plutonium from its 50-MW reactor. In 1990 it tested bomb components, opened a plutonium processing plant, and inaugurated a new uranium processing plant. As calls for international inspections rose, North Korea denied that it had a program and resisted any oversight, rejecting a Japanese offer of recognition in return. When evidence of an atomic research complex seemed irrefutable, the issue loomed as the most important on the peninsula. Northern intransigence soon led to proposals for more than negotiations. Among the options discussed at the annual U.S.-ROK (Republic of Korea) security talks in November 1991 were economic sanctions and a naval blockade. More ominously, officials also began to discuss potential military remedies, which some called the "Israeli solution," named after the Israeli strike on Iraq's Osirak reactor in 1981.

The DPRK originally justified its refusal to allow IAEA inspections by citing the presence of U.S. tactical nuclear weapons in the South.[6] In October 1991, DPRK foreign minister Kim Yong-nam stated that inspections would be allowed "if such a nuclear threat is removed."[7] However, after Washington announced its intention to withdraw the bombs, Pyongyang quickly added new conditions. Then, in December 1991, the North concluded an agreement with South Korea providing for even more intrusive inspections than those typically carried on by the IAEA, which itself reached an accord with Pyongyang two months later. Hope of a real détente between the two bitter enemies blossomed.

Unfortunately, the two Koreas almost immediately deadlocked over implementation of their agreement. As is so often the case with North Korea, it is hard to separate genuine objections from implausible excuses. During my visit to Pyongyang in August 1992, DPRK officials complained that the South Koreans sought to include inspections of conventional military installations, a matter to be handled by a separate negotiating committee, but could not grant the DPRK the right to visit U.S. bases, which the North Koreans believed to be necessary because the United States had introduced nuclear weapons on the peninsula.

Nevertheless, the IAEA made its first inspection in May 1992 and by the end of the year had conducted six examinations of North Korean nuclear facilities. Although the IAEA was skeptical of some of Pyongyang's explanations, the North was surprisingly cooperative. In November 1992, Ronald Lehman, head of the U.S. Arms Control and Disarmament Agency, stated that international efforts had "stopped" the DPRK program and "blocked" its ability to amass "a sizable number of nuclear weapons over time."[8]

But in January 1993, North Korea refused the IAEA access to two suspected nuclear waste depositories, and tests showed that the North had lied about how much plutonium it had extracted.[9] Pyongyang tied its refusal to the ongoing Team Spirit military exercises in the ROK. When the IAEA made an unprecedented demand for a special inspection of the two sites, North Korea denounced the agency for allegedly fronting for the United States and announced that it was refusing to allow any further IAEA visits, withdrawing from the NPT (no other nation had ever done so), and abrogating the inspection agreement. The IAEA declared the North to be out of compliance and the international crisis flared again.

It remains unclear why the North acted when and how it did. Presumably, it feared that the IAEA inspectors would discover further evidence that it had lied about its production of plutonium; it may have also underestimated the intrusiveness and effectiveness of the IAEA. Or Pyongyang may have decided to test the new governments in both South Korea and the United States. Another possibility is that the regime decided it had received too few tangible benefits from its decision to forgo nuclear weapons, other than demands for yet more inspections. The joint U.S.-ROK military exercises, long a sore point with the North, may have triggered an internal political battle. Perhaps the decision reflected the perceived need by designated successor Kim Jong Il, reputedly in charge of the nuclear program, to demonstrate his commitment to the military. Or the regime may have simply decided the time was right to play the nuclear card yet again.

In any case, fears of a DPRK nuclear bomb rose to a fever pitch. The CIA warned that the North might have enough plutonium to develop a nuclear weapon. South Korea suspended economic activities in the North, and Japan backed away from discussions about improving relations with Pyongyang. Although the Clinton administration generally reacted with circumspection, as the IAEA's March 31 deadline approached, U.S. secretary of state Warren Christopher told a House of Representatives appropriations subcommittee: "There will be enforcement action taken within the U.N. Security Council."[10] Christopher focused on economic sanctions, though there was no guarantee that such measures would have much effect on North Korea's already isolated economy. This course was complicated by the fact that UN action requires the acquiescence of China—long the North's closest ally—which said that it would not penalize Pyongyang. Moreover, Pyongyang warned that sanctions could mean war.

Pyongyang's warnings did not, of course, bother advocates of military action. Joining a plethora of armchair warriors was House Defense Appropriations Subcommittee chairman John Murtha (D-Pa.), who called for destroying the North Korean facilities even though, he admitted, "there is no question we would have to be prepared to go to war."[11] Over time, Senator John McCain (R-Ariz.), former secretary of state Henry Kissinger, and many others argued for a similarly belligerent response.[12] More important, the administration refused to discount such a possibility. But the North "suspended" its withdrawal from the NPT and talks continued: The United States and South Korea agreed to defer their Team Spirit exercises to later in the year, and North Korea accepted restricted IAEA inspections to maintain the continuity of safeguards by replacing batteries and film in the North's nuclear facilities. Alas, the ensuing months were dominated by painful negotiations, broken agreements, recriminations, frustrated inspections, threats (from Washington as well as Pyongyang),[13] reports that the North had already constructed one or more bombs, and ultimately a breakdown in the IAEA monitoring process.

Again, a showdown seemed imminent as the Clinton administration began preparing the public for the worst. But this official jingoism went over far less well in South Korea and Japan than in the United States. As James Fallows of the *Atlantic Monthly* pointed out: "The closer you got to Ground Zero of the North Korea nuclear threat, the less panicked the mood became."[14]

Then came visits to Pyongyang by Selig Harrison of the Carnegie Council and former U.S. president Jimmy Carter, and Kim Il Sung's offer to freeze the North's nuclear program.[15] In return, the United States halted its campaign for sanctions. More negotiations followed, proving to be simultaneously tortuous and torturous. The U.S.-DPRK talks, though not the agreed-upon North-South summit, continued despite the death of Kim Il Sung on July 8, 1994. The result, signed on October 21, was the so-called Agreed Framework, which committed North Korea to remain within the NPT and freeze operations at its reactors and other facilities. The IAEA was to recommence inspections, including ad hoc visits to other sites. Pyongyang was to satisfy IAEA needs for access to sites to resolve discrepancies concerning the North Korean production of plutonium (i.e., the two waste disposal facilities) within five years, begin shipping abroad the eight thousand spent fuel rods now stored in cooling ponds within seven years, and dismantle its old nuclear plants within ten years. North Korea also promised to participate in bilateral talks with the South on economic and political relations and on the implementation of the 1991 North-South Joint Declaration on the Denuclearization of the Korean Peninsula.

In return, the United States—representing the Korean Peninsula Energy Development Organization (KEDO), to be largely funded by South Korea and Japan—was to provide the North with 500,000 tons of heavy oil annually to make up for its loss of electrical power, as well as two light-water reactors to replace the older gas graphite models under construction. Washington also promised not to use nuclear weapons against North Korea as long as the DPRK remained a member of the NPT, to eliminate economic sanctions against Pyongyang, and to move toward diplomatic relations.[16] The reactors alone could run $4 billion (though this estimate is based on the cost of building a comparable unit in South Korea), of which $2.8 billion was to come from the South, $800 million from Japan, and the rest from the United States and other nations.

The Agreed Framework was a compromise: In essence, it put to the side questions about the North's past activities in order to prevent the expansion of its atomic capabilities and create an environment in which regional relations could improve. The issue of inspection of the disputed sites would perhaps come to the fore later. Not surprisingly, the Agreed

Framework has come under sharp criticism, some of it hysterical. For instance, Frank Gaffney from the Center for Security Policy called it an act of "appeasement" ranking with Neville Chamberlain's abandonment of Czechoslovakia in 1938.[17] U.S. Senate majority leader Robert Dole complained that the accord "shows it is always possible to get an agreement when you give enough away."[18] However, none of the many critics suggested any alternative—except for Gaffney, who had long wanted to send in the bombers and hope for the best—let alone a better alternative.

So far the agreement has held. The North has left its nuclear program in deep freeze, KEDO succeeded in its first round of negotiations, the initial load of equipment has been shipped from South to North (via a Chinese ship), and Washington and Pyongyang have discussed establishing a liaison relationship. Of course, North Korea has continued to make new demands.[19] But the process has not collapsed, as predicted by some. The DPRK even expressed its "regret" over the bloody incident resulting from a submarine running aground on the South Korean coast. As one U.S. diplomat told the *Washington Post,* "The baby's healthy, but also prone to a lot of infections."[20]

Alternative Hypotheses

Where do the United States and its East Asian allies go from here? One of the problems in developing policy toward the North is that there is an information vacuum. Very little is known about the North, its government, and the regime's decisionmaking processes. The lengthy transition following the death of Kim Il Sung only exacerbates the problem. It appears that Kim Jong Il is in charge and remains committed to the flexible policies approved by his father shortly before his death. But this is only an assumption, albeit a reasonable one.

What does Pyongyang really intend to do with its nuclear program? CIA director R. James Woolsey argued in early 1993 that "an obvious reason for the standoff is that North Korea has something significant to hide."[21] But this is not the only interpretation. To the contrary, there are at least five possible reasons for Pyongyang's nuclearized course. The first, and most threatening, is Woolsey's thesis, that the North has a nuclear development program under way *and* remains committed to building a bomb. In this scenario, Pyongyang balked at inspections in 1993 because it figured the IAEA would uncover its efforts, and the October 1994 agreement was a mere sham that has not really halted North Korea's program (or will soon be violated).

This is a reasonable hypothesis, but not one compelled by the facts. We actually know very little about the North Korean effort. Reports a U.S. Institute of Peace working group: "What all this adds up to is a nuclear program whose only purpose seems to be to produce weapons-grade plutonium but which, to date, may not have succeeded in producing substantial amounts of such plutonium or weaponized nuclear devices."[22] We do not even have evidence that the North has reprocessed its plutonium, let alone tested a weapon or created an effective delivery system.[23]

Thus, we should consider the other possibilities. For instance, North Korea may have had a nuclear program under way but decided in late 1991 to drop it in exchange for the expected benefits: diplomatic recognition by Japan and the United States, aid from South Korea and Japan, and investment from and trade with South Korea and the United States. In this way, suggests one analyst, the nuclear program (and the continuance of the armistice regime, which North Korea made an issue in 1995) may be viewed by Pyongyang "more as instruments to build ties to the U.S. than as goals in themselves."[24] In a move perhaps triggered by the Team Spirit exercises, however, more hard-line elements may have attacked, contending that all the North had received for its more conciliatory course were ever-escalating demands and that the regime should therefore "just say no" to more inspections. Some DPRK diplomats and officials have apparently suggested just such a policy struggle in conversations with Westerners.[25] This scenario differs significantly from the first in that it suggests that the North may intend to live up to the framework's conditions, though undoubtedly all the while attempting to squeeze ever more benefits out of Washington.

The third possibility is that a frustrated North has been sporadically playing the nuclear card, irrespective of the actual state of its program, in an attempt to wring more concessions from the United States, South Korea, and Japan. Since those nations have shown that nothing else gets their attention, the North may believe that it must revive the nuclear threat from time to time. That could account for the temporary dispute over ROK participation in the reactor project.

The fourth scenario is that North Korea's intransigence in 1993 reflected an effort by heir apparent Kim Jong Il to shore up his rather thin military credentials by proving that he would protect the defense establishment's and his nation's interests. His father's decision to negotiate a settlement cleared the way for a peaceful accord, and economic desperation as well as foreign concessions allowed the younger Kim to return to the NPT process in a strengthened political position.

Finally, the fifth possibility is that North Korea has little or no program but has brilliantly exploited the West's fears as part of a blackmail campaign. It would be risky to base policy on such an assumption, but it cannot be discounted entirely.

Unfortunately, it is impossible to know which of these explanations is accurate. The critical point, however, is that only the first scenario represents a serious problem to which there is no diplomatic solution. The other four are susceptible to negotiation, however hated that course may be for students of the "start bombing" school.

And even the worst case—that North Korea has or remains committed to building an atomic weapon—does not mean that the DPRK is intent on aggressive war. There are, of course, some who seem to see no difference between the North's possession of one or two nuclear weapons and a world in flames. Columnist Charles Krauthammer, for instance, said in mid-1994 that the administration's "appeasement" of Pyongyang had brought us to a "time of acute danger."[26] Of course, the United States' preference would be that the North not acquire nuclear weapons. The regime's prior behavior suggests that it is fully capable of using an atomic bomb, but one or two crude weapons with questionable deliverability would not dramatically change the peninsula's balance of power.[27] Moreover, the simple desire for a nuclear capability is not itself evidence that Pyongyang plans to develop one. Although Pyongyang's contentions may be self-serving, they cannot be dismissed out of hand. Observes the International Institute for Strategic Studies: "It can be argued that North Korea had good cause to embark on a nuclear weapons programme."[28]

Bitter Competition

Since their creation, the two Koreas have competed bitterly in the economic, military, and political arenas. In the early years Pyongyang held the advantage on almost all fronts. But the North's economic edge disappeared during the 1960s; in the following decade Seoul was outstripping its rival in the political realm as well. By the 1980s the game between the two was essentially over: The South was twice as populous, dramatically more prosperous, a serious player in international economic and technological markets, and one of the globe's leading trading nations. Only on the military side did Pyongyang retain a lead, one largely reflecting the fact that the United States' security guarantee made additional defense spending by the South unnecessary.

Today the gap between the two nations is even starker. The South possesses a gross national product estimated to be twenty times that of its Northern rival.[29] Although a sudden onslaught by the North's million-man military might succeed in capturing or destroying Seoul, which lies just thirty miles south of the border, even many South Korean analysts now discount the likelihood of a northern invasion.

Thus, the North's only potential edge is the development of a nuclear weapon. And, in fact, Pyongyang's original objective in pursuing a nuclear program might have been honestly defensive: Over the past two decades it has been steadily losing its military edge. Its decline has accelerated with the end of the Cold War, which resulted in the collapse of the Soviet Union and China's steady move toward the ROK. By the early 1990s, North Korea found itself at a particular disadvantage, given the presence of tactical U.S. nuclear weapons (since withdrawn) in the South and the defection of its allies. In short, in the DPRK view, there may be little to prevent an invasion backed by U.S. nuclear weapons other than continuing U.S. restraint.

Although, understandably, the United States views North Korean fears as paranoid, they are not completely irrational. After all, Washington explicitly threatened to use nuclear weapons to halt a North Korean invasion in 1950. Moreover, DPRK officials allegedly cited the potential U.S. threat when they sought Soviet assistance in 1963 to build a bomb.[30]

Indeed, in an already unsettling environment the North finds itself with a shrinking economy as it faces an adversary whose economic lead grows hourly. In time, Pyongyang's military capabilities are going to be severely degraded and its ability to defend itself, let alone threaten the South, will be concomitantly reduced. For this reason, concluded *Jane's Intelligence Review,* "nuclear weapons are also a relatively cheap form of deterrent and the cost of deterrence became an important consideration in the 1980s as the North Korean economy began to collapse. . . . North Korea is increasingly incapable of supporting its massive conventional forces. The logic of nuclear weapons as an ultimate deterrent has never been more clear."[31]

Under these circumstances, Kim Il Sung and Kim Jong Il may have come to view the atomic bomb as a means (perhaps the only means) of ensuring the regime's survival, whether against a military attack or more general political pressure. In fact, this is a more widely understood lesson than some might think. After the Gulf War, the chief of staff of India's military reportedly cautioned: "Never fight the U.S. without nuclear weapons."[32]

Along the way, North Korea undoubtedly has also recognized the potential political and economic value of a nuclear weapon. After all, only the threat of a DPRK bomb has caused Japan and the United States, in particular, to treat North Korea seriously. Development of a nuclear capacity would allow either international sales of the technology or a further shakedown of Western nations to prevent such sales. Observes Joseph Bermudez: "The nuclear arsenal is North Korea's only bargaining chip, and one it can be expected to continue to use both skillfully and effectively."[33]

None of this is to suggest that North Korea's possession of nuclear weapons would be a good thing, but it would also not likely be cataclysmic. It is for this reason that many South Koreans and Japanese view the possibility with so much greater equanimity than do many U.S. analysts. Thus, the United States should exercise care in the risks it runs in attempting to prevent the North from developing or possessing a nuclear weapon.

Most important, Washington should consider the regional context of what is much more than an abstract issue of nonproliferation: developing a strategy to promote simultaneously DPRK compliance with the Agreed Framework and détente with the South.[34] The first step would be for the U.S. Congress to continue appropriating the necessary funds for promised oil shipments; otherwise, the United States could be in default under the accord.[35] And despite future disputes sure to occur, the United States should continue to rely on diplomacy. Pyongyang may be exceedingly difficult to deal with, but it does appear to respond to positive incentives. The North's ratification of the safeguards agreement, acceptance of IAEA inspections, cancellation of its threatened withdrawal from the NPT, and agreement to the framework were all achieved diplomatically. Observes one group of experts: "While cause and effect are hard to assess with assurance, this pattern of behavior suggests that U.S. actions can have at least limited effect on the decisions of a North Korean leadership that may be uncertain about how to deal with its parlous condition."[36] And the pact does not depend on trust. Should the North reactivate its nuclear program or fail to allow IAEA inspections, the United States could cut off oil shipments, drop work on the light-water reactors, and stop the move to diplomatic recognition. The result would simply be to return to the mid-1994 status quo. That's not good, but it hardly suggests "appeasement" like the irrevocable remilitarization of the Rhineland or the dismemberment of Czechoslovakia, for instance.

Moreover, even the pact's severest critics have offered nothing better, because they have nothing to offer. The most important purpose of the Agreed Framework is to freeze in place the North's nuclear program. Before, North Korea appeared to be moving toward production of a bomb, and South Korea and its allies were moving toward a confrontation with the North and possibly China. Both of those processes have stopped. It is hard to imagine any policy other than engagement that is likely to moderate the North's actions. The alternatives—economic sanctions and military action—offer no guarantee of success, and they are far riskier.

To enhance fulfillment of the accord, Washington should continue the process of establishing diplomatic ties with the North, allowing investment and trade, and offering modest amounts of humanitarian food shipments.[37] This would provide the North Koreans with a continuing, positive reason to remain in the process. Is that a "concession"? Of course, but it is a minimal one, and it would offer some small benefits to the United States as well: access to DPRK mineral exports, for instance, and a larger window into the secretive "hermit kingdom." At any rate, other nuclear states, such as Kazakhstan and Ukraine, received aid tied to their compliance with the NPT, and the North has agreed to do more than usual through the planned IAEA special inspections (never carried out elsewhere) and the separate nuclear agreement with Seoul.[38] Surely it is better to offer some cheap carrots to reduce the chance of a disagreement that might plunge the Korean peninsula and its more than sixty million people into war.

South Korea's role is equally significant. Although Pyongyang's recalcitrant reputation is well earned, Seoul has also at times impeded meaningful dialogue. Thus, suggests Robert Manning, Seoul must choose "whether it is retribution or conciliation that is ultimately in the best interest of the Korean people."[39] However tempting the former course, the latter is more likely to lead to the sort of "soft landing" that most South Koreans believe to be in their interest. And this probably requires a relaxed attitude toward aid to, investment in, and trade with the North.[40]

More significant, the diplomatic option should include a commitment to three-way talks to implement the two Koreas' independent nuclear inspection agreement signed in late 1991.[41] South Korean and U.S. officials argue that such talks would allow the North to divide the allies, but Pyongyang has little leverage to promote a split; in any case, Washington and Seoul should not paper over the gap when they find that their interests diverge. Another complaint is that the talks would be yielding to Northern extortion, but negotiations are a cheap price to pay for attempting to both avoid war and denuclearize the peninsula. The ultimate objective in such talks should be a willingness by all sides to allow investigation of any suspected facility, though the initial inspections could be more modest; for instance, Washington could offer to open several U.S. bases where it once deployed nuclear weapons in return for IAEA access to the two North Korean waste facilities and South Korean perusal of Yongbyon. Additional bases and facilities could be opened for view over time.

The United States should also offer to help jump-start talks between North and South through a joint military committee in order to promote inspections of conventional facilities. As part of that process, the United States and South Korea should announce a permanent cancellation of joint exercises, a phased withdrawal of Washington's thirty-seven thousand soldiers, and a willingness to pledge no-first-use (by the United States) of nuclear weapons[42] and replace the armistice with a peace treaty. The two nations should then invite the North to respond by entering into three-way talks, demobilizing some of its forces, and pulling them back from their advanced, threatening positions on the border. A variety of confidence-building measures are possible. If Pyongyang refused to respond positively, the South could undertake whatever military buildup it deemed necessary. With its enormous economic, political, and technological edge, South Korea is fully capable of defending itself. (Broader talks involving China and even Japan and Russia might also prove fruitful, but only if they were not intended to result in a new, extended U.S. security guarantee for the peninsula.)

The basic objective is to convince the North that it will gain more by staying within the process. Observes Kim Kyong-won, president of the Institute of Social Sciences: "While we cannot count on the Pyongyang leadership's conscience, we can assume that it will not act against what it considers its own best interests."[43]

The Risks of Coercive Nonproliferation

If the Agreed Framework survives, the crisis will be defused and détente may flourish on the Korean peninsula. But what if Pyongyang threatens to restart its nuclear effort?

The West should nevertheless avoid taking precipitous action and look for evidence as to why the North acted as it did—essentially to decide whether the Kim Jong Il regime is irrevocably committed to the acquisition of nuclear weapons or is opening yet another negotiating round. As long as it might be the latter case, in which negotiation could prove fruitful, Washington should pursue the diplomatic option.

Even if the former conclusion seems more likely, however, restraint would remain a virtue, especially if Pyongyang did not appear to be attempting to construct a large arsenal. In the long term, North Korea is likely to find a nuclear capability to be more useful in guaranteeing the survival of the North Korean state and as political leverage than as an offensive weapon for use against the South, especially as economic ties between Seoul and China, Pyongyang's closest friend, increase.

The prospect of a North Korean bomb would be an unpleasant example of proliferation, certainly, but not unprecedented. After all, in the early 1960s Washington faced the likelihood of Maoist China—secretive and factious, unpredictable and irrational, belligerent and threatening—gaining nuclear weapons. The Johnson administration seriously debated preemption, a step advocated publicly by some politicians and journalists. For instance, in 1968 James Buckley, the soon-to-be-elected conservative candidate for the U.S. Senate, argued that bombing China's nuclear facilities would "have been a prudent" idea because it would have eliminated "an atomic capability which is now increasingly threatening."[44] Three years earlier, the *National Review,* edited by his brother, William F. Buckley, Jr., had observed: "There is something to do, now. We can destroy—destroy literally, physically—the present Chinese nuclear capability, and thereby guarantee, since their underlying industrial recovery power is meager, that they cannot become a nuclear power for a good many years ahead."[45] Cooler heads prevailed, almost certainly for the best. It seems that nothing has changed, however. William F. Buckley, Jr., wrote in 1993: "That we are obliged to abort the nuclear bomb is axiomatic."[46] But the potential of a North Korean nuclear bomb no more warrants war than did the potential of a Chinese bomb.

Economic sanctions would be little better. Trade restrictions have demonstrated only limited efficacy throughout history. Sanctions against outlaw regimes, like Iran and Libya, have generally proved to be least successful. North Korea is poor, vulnerable, and alone, and its economy is probably already the most isolated on earth. Whether the additional pressure would be sufficient to force compliance is unknowable.

The threat of hardship alone is not likely to be enough. The Kim regime has long survived with very little; presumably, it can survive with less for at least some time. And it will not even have to do with less if sanctions do not gain the support of Iran, a major oil supplier already operating under a U.S. embargo, and China, which supplies Pyongyang with both food and oil and could veto any UN measure. Even if Beijing allowed sanctions to take effect—perhaps with a promise from the United States to drop pressure on human rights and from Seoul to increase investment—it would also have to be willing and able to suppress the widespread yet informal border trade between Koreans and neighboring Chinese of Korean heritage.

Similarly, Japan, home to some 800,000 residents of Korean descent—about 250,000 of whom are active in the pro–North Korean Chosen Soren (Choch'ongnyon)—would have to end trade and financial transfers worth as much as $4 billion annually. Particularly hard to stop would be money, much of it transported in cash, provided by the seven thousand Korean-Japanese who visit North Korea every year.[47] Enforcing UN sanctions, as well as allowing Washington to use Japanese bases to enforce an embargo, would raise complicated political questions for the Japanese government, especially for one backed by the Socialist Party, which has traditionally maintained close ties with the North.[48] Moreover, Tokyo, shaken by the 1995 gas attack in its subway, also fears that its enforcement of sanctions might touch off terrorism by pro-Pyongyang Korean-Japanese.

Ironically, sanctions also have the potential to work too well. If China and Japan seriously enforced an embargo and the United States interdicted Iranian oil shipments, the policy would significantly increase the pressure on the North. The DPRK might simply implode, a possibility that scares South Koreans, especially since the regime in Pyongyang could choose to strike out rather than surrender. Consider recent history: Although obviously complex, Japan's decision for war against the United States in 1941 was triggered in part by sanctions against the sale of petroleum and other critical products, as well as the freezing of Japanese assets. In particular, the Japanese military feared that sanctions would degrade its ability to fight.[49] Thus, Tokyo took what many officials even then recognized to be a wild gamble, but they viewed the risk as preferable to succumbing to U.S. economic pressure.

Although Communist North Korea differs substantially from imperial Japan, the former is paranoid, possesses an oversize military, and could see sanctions as threatening its ability to act as a nation and even to defend itself. Pyongyang might therefore choose to react in a similar way. In fact, the North warned both the United States and Japan that sanctions would be considered a "declaration of war" and that "sanctions mean outright war"; Pyongyang also informed Japan that it "would be unable to evade a deserving punishment."[50]

Proposals to destroy the DPRK nuclear facilities are even more foolhardy. What makes such saber rattling so disturbing is that military action is likely to be neither effective nor safe. First, destruction of the North's reactors could lead to radioactive releases over China, Japan, Russia, and South Korea. Second, it is not clear that such a strike would obliterate the North's nuclear program, especially if there are underground nuclear sites. The only other option would be to use nuclear weapons, as advocated by Mark Helprin of the Hudson Institute, though perhaps by no one else.[51] Yet an unsuccessful strike, nuclear or non-nuclear, would actually encourage the regime to persevere—rebuilding its reactors, if necessary, as did Iraq after Israel's 1981 raid on the Osirak reactor—because such a raid would prove that *only an atomic bomb would allow the North to effectively defend itself.* Third, though proponents of military action may be right in believing both that Washington and Seoul could successfully eliminate unknown facilities at unknown locations and that Pyongyang would quietly acquiesce to such a devastating and very public international humiliation, the odds are against such a result. At a minimum, the North would likely restart its terror campaign, apparently dormant since 1987, which once blew airline passengers out of the sky and massacred South Korean cabinet members. This time, however, U.S. citizens would almost certainly become targets.

Far worse is the possible ignition of what remains perhaps the world's most dangerous flashpoint: the 1.5 million soldiers, almost as many as once manned the 4,600-mile China-USSR border, who currently sit astride the 155-mile Demilitarized Zone (DMZ) within a short drive of Seoul, with its population of 16 million people. An attack could easily goad Pyongyang, long considered one of the least predictable and most threatening regimes on earth, into launching a full-scale invasion of the South. The consequences of a new war would be ruinous to all concerned, despite the prospect of ultimate victory for the South and its allies.

Of course, given the cost of war to the North, any rational calculation by its leadership would result in restraint. In fact, this particular assessment has kept the peace for the past forty years. But air strikes by the United States or a commando operation by the South would be an act of war that Kim Jong Il could not easily ignore, even if he is committed to maintaining an opening to the West, as suggested by recently released tapes of his conversations with two defectors.[52] It would prove particularly difficult for Kim Jong Il to face down the military if it has gained influence since the death of Kim Il Sung, as theorized by some.[53] Indeed, the ruling elite might decide that if the United States and South Korea appear to be dedicated to the regime's destruction, then it would be better to have war now rather than later, when the North would be weaker and the South stronger.

In the end, patience is a virtue. It worked with the Chinese nuclear program and with the Soviet empire, and it has so far worked with North Korea. Instead of moving to coercion, Washington should seek to generate a new package of carrots and sticks while limiting the amount of public pressure, which may very well encourage the status-conscious North Koreans to be more recalcitrant. Time is against North Korea. The longer Washington is able to keep Pyongyang talking, the greater the chance that internal changes in the DPRK will alleviate the problem.

Thus, if Pyongyang appears ready to abandon the Agreed Framework, the United States should emphasize that stronger diplomatic and cultural relations, growing trade, and increased participation in international organizations all depend on resolving the nuclear issue. Similarly, South Korea, too, should emphasize that investment and trade, emergency assistance, and improved relations are all predicated on Pyongyang fulfilling the Agreed Framework. (This argument would, of course, be more credible if contacts had been increasing.)

Washington and South Korea should continue to work with other regional powers, particularly China, though relations between Washington and China are currently strained. To increase Chinese willingness to cooperate, Washington might point to the risk of North Korean and possibly South Korean bombs leading to a Japanese bomb, something Beijing, which has opposed virtually any Japanese rearmament, surely would not welcome.

Japan is also an important player. The North wants diplomatic recognition from and trade with Tokyo, as well as reparations for Japan's colonial misrule earlier this century. South Korean analyst Kim Kuk-chin even argues that "Japan is the only real option" as leverage with the North.[54] Although he probably overstates the case—the South's contacts with Pyongyang have been growing (South Korea, not Japan, ended up providing rice to North Korea, for instance)—only Tokyo seems a likely source of large-scale financial transfers.

As part of this process, the United States should encourage the regional powers, who have most at stake in a nuclear-free peninsula, to take the lead in negotiations with North Korea. Self-aggrandizement tends to be a U.S. weakness: Officials in both Seoul and Tokyo state that they felt they were informed, rather than consulted, about the Agreed Framework negotiations and were simply handed a bill at the end.[55]

Further, Washington should be prepared to brandish the "stick" of a regional nuclear arms race. If Pyongyang moves ahead to develop an atomic bomb, it will be because Kim Jong Il believes that his nation or his political dynasty, or both, will be more secure as a result. Washington might help disabuse him of that notion by warning the North that if it develops a nuclear capability, the United States will no longer discourage the South, which under U.S. pressure dropped its program in the mid-1970s, from acquiring a countervailing weapon. Indeed, if necessary, the United States could threaten to provide the South with a small nuclear inventory, sufficient to cancel the North's advantage, in addition to whatever antimissile technology is available.[56] Washington should also point out that Japan would likely follow suit. Thus, North Korea would end up less, rather than more, secure. Obviously, such a spread of weapons would be undesirable, but it might be the lesser of evils. Still, such a threat, communicated privately, might make such a decision unnecessary.

What If?

What of the U.S. presence in the South if the North still refused to eschew nuclear weapons? Under no circumstances should Washington begin a conventional buildup, as proposed by policymakers and analysts who want to use the nuclear controversy as an excuse for increasing U.S. troop presence. Senator McCain, for instance, proposed a "Desert Shield" sort of buildup in summer 1994. This step is unnecessary, given the South's ability to supplement its own defenses. Richard Fisher of the Heritage Foundation declared, "South Korea must be defended."[57] This is certainly true. But why not let it be defended by the South Koreans? A U.S. buildup would be dangerous because it might convince Pyongyang that war was coming— that the new Desert Shield was about to be followed by a new Desert Storm. The Gulf War may very well have taught the North that its only hope in a conflict would be to attack before Washington is ready. As one U.S. official puts it: "Don't let the Americans build up their forces; don't let them put in air power; don't let them take the initiative; don't let them fight a war with low U.S. casualties."[58] If North Korea comes to view a conflict as inevitable, it is likely to strike preemptively.

What, then, to do if the North forges ahead with its nuclear program? The United States should not retain, let alone strengthen, nuclear guarantees to Korea and Japan and possibly to other nations in the region.[59] The United States' past conventional intervention on behalf of tangential interests—as in Vietnam, for instance—proved costly, but the risks from the fighting that would accompany a nuclear contest between U.S. allies and their antagonists is far worse.

Already Washington finds itself dangerously entangled in the affairs of India and Pakistan, which have fought conventional wars against each other and possess at least threshold nuclear capabilities.[60] Moreover, Washington now risks involvement on Russia's doorstep through its pressure on Ukraine to dismantle Kiev's nuclear arsenal (inherited from the USSR). When asked if the United States was ensuring Ukraine's borders, Secretary of State Christopher stated: "The security guarantees do relate to that subject and provide assurance in that connection."[61] These connections are dangerous enough. There is no reason for the United States to risk nuclear exposure in East Asia as well.

South Korea, understandably, would be reluctant to sit atomically naked if it had no U.S. umbrella while the North possessed the bomb; Japan and even Taiwan would also have cause for concern. The possibility of proliferation involving these powers would be unpleasant, to be sure, but not necessarily catastrophic, because it would increase the price of aggression by any regional power.

In any case, for a variety of reasons, an increasing number of nations are likely to acquire atomic weapons in the years ahead, despite the NPT. In fact, both South Korea and Japan may very well decide in time that their national interests require acquisition of nuclear weapons irrespective of the present U.S. guarantee, especially if they begin to doubt Washington's willingness to risk nuclear retaliation and terrorism to defend distant allies that lie next door to the major, nuclear-armed powers of China and Russia.[62]

Moreover, for purposes of negotiation, the threat that Seoul and Tokyo might acquire nuclear weapons would probably have a far greater deterrent impact on the North than would the threat of a permanent extension of the U.S. nuclear umbrella. Not only will the credibility of the U.S. commitment decline as Washington withdraws or reduces its military forces abroad, which is inevitable, but any continuing U.S. nuclear presence in the region, however limited, will encourage Pyongyang to create its own countervailing weapon. North Korea needs to be convinced that acquisition of an atomic bomb would leave it less, rather than more, secure. Even Kim Jong Il might pause at the prospect of both South Korea and Japan developing their own nuclear forces.

Outside of the particular consequences of proliferation in East Asia, some observers fear the broader impact on the nonproliferation regime. Yet proliferation occurs on a case-by-case basis, and in the coming years, the United States is likely to face a number of challenges to its preference for nonproliferation. Many analysts seem to be proposing coercive nonproliferation, particularly through the use of military force, but the problems of such a course are manifold, ranging from the difficulty of destroying the most important sites to the danger of radioactive leaks to nearby states and local civilian populations, the threat of terrorist retaliation, and significant political difficulties in mounting Osirak-type operations. The case of North Korea presents all of these problems, as well as the possibility of full-scale war.[63]

As a result, it would be better to examine how the United States can best adjust to a world in which nuclear weapons do proliferate. That does not mean that there is no value in attempting to stop some states from acquiring nuclear weapons or to slow other nations' programs. But

Washington should replace today's all-or-nothing approach—the United States either prevents a state from acquiring weapons, by war if necessary, or extends its nuclear umbrella—with a mixture of strategies, including development of antimissile technologies,[64] expansion of anti-aircraft capabilities, maintenance of a sufficient U.S. nuclear deterrent, and judicious provision of deterrent forces to friendly states. Observes the Cato Institute's Ted Galen Carpenter: "Without the threat posed by a would-be hegemon, it is difficult to imagine what interest could be important enough for the United States to risk the consequences of a nuclear war to defend NATO member Turkey from a nuclear-armed Iran or to defend South Korea from a nuclearized North Korea."[65]

Conclusion

With the demise of the USSR, Pyongyang is left as perhaps the most unstable and potentially threatening actor on the world stage. The possibility of North Korea acquiring nuclear weapons rightly unsettles not only its neighbors but also the United States. Nevertheless, the Agreed Framework appears to be working. Should it fail, there would be no imminent crisis, let alone one that justified turning the possibility of future conflict into the far greater likelihood of war today. Replacing an unpleasant Korean Cold War with a very hot war by launching a preemptive military strike against the North's nuclear facilities would be particularly foolish.

Instead, the United States and South Korea should continue to pursue diplomatic options to reinforce Pyongyang's apparent decision to forgo its nuclear course and to improve its relations with its neighbors. What if the North is firmly committed to acquiring an atomic bomb? There are no good options and plenty of bad ones, but this is also the case in Iran, Pakistan, and elsewhere around the globe. Despite the temptation to adopt a more vigorous—but ultimately more dangerous—course, all the United States may be able to do is choose a second-best plan of action. For four decades the United States' response to potentially threatening nuclear antagonists has been to pause rather than preempt. Such circumspection should remain the touchstone of policy today.

Notes

1. Robert Manning, "The US, ROK and North Korea: Anatomy of a Muddle," paper presented at conference on "Peace and Stability in Korea: Prospects and Pitfalls," Carnegie Council on Ethics and International Affairs, October 31, 1995, p. 1.
2. For a more detailed listing, see Ministry of National Defense, *Defense White Paper, 1994–1995* (Seoul: Ministry of National Defense, 1995), p. 6.

3. Quoted in John Fialka, "North Korean Nuclear Effort Tests U.S.," *Wall Street Journal,* November 14, 1991, p. A10.

4. Among the summaries of the painful process of negotiations, promises, inspections, denunciations, threats, and negotiations are Michael Mazarr, *North Korea and the Bomb: A Case Study in Nonproliferation* (New York: St. Martin's Press, 1995); William Berry, *North Korea's Nuclear Program: The Clinton Administration's Response* (Colorado Springs, Colo.: Institute for National Security Studies, 1995), pp. 2–31; Hakjoon Kim, "North Korea's Nuclear Development Program and the Future," in *US-Korean Relations at a Time of Change* (Seoul: Research Institute for National Unification, 1994), pp. 53–64; "Promises, Promises (While Building the Bomb)," *New York Times,* March 20, 1994, p. E4; Byung Chul Koh, "Confrontation and Cooperation on the Korean Peninsula: The Politics of Nuclear Nonproliferation," *Korean Journal of Defense Analysis* 6 (Winter 1994):53–83.

5. The IAEA monitoring process is described in F. R. Cleminson, "Ongoing Monitoring and Verification: Learning From the IAEA/UNSCOM Experience in Iraq," *Korean Journal of Defense Analysis* 7 (Summer 1995):129–154.

6. For years the United States refused to formally confirm the presence of such weapons, but it was generally believed that Washington maintained between 100 and 150 nuclear artillery shells and air-delivered bombs on South Korean soil.

7. Quoted in David Rosenbaum, "U.S. to Pull A-Bombs from South Korea," *New York Times,* October 20, 1991, p. 3.

8. Quoted in Don Oberdorfer, "North Korean A-Arms Danger Is Downgraded," *Washington Post,* November 1, 1992, p. A34.

9. Pyongyang went to great lengths to camouflage the two waste depositories in an unsuccessful attempt to fool the IAEA; see Nayan Chanda, "Bomb and Bombast," *Far Eastern Economic Review,* February 10, 1994, pp. 16–17.

10. Quoted in Warren Strobel, "North Korea Risks Sanctions, Christopher Warns," *Washington Times,* March 26, 1993, p. A7.

11. Quoted in "What to Do About North Korea's Nuclear Threat: Execute the 'Osirak' Remedy," Center for Policy Security, no. 93-D 20, March 19, 1993, p. 3.

12. See, e.g., Jack Anderson and Michael Binstein, "McCain's Korea Warning," *Washington Post,* May 29, 1994, p. C7; Frank Gaffney, "What to Do About North Korea's Nuclear Threat: Hold the 'Carrots,' Apply the 'Stick,'" speech to the American Enterprise Institute, November 2, 1993; Paul Greenberg, "Unhappy Precedent," *Washington Times,* March 19, 1993, p. F3; Henry Kissinger, "No Compromise, but a Rollback," *Washington Post,* July 6, 1994, p. A19; Charles Krauthammer, "North Korea's Coming Bomb," *Washington Post,* November 5, 1993, p. A27; William Safire, "Reactor Roulette," *New York Times,* June 2, 1994, p. A23; Brent Scowcroft, "Korea: Time for Action," *Washington Post,* June 15, 1994, p. A25; and Lally Weymouth, "North Korea and the Specter of War," *Washington Post,* April 6, 1994, p. A19.

13. For some of the president's remarks, such as threatening "the end of their country as they know it," see "Clinton's Warning Irks North Korea," *New York Times,* July 13, 1993, p. A6; and Berry, *North Korea's Nuclear Program,* pp. 13–14.

14. James Fallows, "The Panic Gap," *National Interest* (Winter 1994/1995):41.

15. Harrison describes his trip in "The North Korean Nuclear Crisis: From Stalemate to Breakthrough," *Arms Control Today* (November 1994):18–20. For a detailed discussion of the Carter mission, see Young Whan Kihl, "Confrontation or Compromise on the Korean Peninsula: The North Korean Nuclear Issue," *Korean Journal of Defense Analysis* 6 (Winter 1994):112–118.

16. "Agreed Framework Between the United States of America and the Democratic People's Republic of Korea," October 21, 1994; "Agreement on the Establishment of the Korean Peninsula Energy Development Organization," October 21, 1994; and "US-DPRK Framework Agreement Time Line for Implementation (Briefed to Foreign Embassies on 10/20/94)," October 20, 1994. All were provided by the U.S. Department of State.

17. Frank Gaffney, "Whistling Past Galluci Gulch," *Washington Times,* October 24, 1994, p. A20.

18. Office of Robert Dole, "North Korea," press release, October 19, 1994.

19. See, e.g., Steven Greenhouse, "North Korea Issues Threat over Reactor," *New York Times,* October 1, 1995, p. 9.

20. Quoted in R. Jeffrey Smith, "Year After Deal, U.S. and N. Korea Debating Details of Reactor Project," *Washington Post,* October 21, 1995, p. A26.

21. Quoted in Douglas Jehl, "U.S. Outlines Concern over North Korean A-Arms," *New York Times,* February 25, 1993, p. A7. The *Washington Post* goes even further, declaring that "the only explanation that makes sense . . . is that the latest inspections demanded by the International Atomic Energy Agency would have uncovered evidence of the bomb the North Koreans deny they're working on"; "Nuclear Cheat," March 25, 1993, p. A24. Similar is the *Wall Street Journal*'s opinion that "the only possible conclusion is the obvious one: North Korea wants to have nukes"; "North Korea's Bomb Threat," March 17, 1993, p. A14.

22. "North Korea's Nuclear Program: Challenge and Opportunity for American Policy," United States Institute of Peace, undated, p. 11. See also "North Korea Suspected of Hiding Plutonium," *Chemical & Engineering News,* April 11, 1994, p. 5.

23. Robert Manning, "Clinton and the Korea Question: A Strategy for the Endgame," Progressive Policy Institute Policy briefing paper, July 7, 1994, p. 4.

24. Manning, "Anatomy of a Muddle," p. 5. Manning believes that "Kim Il Sung made a strategic decision to pursue an opening to the U.S. sometime in 1990 or 1991" (p. 4).

25. Selig Harrison, "Breaking the Nuclear Impasse: How North Korea Views the Nuclear Problem," paper presented to symposium "The United States and North Korea: What Next?" Carnegie Endowment for International Peace, Washington D.C., November 16, 1993, pp. 4–8.

26. Charles Krauthammer, "Get Ready for War," *Washington Post,* June 3, 1994, p. A23.

27. Chung Min Lee, "The North Korean Nuclear Issue and the Korean-American Alliance," *Korean Journal of National Unification* 4 (1995):43.

28. International Institute for Strategic Studies, *Military Balance: 1993–1994* (London: Brassey's, 1993), p. 232.

29. All numbers involving the North are rough estimates, and work by Nicholas Eberstadt of the American Enterprise Institute shows a smaller gap between the two; Eberstadt, *Korea Approaches Reunification* (Armonk, N.Y.: M. E. Sharpe, 1995), p. 12. However, other analyses consistently show a larger difference. For example, Bank of Korea estimates the respective GNPs in 1995 to be $451.7 billion and $22.3 billion. And the gap continues to widen. Compare the International Institute for Strategic Studies, which figured the respective GDPs in 1994 to be $379.6 billion and $20.9 billion, with the National Unification Board and Bank of Korea, which estimated $328.7 billion and $20.5 billion for the respective GNPs in the same year. International Institute for International Studies, *The Military Balance: 1995/96* (Oxford: Oxford University Press, 1995), pp. 180, 178; Young Namkoong, "Assessment of the North Korean Economy: Status and

Prospects," in *US-Korean Relations at a Time of Change* (Seoul: Research Institute for National Unification, 1994), p. 26.

30. Harrison, "Breaking the Nuclear Impasse," p. 3.

31. Robert Hall and Ian Kemp, eds., "North Korea: The Final Act," *Jane's Intelligence Review*, Special Report No. 2 (1994):3.

32. Quoted in Haynes Johnson, "Lessons from the Gulf War," *Washington Post*, January 17, 1992.

33. Quoted in Edith Lederer, "Report: N. Korea Sees a Low-Cost Deterrent," *Philadelphia Inquirer*, March 22, 1994, p. 8. For one summary of reasons other than military aggression that the DPRK may have pursued the nuclear option, see H. Kim, "North Korea's Nuclear Development Program" pp. 64–75.

34. The United States and its allies do need a strategy. Robert Manning complains that the Clinton administration has operated largely without one, instead having "lurched from crisis-to-crisis"; Manning, "The US, ROK and North Korea," p. 3.

35. See Robert Manning and James Przystup, "North Korea: Who Is Minding the Store?" *Washington Times*, January 24, 1996, p. A19.

36. U.S. Institute of Peace, "North Korea's Nuclear Program," p. 14.

37. Analyst Scott Snyder writes of a "reconciliation policy"; Snyder, "A Framework for Achieving Reconciliation on the Korean Peninsula," *Asian Survey* 35 (August 1995):707.

38. Manning, "Clinton and the Korea Question," p. 6.

39. Manning, "The US, ROK and North Korea," p. 9.

40. An increasingly promising economic dialogue was essentially halted as the nuclear crisis burgeoned in 1993; see Shim Jae Hoon, "Dangerous Deadlock," *Far Eastern Economic Review*, June 22, 1995, p. 50; Jinwook Choi, "Inter-Korean Economic Cooperation: A Vital Element of Seoul's Unification Policy," *Korean Journal of National Unification* 4 (1995):133–150; *South Korea, North Korea: 1994–95* (London: Economist Intelligence Unit, 1994), pp. 5–7.

41. Various inspection options are covered by Seong Cheon, "North Korea's Nuclear Problem: Current State and Future Prospects," *Korean Journal of National Unification* 2 (1993):100–101.

42. The Agreed Framework includes a provision that appears to offer such a pledge, but its meaning is disputed by some; see, e.g., Seongwhun Cheon, "Some Problems of the US-DPRK Agreed Framework: A South Korean View," paper prepared for RINU-Cato Workshop, September 5, 1995, pp. 1–7.

43. Kim Kyung-won, "Need for a Realistic Approach to North Korea," *Korea Focus* 2, no. 4 (September/October 1994):10.

44. "Buckley's View on Bombing China," *New York Times*, October 26, 1968, p. 16.

45. "Should We Bomb Red China's Bomb?" *National Review*, January 12, 1965, p. 9.

46. William F. Buckley, Jr., "Meanwhile, Over in the East," *Washington Times*, June 11, 1993, p. F3.

47. Much of these funds come from Pachinko gambling shops and export-import firms, which dominate foreign investment in the North; see, e.g., Manning, "Economic Sanctions or Economic Incentives?" Paper presented to symposium "The United States and North Korea: What Next?" Carnegie Endowment for International Peace, Washington, D.C., November 16, 1933, pp. 7–8. However, there is substantial dispute over how much is at stake. Press reports usually run between $500 million and $1.8 billion, but other analysts are skeptical; see Marcus Noland, Chapter 2 of this volume.

48. See, e.g., David Sanger, "Tokyo Reluctant to Levy Sanctions on North Koreans," *New York Times,* June 9, 1994, pp. A1, A7; T. R. Reid, "Japan Weighs Own Embargo of North Korea," *Washington Post,* June 7, 1994, p. A13; David Sanger, "Japan Split over Role in a North Korea Showdown," *New York Times,* April 24, 1994, p. A3; and Willis Witter, "Japan Can Ease Effect of N. Korea Sanction," *Washington Times,* February 11, 1994, p. A18.

49. See, e.g., Robert Dallek, *Franklin D. Roosevelt and American Foreign Policy, 1932–1945* (New York: Oxford University Press, 1979), p. 302.

50. David Hamilton, "North Korea Threatens War Against Japan," *Wall Street Journal,* June 10, 1994, p. A6; Paul Shin, "N. Korea Repeats Threat of War over Sanctions by U.N.," *Washington Times,* June 7, 1994, p. A18; and Teruaki Ueno, "N. Korea Lashes Out at Sanctions," *Washington Post,* February 13, 1994, p. A18.

51. Mark Helprin, "My Brilliant Korea," *Wall Street Journal,* July 25, 1994, p. A14.

52. Kevin Sullivan, "All Eyes—and Ears—on N. Korea," *Washington Post,* October 27, 1995, pp. A27, A30.

53. Shim Jae Hoon, "Empty Driver's Seat," *Far Eastern Economic Review,* October 26, 1995. There has long been much speculation about splits in Pyongyang between moderates and hard-liners; see, e.g., Hyun In-taek and Masao Okonogi, "Security Cooperation in East Asia," *Korea Focus* 2, no. 4 (September/October 1994):53–54, and Yinhay Ahn, "Elite Politics and Policy Making in North Korea: A Policy Tendency Analysis," *Korean Journal of National Unification* 2 (1993):63–84. Although probably true, most North Korean "moderates" would likely look rather hard-line to anyone living in the democratic, capitalist West.

54. Quoted in Damon Darlin, "Roh's Nuclear-Free Pledge May Advance Effort to Inspect North Korean Facilities," *Wall Street Journal,* November 11, 1991, p. A10.

55. This sentiment was expressed by several officials during a trip to Seoul and Tokyo in July 1995.

56. The U.S. Defense Department is set to spend about $12 billion on theater missile defense between 1995 and 1999. South Korea first discussed participation in the Reagan administration's Strategic Defense Initiative a decade ago; concerns raised about the impact on relations with the Soviet Union obviously no longer apply; see, e.g., Kang Suk Rhee, "South Korea's Participation in the SDI," *Armed Forces and Society* 14 (Spring 1988):391–406.

57. Richard Fisher, "North Korea's Nuclear Threat: A Test for Bill Clinton," *Heritage Foundation,* no. 190 (March 23, 1993):3.

58. David Ignatius, "The Secret Korean Debate," *Washington Post,* June 12, 1994, p. C2.

59. Naturally, there are those who insist that the United States "must not weaken its remaining nuclear umbrella over South Korea"; see Taewoo Kim, "The United States and North Korea: A South Korean Perspective," paper presented to the Carnegie Endowment for International Peace Symposium, p. 10.

60. For a detailed analysis of the risks of the United States' alliance with Pakistan, see Ted Galen Carpenter, *A Search for Enemies: America's Alliances After the Cold War* (Washington, D.C.: Cato Institute, 1992), pp. 113–125.

61. Quoted in Doug Bandow, "Let 'Em Have Nukes," *New York Times Magazine,* November 13, 1994, p. 56.

62. The nuclear capabilities of China and Russia are discussed in Gerald Segal, "What Can We Do About Nuclear Forces in Northeast Asia?" *Korean Journal of Defense Analysis* 6 (Winter 1994):36–39. See also Gerald Segal, "China's Nuclear Posture for the 1980s," in Robert O'Neill, ed., *Security in East Asia* (New York: St. Martin's Press, 1984), pp. 70–77.

63. Ted Galen Carpenter, "A New Proliferation Policy," *National Interest* (Summer 1992):67–68.

64. This is a matter of some interest throughout East Asia; see Jae Kyu Park and Byung-joon Ahn, eds., *The Strategic Defense Initiative: Its Implications for Asia and the Pacific* (Boulder, Colo.: Westview Press, 1987). For an expression of Japanese interest, see Hisahiko Okazaki, "Thoughts on the North Korean Nuclear Issue," *Korean Journal of National Unification* (Special Edition, 1993):29.

65. Carpenter, "A New Proliferation Policy," pp. 70–71.

7

The Conventional Military Strength of North Korea: Implications for Inter-Korean Security

Edward A. Olsen

Assessing the conventional military strength of the Democratic People's Republic of Korea (DPRK) has been a key concern of the alliance between the United States and the Republic of Korea (ROK) for many years. Those U.S. and South Korean personnel who conduct war games regularly engage in exercises that seek to compare notes on their own and others' perceptions of North Korea's capabilities and intentions regarding conventional arms. Although a great deal of attention has been paid in the 1990s to North Korea's nuclear ambitions, virtually all analysts subscribe to the conventional wisdom about conventional arms, which holds that they remain North Korea's real threat to South Korea and the U.S. forces stationed there. In this chapter, I intend to go beyond a rehash of numerous order-of-battle type of analyses so as to build on them and seek some insights into the rationale behind North Korea's maintenance of major conventional forces.

North Korea is renowned, and in some circles infamous, as a military power, devoting about 30 percent of its budget to national defense. Relative to its population of 22 million (versus 44 million in South Korea) and its economy, estimated as of 1992 to be $23 billion in gross domestic product (versus $283 billion in South Korea), North Korea is certainly the most militarized society on earth. About 23 to 30 percent of its population (or 5 to 6.5 million people) are in either the Korean People's Army or a kind of national guard called the Workers-Peasants Red Militia.[1] These proportions amply justify the long-standing description of North Korea as a "garrison state."[2] I will outline what North Korea has acquired quantitatively with those expenditures and will then qualitatively assess North Korea's desire for such armed forces and what it may intend to do with them.

In the early 1990s, North Korea's nuclear ambitions and aspirations attracted enormous international attention.[3] This chapter assesses the conventional armed strength of the DPRK, examines its meaning for the durability of Kim Jong Il's successor regime, and evaluates the implications of those forces for the future of inter-Korean security. For present purposes, "conventional" is interpreted in an unorthodox fashion as "non-nuclear" and therefore incorporates a range of threat perceptions normally considered to be "unconventional" forms of preparation for conflict.

Conventional Forces of North and South Korea

Using two solely unclassified, but credible, descriptions of DPRK contemporary armed forces, Table 7.1 compares the conventional forces of North and South Korea as of 1995–1996. Although the Ministry of National Defense and International Institute for Strategic Studies (IISS) numbers for the DPRK forces differ slightly, the important features are that they both greatly exceed the numbers for the ROK and that both sets of numbers are disproportionately large for a state with North Korea's population and economy. As strategists routinely concede, such numbers can be misleading because of the qualitative advantages South Korea enjoys in terms of technological sophistication. Because of South Korea's economic advantages, Seoul is much better positioned to create and pay for more advanced

Table 7.1   Comparison of ROK and DPRK Armed Forces

	ROK[a]	DPRK[a]	DPRK[b]
Personnel			
Army	540,000	910,000	1,000,000
Navy	60,000	46,000	46,000
Air force	55,000	84,000	82,000
Total	655,000	1,040,000	1,128,000
Ground forces			
Corps	11	19	16
Divisions	50	53	49
Brigades	21	99	n.a.
Ground equipment			
Tanks	2,050	3,800	3,700
Armored vehicles	2,200	2,500	3,000
Field artillery	4,650	10,850	9,080
Naval forces			
Combatants	180	434	390
Support vessels	60	320	n.a.
Submarines	2	26	25
Air force			
Tactical aircraft	520	850	770
Support aircraft	160	500	485
Helicopters	630	290	340

Notes: a. *Defense White Paper 1995–1996* (Seoul: Ministry of National Defense, 1996).
b. *The Military Balance, 1994–1995* (London: International Institute for Strategic Studies, 1995), pp. 178–179.

equipment than Pyongyang can provide and sustain. South Korea also benefits enormously from access to U.S. military technology and strategic and
logistical support in ways that North Korea today largely lacks. The North's
former support network with the Soviet Union and the People's Republic of
China has virtually evaporated.

Furthermore, those qualitative factors are magnified by the further
"force multiplier" impact the U.S.-ROK alliance supplies to South Korea in
the form of extended deterrence provided by the world's only superpower.
As if these factors were not sufficient, South Korea also enjoys the old-
fashioned—but still valid—geopolitical and tactical advantages that accrue
to forces on the defensive in inhospitable mountainous terrain. Put another
way, North Korea's numerical advantages do not loom so large when they
are presumed to be for offensive purposes. North Korea's numerical advantages do look impressive on paper, but many mitigating strategic factors
strongly suggest that North Korea's conventional forces and their weapons
systems are not enough to prevail over South Korea.[4]

Beyond such data, there are other facets of North Korea's non-nuclear
capabilities. As past data from the IISS note, that imbalanced proportion is
not new. Moreover, there have been repeated warnings in South Korea and
the United States about intensified North Korean conventional arms
buildups.[5] These continued in 1995 and into early 1996, but they have not
provoked undue anxiety on the part of responsible officials in the U.S.-
ROK alliance.[6] Although the latest reports from the Ministry of National
Defense and the IISS indicate that about 65 percent of DPRK ground forces
and 40 percent of its air forces are forward deployed near the Demilitarized
Zone (DMZ) in an apparently aggressive posture, this is not really new
either.[7] One important aspect of the Ministry of National Defense assessment of the DPRK military buildup is that the North increased its defense
budget by $5.7 billion in fiscal year 1994[8] at a time when its economy was
widely considered to be strapped and its geopolitical network shattered by
the end of the Cold War. This latest version of a North Korean conventional
buildup (along with Pyongyang's diplomatic use of its nuclear option) may
well be a response to the lesson Pyongyang presumably learned from wit-
nessing the display of U.S. military power during the Gulf War.[9]

One cannot be certain precisely as to what lessons North Korean leaders learned from the Gulf War. Moreover, any lessons learned were almost
certainly filtered through the framework of permanent lessons they learned
the hard way during the Korean War, which remains North Korea's key
strategic paradigm. Nonetheless, it is likely that DPRK leaders were atten-
tive observers of the Gulf War. Although North Korea's strategic and tactical situation does not leave the country as exposed as Iraq was and North
Korean military forces are probably better prepared today than the Iraqi
forces were then, neither factor can be very reassuring to North Koreans as
they contemplate testing their abilities against the kind of power demon-

strated to the world via CNN by the United States in the Gulf War. One suspects that the confidence obviously gained by the South Korean allies is mirrored by a lack of military self-assurance in North Korea. It is probably not a coincidence that significant North Korean diplomatic overtures toward the United States, albeit clumsy and stilted, commenced in the wake of the Gulf War.

Pyongyang displayed a renewed appreciation for the ability of the United States to enforce its will militarily. Against this background, the DPRK conventional forces are much less credible for assault purposes and, since there is little prospect of DPRK forces having to defend against a U.S.-ROK attack, they seem useful mainly for deterrence and for domestic control. These subjective factors are crucial in the Korean military balance of power because they provide a context for North Korea's diplomatic and psychological use of its armed forces. The objective elements of North Korea's non-nuclear capabilities are formidable, but Pyongyang's subjective intentions—a critical factor for the political future of the Kim Jong Il regime and for strategic stability on the Korean peninsula—remain uncertain.

ROK and U.S. defense officials must rely on worst-case assumptions and base their defensive preparations accordingly. They have to keep one eye on capabilities and the other on the conditions that could compel North Korea to risk using its forces. With North Korea's presently constrained nuclear potential very much in mind, these planning scenarios must include preparations for coping with North Korea's presumed missile capabilities. According to an open literature source, North Korea's Scud C (500-kilometer range) can reach all of Korea; its Nodong 1 (1,300-kilometer range) can reach all of Japan and most of eastern China; its Taep'odong 1 (2,000-kilometer range), which is in development, could reach even more of China; and its Taep'odong 2 (3,500-kilometer range), due in the early twenty-first century, could reach virtually all of China and most of Southeast Asia.[10] These capabilities may induce North Koreans to believe that their strategic reach might permit them to check the aspirations of the United States and South Korea—as perceived in Pyongyang. Consequently, U.S.-ROK alliance leaders must also be wary of misreading North Korea's intentions because Pyongyang may well feel that the daunting combined power of South Korea and the United States—which is also forward deployed and includes openly discussed intentions of a counterattack against Pyongyang[11]—constitutes a genuine threat to its interests in an era of economic and strategic stress.

There are other aspects of North Korea's non-nuclear military offensive positioning that are seen as a threat by ROK-U.S. allies but which may also have defensive qualities. North Korea is widely and fairly deemed a terrorist state that engages in the export of terrorism, recklessly sells arms (including missiles) that escalate tensions in diverse regions, and trains revolutionary Third World groups.[12] Although undoubtedly dangerous and destabilizing, these activities also constitute a form of forward-deployed activity predicated on the notion that the best defense is a good offense. This does not justify what North Korea has done, but it may explain it. The same can be said for unconventional activities within the confines of the Korean peninsula: North Korea's tunnel building;[13] its almost farcical exercise in strategic dam building in the 1980s at Kumgang Mountain, supposedly to inflict a flood on Seoul (which was to be countered by a purported "Peace Dam" designed to intercept the water assault until it was called off)—a vivid example of mutual infliction of a strategic disinformation hoax;[14] and its repeated efforts at espionage designed to topple the government in Seoul.[15] These activities could each be aimed at gaining a military advantage, but they could also be valuable primarily as a kind of psychological warfare.

This context of strategic game playing was reinforced in 1995 by developments in the North that—coming in the wake of seeming progress on the nuclear negotiations front—were a cause of renewed anxiety. Despite expectations that North Korea would not want to damage its prospects for improved relations with the United States and Japan by doing anything reckless vis-à-vis South Korea, several cross-border incursions occurred.[16] Almost certainly these were designed primarily to keep the U.S.-ROK allies off balance and secondarily to strike at targets of opportunity. Although dangerous business, these incidents probably are not precursors of expanded conflict. Somewhat similar were North Korea's attempts to change the way the Military Armistice Commission and the Neutral Nations Supervisory Commission had regulated the truce that halted the Korean War. These efforts were clearly designed to alter the dynamics between the United States and the two Koreas at Panmunjom in ways that might reduce South Korea's influence on the United States.[17] Such meddling helps keep the U.S.-ROK alliance off balance and, from Pyongyang's perspective, could lead to more direct military-to-military contacts with the United States. In addition to indicating that North Korea's conventional deterrence requires shoring up by nonmilitary means, these incidents also raise possibilities for an expanded dialogue over the Korean balance of power.

Two other factors that have emerged in 1995–1997 are significant in conditioning the context in which North Korea's armed forces are perceived. The first concerns the role of the Korean People's Army (KPA) in North Korean society and the likelihood that it is gaining more influence than the Workers' Party of Korea (WPK). Both Seoul and Washington have openly acknowledged that this shift toward the KPA is occurring.[18] As the *Economist* noted, the shift is understandable given that "North Korea's massive military establishment constitutes an economy within an economy, with lucrative sidelines of its own—such as selling SCUDs to Syria and

Iran."[19] Although deciphering who's who in the North Korean pecking order is an even more arcane pseudoscience than yesteryear's Kremlinology, three senior KPA generals who seem close to Kim Jong Il and are prominent graduates of the Mangyongdae Revolutionary Institute—O Kuk-yol, Kim Tu-nam, and Kim Kang-hwan—have been described as a geopolitical troika near the apex of power. This may support the view that Kim Jong Il's relations with the KPA are sound despite his lack of military experience.[20]

That support system for Kim Jong Il was strengthened in the spring of 1997 by the defection of Hwang Chang-yop, a senior civilian ideologue, and the deaths of the defense minister, General Ch'oe Kwang, and his deputy, General Kim Kwang-jin. These events reinforced the transitions to a younger generation of leaders and to military leaders who owe their positions to Kim Jong Il. The KPA is not noted as a bastion of liberalism, and there are indications that Kim Jong Il might be tilting toward hard-liners amid a society replete with economic and agricultural problems and that he is concerned about signs of dissent in that Orwellian country.[21] For these reasons there are concerns—as one South Korean commentator put it—about "the emergence of a de facto quasi-military regime."[22]

Further militarization of North Korea is an ominous prospect, and it might prove to be an ill omen, but an increased societal role for the military does not necessarily translate into a more aggressive regime. After all, when the military seized power in South Korea, the result was greater discipline and a more pragmatic and technocratic approach to developmental issues. It is possible that North Korea could experience something similar at the hands of a military regime.

The Role of the Korean People's Army

The future societal role of the KPA warrants close attention. It is extraordinarily difficult today to gauge the actual internal clout of the army because any such measures—the morale and quality of training of the KPA, the ratio of key officers to the rank and file, the technological and organizational sophistication of the KPA, and its involvement in the civilian sector of the economy—are closely guarded state secrets in a society that tends to be paranoid about disclosure of sensitive facts. Although this secretiveness is at least partially designed to conceal North Korea's weaknesses, it also camouflages its strengths and assets.

The growth of the military as an institution in North Korea is significant in light of Korea's pre-twentieth-century tradition of civilian-dominated civil-military relations. South Korea's deviation from that norm seems to have been decisively reversed by the Kim Young Sam government. This stands in contrast to North Korea's continuation down the path toward militarization. This is not surprising for a country in which the military predates (by seven months) the founding of the state, but the same can be said of the United States and other countries with revolutionary origins.

Despite the reasons for South Korea's anxiety about North Korean militarization, one can also visualize a range of somewhat upbeat consequences. It could be a source of political stability in an otherwise shaky regime—permitting the KPA to act as the conscience of the regime and perpetuating Kimilsungism as the means for regime survival. It could foster a developmental model in North Korea that might resemble South Korea in the 1960s or today's Indonesia or Burma. It could emulate the People's Liberation Army (PLA) more explicitly than it already does implicitly, potentially a very positive step, given the PLA's cooption of capitalism. Or it could formulate an admittedly odd combination of all of the above, which might be described as a military regime in pursuit of market Leninism with Kim Il Sung characteristics.

Although the growing political role of the military remains a bit tenuous and may be a longer-term cause for concern, the second societal factor that has emerged in 1995–1997 to cause strategic anxiety threatens to have a shorter fruition period. The threat of a DPRK attack on the South has long been held in check by a sense that North Korea, for all its authoritarian excesses, was a stable regime. But with the end of the Cold War came apprehension that the loss of key allies could push North Korea into a geopolitical corner, causing it to strike out at the South in desperation. Using the silver lining in a dark cloud (i.e., the DPRK nuclear option) was a way for Pyongyang to transform a vulnerability into creative diplomatic leverage to prevent it from being cornered. In the midst of these diplomatic games, anxieties arose that North Korea's military hand could be forced by economic setbacks and stagnation, which would in turn threaten it with collapse.

Even as that danger persisted, a new and unexpected circumstance arose that threatened to corner North Korea: the much discussed dangers of serious famine.[23] Whether a cause of desperate military action against South Korea or of domestic turmoil that could provoke the dangers of collapse, these conditions may precipitate the kind of instability that those who express confidence in the stability of the military status quo cannot adequately factor into their calculations. This situation may pass without leading to a crisis, but it is the kind of uncertainty[24] that no strategist on the U.S.-ROK side relishes or can afford to discount.

Returning to the more narrowly defined military arena, the forms of non-nuclear arms capability that are least excusable in terms of this kind of gamesmanship are North Korea's endeavors in chemical and biological warfare[25] and its special forces.[26] Although possession of such forces fosters elements of deterrence on the part of South Korea and the United States, they are (like a nuclear capability) likely to engender severe threat perceptions. It is therefore difficult to account for such forces in terms of psychological warfare short of Pyongyang playing a very risky game in which it might hope that Seoul and Washington would perceive and understand the utility of calculated and intentional "irrationality," in which more powerful foes can be deterred by concerns over displays of creative belligerence and obstreperousness. Although fundamentally a cause of genuine concern among the ROK and U.S. defenders against North Korea, there are reasons to view these special-function conventional forces with a kind of perverse optimism.

Effectiveness of the Korean People's Army

The effectiveness of North Korea's non-nuclear forces vis-à-vis the U.S.-ROK allies has not been seriously tested for many years. Given the post–Cold War appraisals of the Soviet Union's armed forces, which suggest that the Western allies probably grossly exaggerated their effectiveness, it is tempting to explore similar appraisals of North Korean conventional capabilities. It is entirely possible that the DPRK armed forces are not as formidable as the U.S.-ROK allies assume. This possibility is reinforced by a widespread sense that North Korea's numerical advantages are more than compensated for by the qualitative military and economic advantages enjoyed by the U.S.-ROK alliance. Because the North tightly controls the flow of information—particularly about its military strengths and weaknesses—it is impossible to know how accurate the levels of apprehension or confidence may be.

This, of course, suits Pyongyang just fine. North Korea's ace in the strategic hole is its opponents' uncertainty about just how strong the adversary may be. The political uncertainties introduced by Kim Jong Il's ongoing succession and solidification of power, which are generally perceived as a weakening factor, perversely compound North Korea's strategic advantage because of the additional uncertainties they inject into U.S. and ROK assessments of their adversary's capabilities and intentions. As a consequence, the U.S.-ROK alliance must face periodic expressions of doubt that it could prevail in a ground war against North Korea or that a sea blockade could be effective against North Korea.[27] Therefore, the prudent military leaders of the alliance continually reassert the need for steadfastness in the face of North Korea's conventional capabilities. Similarly, the 1995 version of U.S. strategy for the Pacific responds directly to the North Korean threat: "The continuing tensions on the Korean Peninsula remain the principal threat to peace and stability of the Asian region."[28]

Washington and Seoul pointedly treat their alliance as a very stable and predictable relationship. In the face of a continuing North Korean threat, there has been a gradual maturation of the alliance and a recognition that

South Korea can assume a proportionately larger share of the responsibility. This development has produced shifts within the Combined Forces Command structure and a growing South Korean appetite to develop the leadership wherewithal to share greater power with the United States.[29] It also has yielded some South Korean interest in regional security cooperation[30] and in specific efforts to control the inter-Korean conventional arms race.[31] To date, little progress has been achieved, but it remains the central issue of the conventional arms balance in Korea. Although North Korea has so far rejected such efforts, in part because of its suspicion of Japan's motives,[32] this issue is by no means closed. In fact, the changing balance of power in post–Cold War East and Northeast Asia promises to accelerate consideration of such regional fora.

That balance is also being influenced by the changing nature of U.S.-DPRK relations, which are on the road to diplomatic recognition; the growth of anxieties in Seoul over U.S. contacts with North Korea (and Pyongyang's ability to drive a wedge between the United States and South Korea); and the emerging reality that a de facto, if unspoken, negative security guarantee has been spawned by the U.S.-DPRK Agreed Framework. Because the last facet of the Northeast Asian regional security system adds one more spoke in the fan and effectively provides North Korea with incentives to perceive the double containment value of the United States' relationships with South Korea and Japan in which the United States acts as a restraining influence on North Korea's neighbors,[33] it harbors enormous potential to compound regional stability by giving North Korea and the United States a set of overlapping mutual security interests. Clearly, the strategic future of Northeast Asia is becoming more complex and nuanced, in keeping with overall trends of the post–Cold War era. North Korea's strategic posture is becoming more like the late–Cold War situation of China, in that Pyongyang can visualize itself as a reactive regional balancer, using its weaknesses as assets and leverage.

As long as the United States perpetuates its supportive security roles with Japan and South Korea, North Korea will be able to rely on a negative security guarantee to ensure its strategic stability and survival as a state. Perversely, the key to this form of stability is the persistence of North Korea's conventional armed forces positioned in a deterrence mode. As long as the North Korean economy can sustain such forces and North Korea can count on the United States to regulate the balance, Pyongyang may have reason to want to retain the status quo. It is odd, but the greatest "threat" to this systemic stability may come from non–North Korean sources. Although South Korea and the United States are accustomed to worrying about dangers to peace emanating from North Korea, the evolution of U.S.-ROK security relations could prove more disruptive to the existing system. Any U.S. effort to redefine the security commitment to South Korea could be destabilizing.[34]

Because South Korea is well aware that the United States might some-day reduce its high levels of strategic support, there is a lively debate over the possibility of the South pursuing an autonomous defense policy independent of the United States.[35] Beyond South Korea's annual defense budget increases, which are largely designed to maintain the status quo with some qualitative improvements (a 10.7 percent increase for fiscal year 1996),[36] a Ministry of National Defense report in mid-1995 called for a doubling of the defense budget over the next six years to keep up with North Korea and with other arms increases in the region.[37] Such an agenda appears to have popular support; a spring 1995 Sejong Institute opinion survey of South Koreans indicated that more than 53 percent supported ROK self-defense as opposed to dependence on the United States, the UN, or a regional security arrangement.[38]

Although the desire for change by the United States and South Korea may be legitimate and persuasive, it may have an adverse impact on North Korea's conventionally armed deterrence. In short, if North Korea perceives the possibility of significant military upgrades by its key adversary and a reduction in the U.S. role as a restraining factor, this could provoke an escalation in the inter-Korean arms race. Such a prospect could be militarily destabilizing, but it would almost certainly be economically destabilizing and would thus influence Pyongyang's threat perceptions. This is not to suggest that Seoul should necessarily refrain from such options; after all, that kind of escalation is exactly what enabled the United States to force the Soviet Union into insolvency en route to losing the Cold War. Moreover, the United States continues to utilize that approach against the Castro regime in Cuba. It could work in Korea, too, but the risks are all too real—particularly because North Korea is well aware of what caused the Soviet Union to lose the Cold War.

As important as the nuances of inter-Korean strategic maneuvering are to North Korea's ability to preserve its conventionally armed deterrence, the DPRK also has to contemplate broader themes that will influence the future of its forces. Two of those themes are narrowly military in nature. First, the Korean conventional arms balance and the form of deterrence it sustains have been, and will remain for the near term, a continental balance predicated overwhelmingly on ground forces supplemented by ground-based air power. Naval power has not been central to the peninsular balance, although U.S. logistical and maritime support is of prime importance to South Korea in keeping the sea lanes of communications open.

In the Asia Pacific region, however, there has been a larger shift in the balance of power among the United States, Japan, and China in which sea power is a central factor. As a consequence, South Korea has begun to take seriously the task of carving out a maritime role that is only indirectly motivated by inter-Korean tensions.[39] The big loser in this changing power balance is North Korea, which cannot afford to be a serious naval player and is not well positioned economically or geographically to entertain such an ambition. Although this is a long-term trend, it portends a dramatic movement by South Korea into the full-fledged conventionally armed big leagues while North Korea remains behind without a truly competitive naval branch. This prospect should be considered carefully by Seoul, Washington, Tokyo, Beijing, and Moscow. How might Pyongyang react strategically, with its ground and air power, as it discovers that it will be relatively marginalized on the maritime front?

A second military theme concerns the unconventional facets of North Korea's conventional forces—its special operations forces. To date, most defense analysts have been concerned by the North's willingness to resort to a nuclear option in response to efforts to obstruct its conventional forces. Now that the DPRK nuclear option has been blocked through negotiations that also helped reduce the overall tension on the peninsula, concern has shifted to another alternative open to North Korea. In part because of geopolitical deterrence by South Korea and the United States, and in part because of some axioms about defense economics (i.e., nuclear weapons are cheaper than conventional forces, and chemical and biological weapons are the poor man's nuclear weapons), there is renewed unease about North Korea's ability to resort to chemical and biological warfare. These concerns are heightened by the great difficulty of verifying such forces and weapons. Although North Korea's overt conventional forces and its residual nuclear leverage are useful to preserve deterrence, these two key levers have now been relatively contained by its adversaries, effectively eclipsing Pyongyang's ability to manipulate anxieties about their escalation. North Korea's best remaining arsenal consists of those measures that appear irrational and desperate. These defense systems may be perfect for the North because of the uncertainty they generate among opponents.

Revolution in Military Affairs

The political and societal uncertainties noted previously contribute to this grand strategic mix, but on the narrow military front, Pyongyang is well served by retaining its edge in unconventionally used conventional forces and in the potential of a chemical-biological threat. For some time North Korea has been engaging in what the U.S. Department of Defense calls a "revolution in military affairs." When the United States uses this term, it is usually thinking about what future high-tech wars will be like, what circumstances may provoke them, and how to cope with them.[40] The North Korean equivalent is distinctly different and points to an evolution in the DPRK's strategic way of thinking as much as it does to an adaptation to different technologies. The North increasingly uses military and paramilitary capabilities for a kind of diplomatic psychological warfare whose net result is to perpetuate conventional deterrence and ensure the survival of the DPRK state. This North Korean "revolution in military affairs" deserves much closer attention by the United States and South Korea because, in their own terms of reference, the North Koreans are on the cutting edge and are preparing to cope with the next generation of inter-Korean conflict. In fact, this theme could be a crucial determinant of North Korea's emerging national security policy. Just as it is important to understand how U.S. and ROK ways of thinking about strategy are evolving toward greater interdependence and multilateralism, so, too, is it essential to grasp the nuances of the adversary's way of thinking.

Beyond these two relatively specific, broader military themes, North Korea also confronts the core future issue of the Korean nation: how the Korean people eventually will integrate themselves into a single state. That issue is too broad to be addressed here, but one facet of the unification question is how the DPRK military may fit into that puzzle. Precisely what role(s) North Korea's armed forces might play in reducing inter-Korean tensions and in the process of national unification is anyone's guess. The only thing certain is that they cannot be ignored, and they may prove to be decisive decisionmakers. Similarly, once Korea is unified, it is also certain that what will then be the former DPRK armed forces will have to be integrated into a united Korean society. If unification comes about through some cooptive process, presumably the South Korean–led successor state will deal with the former adversary's forces in a manner reminiscent of West Germany's absorption of East Germany's military. However, if the two Korean states negotiate a reconciliation on the basis of rough parity, then the task of incorporating the 1.5 million combined armed forces within a united Korean state promises to be far more complicated. In either case, a united Korea must also address the question of what to do with North Korea's massive paramilitary forces.

Although much of that task will necessarily be the purview of Korean leaders on both sides, the long-standing U.S. commitment to South Korea inevitably will inject U.S. decisionmakers into the resolution of Korea's division. The broader aspects of any such U.S. role also are beyond the scope of this chapter, but there is one aspect in which U.S. authorities should have a major role: namely, helping to plan for a profound military transition stemming from the end of the inter-Korean Cold War. Contingency plans for ending the tensions and for coping with the aftermath are needed. In this regard, U.S.-ROK efforts to deal with North Korea on the political, economic, and nuclear fronts are adequate, but they are inadequate on the conventional arms front. As the nuclear arrangements are proved workable and engender greater confidence among all parties involved, sufficient mutual trust will have been created to move on to conventional arms control and reduction negotiations. Both of these approaches should be treated as instruments in a larger game, that of helping to transform North Korea and setting the stage for merging the two Koreas into one.

Conclusion: Conventional Arms Control

Partly because the United States prefers to abstain from inter-Korean normalization talks, it has shied away from interjecting itself into negotiations that could lead to reduced tensions about conventional arms. This is not a tenable posture, because U.S. forces in Korea and its environs are a key portion of the conventional arms balance. In effect, U.S. conventional arms amount to potential bargaining chips to the North Koreans as they cope with South Korean bargaining efforts, and it is unrealistic to leave them off the table when the two Koreas talk. Although it is a sensitive topic among South Koreans who are nervous about the United States' strategic steadfastness and its preoccupation with the Middle East and the Balkans, North Korea has provided an opportunity for the United States to engage the DPRK on military-to-military issues that might include arms control if handled skillfully. For example, the North Korean overture transmitted in fall 1995 through Selig Harrison could be treated as an opportunity instead of a manipulative ploy.[41]

Clearly, Seoul and Washington have to be extremely careful about responding to any DPRK initiatives that are intended to divide their alliance. Just as clearly, however, the allies should have enough confidence in their strength to explore opportunities that might be imbedded in North Korean peace campaigns. There is a need for greater creativity toward North Korea, and conventional arms reduction is a topic that seems ripe. One topic that is particularly ripe is the United States' role as a mediator between the two Koreas on conventional arms reduction and on broader tension reduction.[42]

U.S. diplomacy at the Balkan summit, held at Wright-Patterson Air Force Base in Dayton, Ohio, may have been successful as a catalyst bringing bitter enemies together en route to a peaceful future. Only time will tell as the peace process evolves in the coming months. There was, of course, a precedent for this exercise—the 1977 Camp David summit between Anwar Sadat and Menachem Begin organized and hosted by U.S. president Jimmy Carter. Both efforts at bringing together seemingly intractable adversaries deserve praise. Why has Washington not applied this same U.S. catalyst role to the Korean conundrum? Is it not time to pursue the possibility of a "Camp David II" or "Dayton II" in pursuit of conventional arms control and reductions in Korea?

Surely Korea is at least as important as the Middle East or the Balkans. After all, the United States did not fight a war on behalf of either the Arab or Israeli protagonists, and it is doing its utmost to avoid being entangled in a Balkan war as a result of the Dayton agreement. Yet the United States did fight in Korea, suffered many casualties, has been engaged there strategically for more than four decades, and has a widely acknowledged interest in regional peace and stability. But the United States has remained passive about the inter-Korean peace process, largely relegating that agenda to the Korean participants. Washington is remiss when it avoids the opportunity to insert U.S. diplomacy as an intermediary between North and South Korea. The Korean problem will almost certainly remain stagnant if the two Korean states are left to resolve their differences bilaterally.

The Korean antagonists could benefit greatly from a U.S. diplomatic catalyst en route to conventional arms reduction. The first step in that direction was indirectly taken when former president Carter acted as a de facto intermediary with Pyongyang during the critical phase of the nuclear crisis, which threatened to escalate tension in Korea to the breaking point. In effect, Washington has already violated its former prohibition against interfering in inter-Korean diplomacy by arranging the Agreed Framework with North Korea. The agreement in turn sustains the Korean Peninsula Energy Development Organization, which is supposed to be a vehicle for a North-South dialogue over the nuclear issue. Washington need not shy away from further activism as a broker in inter-Korean military affairs.

Although some in the United States and South Korea have deep reservations about the outcome of that round of U.S. mediation, notably because it set precedents for global nuclear proliferation, the agreement was highly productive in terms of enhancing the broader process of reducing tensions in the Koreas. It is now time for the United States to take a further step by interjecting itself into the inter-Korean peace process through the mechanism of a Camp David/Dayton–style tripartite military summit. A major reason that such a summit has not yet occurred is that North Korea has advocated a tripartite approach to other aspects of the Korean question, clearly intending to use it to undercut U.S.-ROK solidarity and to establish more direct U.S.-DPRK relations. Some in South Korea and the United States perceive the tripartite formula as a trap that Seoul and Washington should carefully avoid. But the United States would by no means be reducing its commitment to South Korea through such summitry, any more than the Camp David formula minimized U.S. support for Israel. On the contrary, the United States would be strengthening its overall bond with Korea.

So, as the Middle Eastern and Balkan peace processes follow sometimes arduous paths, the United States should seriously consider facilitating similar opportunities for the long-divided Korean nation. The United States has a moral responsibility, dating from its role in Korea's original division in the 1940s, to take a proactive stance designed to bring Korea together again peacefully through negotiations on conventional arms control and reduction. This process would be given a major boost if Washington were as willing to do for the Koreans what it has been willing to do for the Israelis, the Egyptians, the Palestinians, the Bosnians, the Serbians, and the Croatians. Given U.S. interests in Asia and the potential post–Cold War benefits that would stem from genuine peace in the region, can the United States really afford not to do as much for Korea?

Notes

1. The lower figures are from Kim Hak-joon, "On the Nature of the North Korean State," *Korea and World Affairs* (Winter 1995):695, and the higher figures are from the Ministry of National Defense, *Defense White Paper, 1995–1996* (Seoul: Ministry of National Defense, 1996), p. 57.

2. Gregory F. T. Winn, "North Korea: A Garrison State," in Edward A. Olsen and Stephen Jurika, Jr., eds., *The Armed Forces in Contemporary Asian Societies* (Boulder, Colo.: Westview Press, 1986).

3. It should be noted that South Korea's aborted efforts to acquire a nuclear capability dated from the early 1970s and that North Korea's more recent nuclear efforts were known to the United States in 1985. For a brief overview of those moves, see the *Far Eastern Economic Review,* February 2, 1989, p. 15. For a detailed analysis of North Korea's nuclear efforts, see Michael Mazarr, *North Korea and the Bomb: A Case Study in Nonproliferation* (New York: St. Martin's Press, 1995). It also should be noted that some South Koreans are seriously annoyed by U.S. policies toward Korean nuclear options, which they claim undermine Korean "nuclear sovereignty"; see Kim Tae-woo and Kim Min-seok, "The Nuclear Issue of the Korean Peninsula," *Korea Focus* 1, no. 6 (1993):47–70.

4. For analyses of the weapons systems, military strategy and tactics, and contextual factors that indicate North Korea's conventional arms inadequacies, see Greg J. Gerardi and James A. Plotts, "North Korea—to the Brink and Back," *Jane's Intelligence Review, Year Book,* December 31, 1994; James Goodby and William Drennan, "Koreapolitik," *Strategic Forum,* no. 29 (May 1995); Nick Beldecos and Eric Heginbotham, "The Conventional Military Balance in Korea," *Breakthroughs* 4 (Spring 1995):1–8; and Bruce W. Bennett, "The Prospects for Conventional Conflict on the Korean Peninsula," *Korea Journal of Defense Analysis* 7 (Summer 1995):95–127.

5. For some examples, see *Washington Post,* January 14, 1979, p. A9; *Christian Science Monitor,* May 18, 1982, p. 5, and March 21, 1986, pp. 9–14; *Foreign Broadcast Information Service (FBIS),* November 23, 1984, p. E3, and April 19, 1989, p. 18; *Korea Herald,* May 11, 1985, p. 3, November 2, 1985, p. 1, September 9, 1992, p. 3, and October 14, 1993, p. 3; *Far Eastern Economic Review,* May 13, 1993, pp. 10–11.

6. For the confident views of Secretary of Defense William Perry and Generals John Shalikashvili (chairman of the Joint Chiefs of Staff) and Gary Luck (CINC/USFK), see *Korea Herald,* December 23, 1995, p. 1.

7. For some alarmist reactions to earlier reports of forward deployments, see *Sankei shimbun,* December 3, 1987, p. 2, and February 6, 1988, p. 5. For more recent press coverage of forward maneuvers as of early 1996, see *Korea Herald,* December 13, 1995, p. 2, and December 16, 1995, p. 1.

8. Ministry of National Defense, *Defense White Paper, 1994–1995* (Seoul: Ministry of National Defense, 1995), p. 74.

9. *Korea Herald,* March 15, 1991, p. 3; and *Far Eastern Economic Review,* May 2, 1991, pp. 18–19.

10. *Jane's Intelligence Review* reported in *Korea Herald,* September 2, 1994, p. 3.

11. *Korea Herald,* February 8, 1994, p. 1.

12. For background on this terrorism, see Asian Studies Backgrounder No. 74, *Heritage Foundation,* February 25, 1988; and *Far Eastern Economic Review,* February 18, 1988, pp. 32–33. On arms exports, see Peter Hayes, "International Missile Trade and the Two Koreas," Working Paper No. 1, Program for Nonproliferation Studies, Monterey Institute of International Studies, March 1993. On training in Africa and the Philippines, see *Korea Herald,* August 9, 1984, p. 1, and September 15, 1984, p. 1; *FBIS, East Asia,* November 13, 1989, p. 22; and *Far Eastern Economic Review,* January 11, 1990, p. 20.

13. *Far Eastern Economic Review,* December 11, 1986, p. 29; and *Korea Herald,* March 20, 1992, p. 3.

14. *Far Eastern Economic Review,* November 20, 1986, p. 29, December 11, 1986, pp. 30–31, and May 26, 1988, p. 17; *Washington Post* (weekly), November 24, 1986, p. 16; *Korea Herald,* March 3, 1987, p. 5.

15. For examples of accused agents in the 1990s, see *Korea Herald,* December 27, 1990, p. 3, June 6, 1991, p. 3, September 8, 1992, p. 1, and October 7, 1992, p. 1.

16. *Korea Herald,* May 12, 1995, p. 3, October 10, 1995, p. 2, October 18, 1995, p. 1, October 25, 1995, p. 1, October 26, 1995, p. 1, October 27, 1995, p. 3, October 28, 1995, p. 1, and November 10, 1995, p. 1.

17. For coverage of that effort, see *Korea Herald,* May 5, 1995, p. 1, and May 7, 1995, p. 3; *Pyongyang Times,* May 20, 1995, p. 8; and *Far Eastern Economic Review,* May 18, 1995, pp. 14–15.

18. For Seoul's view, see *Korea Herald,* December 12, 1995, p. 1; for the Pentagon's view, see *Korea Herald,* December 24, 1995, p. 1.

19. *Economist,* October 21, 1995, p. 37.

20. See Yossef Bodansky, "North Korea Continues, with Bellicosity, What Appear to Be Preparations for an Imminent War," *Defense & Foreign Affairs/Strategic Policy* (April 30, 1995):10; and Ken E. Gause, "Kim Chong-il's First Year in Power," *Jane's Intelligence Review,* September 1, 1995, p. 420. For additional analysis of North Korean military centers of influence, see *Vantage Point* 10, no. 1 (January 1995):30–31, and 18, no. 3 (March 1995):1–5; and *Far Eastern Economic Review,* March 13, 1997, p. 24. For a Japanese perception of Kim Jong Il's positive relationship with the KPA, see Takesada Hideshi, "North Korean Military Threat Under Kim Jong Il," presented at the conference "North Korea After Kim Il Sung: Continuity or Change?" Hoover Institution, Stanford University, Stanford, Calif., February 27–28, 1996.

21. *San Jose Mercury News,* December 26, 1995, p. 10A.

22. Chung Jong-moon, "Is North Korea's Military Supplanting the Workers' Party?" *Korea Focus* 3, no. 5 (September–October 1995):111.

23. *Korea Herald,* December 6, 1995, p. 5, December 20, 1995, p. 1, and January 26, 1996, p. 3; *San Jose Mercury News,* December 23, 1995, p. 7A; *Far Eastern Economic Review,* December 14, 1995, p. 20; *Christian Science Monitor,* December 22, 1995, p. 6; *Washington Post* (weekly), January 1–7, 1996, p. 16.

24. That uncertainty was heightened when the DPRK deputy foreign minister, Ch'oe Su-hon, said that North Korea was retrenching from its food aid request

because of concerns expressed by the DPRK military about the impression the policy had conveyed abroad; *San Jose Mercury News,* February 8, 1996, p. 13A.

25. See *FBIS, East Asia,* May 25, 1990, p. 35; *Korea Herald,* October 24, 1992, p. 1, and January 17, 1993, p. 2; *FPI International Report,* January 13, 1989, p. 4; and Michael Ertman, "North Korean Arms Capabilities and Implications: Nuclear, Chemical, and Ballistic Missiles," *Korea and World Affairs* 17 (Winter 1993):612–615.

26. Joseph S. Bermudez, Jr., "North Korea's Special Forces," *Jane's Defense Weekly,* January 30, 1988, pp. 173–175; and Michael S. Durtschi, "The North Korean Special Purposes Forces: An Assessment of the Threat," M.A. thesis, Department of National Security Affairs, Naval Postgraduate School, Monterey, Calif., March 1995.

27. For example, on a U.S. admiral's doubts, see *Korea Herald,* May 22, 1993, p. 3; and on skepticism about victory, *Newsweek,* November 23, 1993, p. 3.

28. *A National Security Strategy of Engagement and Enlargement* (Washington, D.C.: The White House, February 1995), p. 28. See also the comments of the U.S. commander in Korea, General Gary E. Luck, *Korea Herald,* February 18, 1995, p. 1.

29. For a description of those shifts and the impact on South Korea, see *Korea Herald,* February 14, 1995, p. 3. See also Oh Kwan-chi, "Koreanization of Korean Defense," *Korea Focus* 2 (November–December 1994):27–35. See also Jonathan D. Pollack and Cha Young-koo, *A New Alliance for the Next Century: The Future of U.S.-Korean Security Cooperation* (Santa Monica, Calif.: RAND, 1996).

30. Although most of these expressions of interest focus on the ASEAN-PMC-ARF model or the idea of a "mini-CSCA" for Northeast Asia (see, e.g., Foreign Minister Han Sung-ju's efforts in *Korea Herald,* July 13, 1993, p. 5), there also are bolder proposals to facilitate ROK-Japan cooperation, such as Hyun In-taek and Okonogi Masao, "Security Cooperation in East Asia," *Korea Focus* 2 (September–October 1994):50–60.

31. See Cha Young-koo and Choi Kang, "Land-Based Confidence-Building Measures in Northeast Asia: A South Korean Perspective," *Korea Journal of Defense Analysis* 6 (Winter 1994):237–260.

32. For example, see *Korea Herald,* January 25, 1995, p. 2; and *Pyongyang Times,* December 2, 1995, p. 8.

33. James A. Baker, "America in Asia: Emerging Architecture for a Pacific Community," *Foreign Affairs* (Winter 1991/92):4. Double containment's ramifications are evaluated in greater detail in E. A. Olsen and David Winterford, "Asian Multilateralism: Implications for US Policy," *Korea Journal for Defense Analysis* 5 (Summer 1994):9–40.

34. For examples of such initiatives, see Doug Bandow and Ted Galen Carpenter, *The US–South Korean Alliance: Time for a Change* (New Brunswick, N.J.: Transaction Publishers, 1992); and Doug Bandow, *Tripwire: Korea and US Foreign Policy in a Changed World* (Washington, D.C.: Cato Institute, 1996). On balance, I support such changes, but if they are ever implemented by Washington, U.S. leaders should be prepared to deal with the repercussions on South Korea and Japan as North Korea perceives those countries being removed from U.S. restraints.

35. See Chi Man-won, "We Should Go Nuclear to Counter North Korean Nuclear Weapons," *FBIS, East Asia,* July 1, 1994; and Rhee Sang-woo, "New Defense Posture for Next Century," *Korea Focus* (March–April 1995):59–69.

36. *Korea Herald,* September 12, 1995, p. 3, totaling 12.26 trillion won ($15.9 billion).

37. Cited in *Jane's Defense Weekly,* July 15, 1995, p. 15.

38. Lee Sook-jong, "Korean Perception on National Security," *Korea Focus* 3, no. 4 (July–August 1995):18.

39. For background on this important issue for Korea's future, see Kim Dalchoong and Cho Doug-woon, *Korean Sea Power and the Pacific Era* (Seoul: Institute of East and West Studies, Yonsei University, 1990); Kang Yong-o, *T'ongil han'guk ui haegun chollyak* [Naval Strategy for a Unified Korea] (Seoul: Yon'gyong ch'ulp'ansa, 1992); and Lee Choon-kun, ed., *Sea Power and Korea in the 21st Century* (Seoul: The Sejong Institute, 1994).

40. For an overview of that issue, see Eliot A. Cohen, "A Revolution in Warfare," *Foreign Affairs* (March–April 1996):37–54.

41. See Selig Harrison "The US-DPRK Nuclear Agreement and the US-ROK Alliance: The View from Pyongyang," paper presented at the International Workshop on the US/ROK Alliance, Institute for Far Eastern Studies, Kyongnam University, Seoul, October 5–7, 1995. See also critics of the idea such as Paek Chin-hyon's article on Pyongyang's new peace plan, *Choson ilbo,* October 5, 1995.

42. For the generic context of the U.S. role, including some insights on the U.S. role in North Korea, see Amitai Etzioni, "Rethinking Peacekeeping," *Washington Quarterly* (Summer 1995). For some insights into the topic of arms reduction, see Robert Manning, "Broader Korean Strategy Needed," *Aviation Week and Space Technology,* February 20, 1995, p. 68.

8

New Security Arrangements Between the United States and North Korea

Patrick M. Morgan

The United States has, for some time, been moving away from its traditional policy vis-à-vis North Korea and toward establishing a much more normal relationship with that government. In turn, North Korea has also been seeking a more normal relationship with the United States. For North Korea this new relationship will inevitably have an important security dimension; security concerns pervade nearly everything the North does these days, just as they have done for years. This chapter examines the contributions the United States might make to establish a greater sense of security for the North Korean government.

Background

Like other members of the Soviet bloc, North Korea was for years subjected to the U.S. global strategy of containment. Indeed, it has now been the target of containment longer than any other nation. That strategy, while flexible in details, was consistent in its fundamentals. The core elements were (1) isolation of Communist states, politically and economically, from the West; (2) nonstrategic extended deterrence practiced through alliances and by situating near or in the states being protected U.S. forces prepared to use tactical or theater nuclear weapons; (3) strategic nuclear deterrence, including the threat to use the ultimate weapons in the U.S. arsenal if necessary; and (4) the planned use of U.S. conventional forces in response to an attack if deterrence were to fail.

Although Washington came to accept the need for limited cooperation with Communist states—particularly in arms control matters and when such cooperation might help fragment the Communist bloc—there was always a distinction between some level of détente and an end to containment.

North Korea has experienced containment quite thoroughly. U.S. forces helped repel its attack on the South, and they remained in South

Korea thereafter positioned (as elsewhere) to serve, in case of an attack, as a trip wire that would trigger a larger response. Thus, they provided both a more credible deterrence and a first-order contribution to any defense that would be attempted. U.S. forces were also stationed at sea and in Japan for possible use in Korea, and others were available elsewhere in the Pacific. All were equipped with nuclear weapons—stored at sea, in South Korea, and on Okinawa (for many years)—and the United States maintained a first-use posture while periodically threatening the North with a nuclear response.[1] Strategic nuclear weapons were available either to use against the North or, more likely, to deter intervention and escalation by its allies.

There was also a thorough isolation of the North, which, like other Communist states, tended to reinforce this situation by avoiding interactions with the West and pursuing autarky. It received no aid, trade, or investment of significance from the West (remittances from Koreans in Japan were an exception) and had no serious political contacts with Western nations.

The North was subjected to containment as an ally of the USSR and China, the primary targets of the policy. It was also a target because of the U.S. commitment to South Korea, which the North had attacked and toward which it maintained unremitting hostility and a constant threat. Finally, containment reflected the U.S. commitment to Japan; hostilities in Korea were deemed highly threatening to Japan's security. As Japan recovered from World War II, an additional objective (a paramount one today) was that it not feel impelled by developments in Korea to mount a much larger defensive effort that would disturb states in the region.

There was always another, long-term dimension to containment. The original version, set forth by George Kennan, emphasized that it was intended to lead to the breakdown of the Soviet bloc; these states and societies were unnatural allies and would experience severe frictions over time if containment penned them up together. Containment was also intended to lead to either the mellowing of Communist regimes—the waning of their revolutionary aspirations and the softening of their totalitarian nature—or their internal collapse. Such systems could preserve their vitality only through expansion, which containment would prevent. U.S. interest in détente, therefore, was always that it might contribute to such mellowing (or collapse), and thus there were limits on how far détente was carried unless Communist states adopted or experienced significant changes.

For a Communist state to mellow sufficiently and gain release from containment required—in the eyes of successive U.S. policymakers—one or more of the following: (1) an explicit political rapprochement with the West in terms of foreign policy and behavior; (2) economic reforms that pointed toward a market economy; and (3) political reforms that eased political repression and constituted steps toward democracy. The first of these steps could produce a considerable easing of containment, but the second and third were far more potent for securing its complete elimination. The desire for internal changes and the insistence that the enemy renounce hostility toward the United States and its allies were prominent in the containment of North Korea. The United States was simply not interested in a truly normal relationship without such changes.

Another aspect of containment in practice and an element in any political rapprochement was the expectation that détente with a Communist state would be accompanied by or lead to cooperation on other security matters, such as making efforts at collective security management, upholding controls on nuclear proliferation, combating terrorism and subversion, and dealing with what are now termed "rogue" states. In this regard the United States sought to persuade North Korea to abandon its provocative military posture, cease development of nuclear weapons, end its terrorism and subversion efforts toward the South, and avoid selling arms or sensitive technology to states such as Iraq and Iran.[2]

Assessing Recent Developments

With such a background in mind, we can better appreciate the shift in U.S. policy toward North Korea in recent years. The shift began in 1988; various low-level contacts were established over the next four years and have been followed by more extensive talks since.[3] The purposes of containment have been significantly adjusted. The United States remains committed to the Republic of Korea (ROK) and Japan and still perceives the North as a threat. However, the United States no longer pursues containment of the Soviet Union/Russia and China and therefore no longer treats North Korea as an extension of Soviet or Chinese power. Hence, the salience of containment of the North is weaker than before. Containment is not a crucial part, in real or symbolic terms, of a larger purpose; it now must be pursued on its own merits. The United States has shifted away from reliance on containment in favor of supplementing and eventually replacing it with a "strategy of inducements," an approach introduced during the Bush administration.[4] Thus the United States has taken nuclear weapons off its naval vessels and out of South Korea, has announced plans to cut further its forces on the peninsula, and has agreed to normalize relations with North Korea.

Why this shift? A number of factors and considerations have been important. There is the decline in the North's relative military strength and thus of its threat to the South, resulting from the loss of the North's major allies, the continued growth in ROK military strength, and the decay of the North's economy. The United States has in recent years received much assistance from China and Russia in pressuring the North, and such cooperation implies that more would be forthcoming if the North misbehaved grievously. Then there is the declining willingness of Americans to bear the costs of extended deterrence and containment now that the Cold War is

over, a political fact of life that has begun to reshape many elements of foreign policy. There is also considerable concern in Washington and elsewhere about the implications of a complete collapse of the Democratic
People's Republic of Korea (DPRK) regime, an outcome that continued
containment might bring about. Most important, U.S. officials now consider the mellowing (or collapse) of the North as inevitable; it is no longer a
required objective of a strict containment policy. History is against the
North; it is running out of time and alternatives. Finally, there has been
concern that containment would not prevent nuclear proliferation by the
North and might even incite it. As Kenneth Waltz has suggested, the more
vulnerable North Korea has felt, the more strenuously it has sought nuclear
weapons, and "the effective way to persuade states to forego nuclear
weapons would seem to be to guarantee their security against conventional
as well as nuclear threats."[5]

With these considerations in mind, the United States has set aside
many of the preconditions for ending containment that were applied to
other Communist states. (The Agreed Framework is not a political/foreign
policy rapprochement, though complete implementation of its provisions
would bring the two governments a good deal closer. The North displays
only limited interest in serious economic reforms and no signs as yet of
political reforms.) Instead, the United States has sought—as the relevant
quid pro quo—the North's cooperation on various security matters, such as
nuclear nonproliferation and an end to the North's sale of sensitive military
technologies to other states.[6] The United States wants the DPRK to cease
involvement in terrorism and not to renew past efforts at subversion in the
South. It welcomes DPRK participation in collective security management
in Northeast Asia, starting with the tense situation on the peninsula.[7]

What is the new U.S. security policy vis-à-vis North Korea? There are
four paramount objectives: (1) to promote the mellowing of the North by
nudging it toward internal reforms and less isolationism. This is not a new
objective, but a pursuit of it by different means; (2) to move the Korean
peninsula toward peaceful unification while understanding that this complex problem must ultimately be resolved by the Koreans; (3) to stabilize
the security situation in the region through peaceful unification, with no
other state dominating the peninsula and Korea not sharply at odds with
any of its neighbors; and (4) to secure a denuclearized peninsula.

Among the elements of the security relationship the United States is
exploring, the following are evident: negotiations as a supplement to and
eventual replacement for confrontation; oil deliveries to ease the North's
severe economic situation; diplomatic relations; substantial economic relations; arrangement of the transfer of two nuclear reactors to the North in
exchange for a halt to the North's nuclear weapons program; insistence on
renewing the North-South dialogue; and retention of the U.S.-ROK alliance
as insurance.

The persistence displayed by the United States in pursuing this policy is impressive evidence of the commitment behind it. The North was a very difficult negotiating partner in the talks that led to the Agreed Framework, but the United States did not give up. Washington refused to let the submarine incident in September 1996 freeze the slow growth in cooperation with the North, a posture that led to serious frictions with the ROK and displayed U.S. readiness to set aside Seoul's reservations.[8] Thus, the United States moved into talks with the North about Korean War soldiers missing in action, and it reopened contacts with Pyongyang about the North's ballistic missile sales in the Third World.[9] Washington insisted on divorcing these negotiations and the slow dance toward four-party negotiations on the future of the peninsula from its commitment to supply food assistance to the North in response to the famine of 1997, thereby opening a rift with the ROK and Japan, both of which wanted to use food aid as leverage.[10]

Even when a high-level North Korean official defected and indicated that Pyongyang might possess nuclear weapons, giving new life to criticism of the policy of engagement, Washington downplayed the matter and made no change in course.[11] It was clearly the United States' intent to keep trying to avoid confrontation or provocation in dealing with the North Koreans.

It is not surprising that debate has continued about this policy[12] and its effectiveness—whether this is what has moved the North to take tentative steps toward better relations with the outside world. On one side are those who see pressure as the key. Their evidence includes the flurry of agreements with South Korea in late 1991 in the wake of the massive U.S. victory in the Gulf War[13] and the North's reopening of negotiations leading to the Agreed Framework just when the U.S. National Security Council was about to approve a large increase in forces in Korea. On the other side are those who see the North as having decided some time ago to make policy shifts and try reforms in response to its mounting problems and the collapse of the Soviet bloc.[14] Evidence supporting this view includes signs that the North wanted a better relationship with the United States back in the 1980s, the late 1991 agreements if depicted as a response to the end of the Cold War and the Soviet Union, the North's efforts to develop a legal framework for foreign investment,[15] and the Agreed Framework. Delay in the full implementation of the framework is blamed on the internal political struggles between the old guard and the reformers,[16] the succession situation, and the North's extreme caution in view of what happened to East European Communist regimes once rapprochement with the West had begun.

There are various implications of this conciliatory U.S. approach for the long run. Let us assume that the Agreed Framework will be fully implemented and that U.S.-DPRK relations keep improving. One implication is that the North will, if it wishes, also sharply improve its relations with China, Russia, and Japan. The chief barriers to such improvement have been the North's nuclear program, which these states have opposed, and the fact that dealing with Pyongyang as long as that program existed meant being at odds with the United States. U.S. fence mending with the North will dissolve these barriers. Each great power wishes to prevent any of the others from being the dominant influence on the peninsula, especially in shaping unification, which may call for ties to the North, not just the South.[17] While its relations with Japan remain frozen, the North has already secured major assistance from China in 1996–1997, and a draft agreement on a better relationship between Moscow and Pyongyang has been drawn up for signing in mid-1997.

Another implication is that, as the North's relations with the great powers improve, so will its odds of avoiding a complete collapse. Judging by the fate of other Communist states, the odds will not be good, just better. Opening up to the outside world has been perilous for closed Communist systems. Still, the chances for survival of the regime will be better than they have been.

An additional implication is that the great powers will explore coordinating their policies vis-à-vis the peninsula with the two Koreas. Although these powers cannot dictate outcomes, they can influence them and be damaged by them. For instance, a unification that resulted in a nuclear-armed Korea would be considered a disaster by the great powers, as would a frantic unification born of the North's complete collapse. The strain might well destabilize the South, generate burdensome refugee flows, lead to significant foreign aid requests, or even incite some form of military intervention. A unified Korea deeply at odds with one or more of the great powers would be very undesirable. Avoiding such difficulties or evading their worst consequences seems far more likely if the great powers act in concert.

These powers have still more reason to coordinate their long-term policies: A decline in the threat posed by the North and gradual progress toward unification will shrink the political leverage of each on the regional security situation. The more the threat fades, the less important alliances with the United States will be to Japan and South Korea; unless another threat emerges, U.S. influence on both governments will decline. By extension, U.S. leverage with China will also decline. Although China is eager to prevent a dominant U.S. influence in Korea, it cannot hope to do so as long as the United States leads the effort to bar nuclear weapons and remains crucial to ROK security. A peaceful peninsula will remove this pressure from China to act in accordance with U.S. desires. Russia's freedom of action has also been curbed by having to attend to U.S. wishes vis-à-vis the North and by U.S. influence in the South.

However, China's leverage will also be reduced. China has been able to exploit the U.S. need for its support on halting the North's nuclear program, but if the nuclear threat fades, this source of influence will dry up. China has had leverage with Japan for the same reason, and this will suffer the same decline.[18] Finally, as North Korea develops more normal relationships with the outside, its dependence on China will be somewhat reduced.

Japan will face a declining U.S. need for its cooperation on North Korea and will have to confront the fact that the one thing on which the two Koreas agree is their fear of Japan. Russia will be able to improve ties with the North, but, because the North (and South) will be in a position to play each of the great powers against the others, it will not regain its former influence.

Likely Problems

Although it has carefully fulfilled its obligations initially, North Korea will at some point make trouble over the implementation of the Agreed Framework. This is its well-established negotiating style for extracting maximum gains. It will drag its feet on interaction with the South, perhaps on arrangements for the nuclear reactors, because relations with the South may pose a domestic threat and because it wishes to defer as long as possible steps that further legitimize the ROK. It will continue to seek a stronger relationship with the United States as a way to gain leverage over the South.

Much has been made of the North's having played the nuclear card well and having retained it through the option to restart its nuclear program during the five years or more needed to implement the Geneva agreement fully. The card was most useful in the context of U.S. concern about the Treaty on the Non-Proliferation of Nuclear Weapons (NPT) Review Conference, but the successful conclusion of the conference has sharply diminished its value. The United States' determination to curb the DPRK nuclear program now has renewed international support. In addition, Washington has adopted Chinese and Japanese advice on how to deal with Pyongyang and is in a much better position to insist on support from these two countries for a hard line if Pyongyang proves unwilling to live up to the agreement. Finally, the more the nonproliferation agreement is implemented, the greater the effort that will be needed to restart the DPRK nuclear program. Thus, the nuclear card is of less value now than many believe.

Another problem is that South Korea dislikes how things have gone thus far, and its displeasure has strained the U.S.-ROK alliance. Some in the South see the agreement as a move to enable the United States to play the two Koreas against each other. These fears are overblown, but the United States will be under strong pressure to insist that the North resume a dialogue with the South, and the North will be alert to possibilities of increasing the strain in the alliance.

If the agreement succeeds, it will be difficult to shift the loose coordination of great-power efforts in recent years into firm cooperation about the future of the peninsula. The glue in their recent cooperation has been opposition to nuclear weapons, fear of another war in Korea, and a desire to avoid the implosion of the North. If the agreement succeeds, this glue will dissolve. The powers will need renewed cooperation to develop a multilateral security arrangement for the peninsula and even for Northeast Asia, in which the Koreas play an important part. Jockeying for influence in Korea may get in the way of developing such an agreement.

A final problem is that the Agreed Framework and normalization of the North's relations with the United States will not determine the North's future development, and it is the North's future that is the key to regional security. The security management problem will be shifted from the narrow matter of the North's military posture to the larger, more complex question of the future of North Korea itself, on which the great powers exercise only limited influence.

Security for North Korea

If the United States is to draw North Korea out of its isolation, it has to take some measure of responsibility for the North's security. The responsibility is limited but real. Just as the United States is assuming some responsibility for the North's future energy supplies because it has insisted that the North cancel an alternative source of energy, it cannot demand that the North stop pursuing security via isolation and a nuclear weapons program without some contribution to their replacement.

In fact, the United States has contributed to the North's security for years through its view that a South Korea that was truly self-sufficient militarily would be bad for stability on the peninsula. Thus, it has always limited ROK access to advanced military hardware, particularly for offensive operations, and has not insisted that the ROK defense budget be large enough to buy military self-sufficiency. Two decades ago, the United States took steps to halt an ROK nuclear weapons program.[19] The United States has also recognized its current responsibility to contribute to the North's security by the provision in the Agreed Framework to give "formal assurances to the DPRK, against the threat or use of nuclear weapons by the U.S."

It is worthwhile to explore the complexities of the United States' involvement in North Korea's security, a link that will extend far beyond the non-nuclear-use guarantee. Defining the parameters of the "measure of responsibility" the United States is undertaking will be a subtle and complex task for policymakers.

Classic Security Concerns

Constructing such an analysis is best done by means of a comprehensive list of North Korea's security requirements. There is no guarantee that the DPRK leaders have exactly the following requirements in mind, but these items have ample plausibility.

Freedom from the Threat of Nuclear Attack

Either a nuclear deterrence capability or a U.S. negative security guarantee could address the North's fear of nuclear attack. A nuclear deterrence capability is probably the North's preferred option in the abstract because it would be permanently reliable, but it would mean antagonizing the great powers, harming prospects for achieving other foreign policy objectives, and risking a U.S. attack on the North's nuclear facilities and a larger war. Although this option has been set aside (but not completely eliminated), the second option has become available: The United States has now provided the non-nuclear-use guarantee, backed up by prior withdrawal of U.S. nuclear weapons from South Korea and (except for sea-to-land ballistic missiles) from U.S. naval forces. The North may well press for further reassurance, via inspection of facilities in the South, but this would pose complications.

In any case, U.S. leaders have indicated for years that they do not plan to use nuclear weapons in any warfare on the peninsula. The United States could, of course, change its mind or react to another war differently than planned, but the likelihood of such a change depends greatly on North Korea's behavior and thus is under Pyongyang's control to a considerable extent. The United States may wish to consider additional steps, such as further public statements of its intentions, to reassure the North, particularly in response to satisfactory behavior on Pyongyang's part, but the first item on this list is now in place.

Reduced Threat of Attack by U.S. and ROK Conventional Forces

Minimizing the threat posed by conventional forces is undoubtedly an important consideration in Pyongyang. Concern about an outright attack is probably, and rightly, minimal, but the North must inevitably worry about military intervention if its political system is seriously disrupted and its control falters.

This security item is not now provided. The United States and South Korea have no plans to reduce their forces seriously, and an intervention capability is inherent in their existence. What the United States and South Korea have done is suspend the annual Team Spirit exercise (while insisting that this suspension is not required under the Agreed Framework).[20] They could do more by reviving the plan to cut U.S. forces in the South, by moving to put U.S. and ROK forces in a strictly defensive mode, by reducing U.S. naval and air assets in the region, and by continuing the suspension of Team Spirit.[21]

These further steps are, however, impossible without a significant redeployment and reduction of the North's forces. Some 60–65 percent of those forces remain close to the border, in a high state of readiness, well primed for an attack on the South.[22] Normally, this arrangement would be taken as clear evidence that the North remains deeply interested in launching an attack should favorable circumstances arise. However, such a deployment is also compatible, in principle, with a strongly defensive orientation. A state that cannot hope to sustain a long war if attacked by a greatly superior opponent may decide that its only possible defense is to carry the fighting immediately to the opponent and its territory, and that only the threat of this intention is an effective deterrent. Nonetheless, even if the North's deployment is for defensive purposes, the United States and South Korea have little choice but to consider it an offensive threat. Without an adjustment in this situation, it would be irresponsible for the United States to reduce its forces, their alert level, and their reaction time, and the same is true for South Korea.

One question is whether, if there is no significant reduction of forces along the Demilitarized Zone, the allies should remain committed to the destruction of the DPRK if they are attacked. There seems little alternative since the North's preoccupation with the survival of its regime makes threatening its existence the best deterrent. All that can be done is to keep the necessary offensive capabilities in reserve, which is the United States' posture today. The North might take comfort if Team Spirit were permanently suspended (though the Pentagon claims that many of its benefits are now achieved in smaller exercises); this would be one way for the United States to signal that no conventional attack is planned.

Still, nothing can be done about the U.S.-ROK capability for military intervention short of a thorough reduction of South Korean forces (in exchange for big cuts by the North) and the departure of U.S. forces. The North ought to be reassured by the fact that the likelihood of sufficient public and congressional support for U.S. intervention in the North would be minimal, but the North's understanding of the U.S. government has not been strong. Thus, the North will be satisfied on the issue of conventional forces only if the peninsula is significantly demilitarized.

Whether this can be done is quite unclear. No progress toward this objective has ever been made. However, the North has proposed for years that forces on each side be greatly reduced (usually suggesting cutbacks to a level of 100,000), and Western and ROK analysts have suggested that the

North feels greatly threatened by the burdens of the heavy defense spending required to compete with the South. One stumbling block in the past was the North's insistence that cuts include the elimination of U.S. forces, but recently the North has signaled that it will no longer treat this desire as a prerequisite.[23] Obviously, the United States must be prepared to explore sharp cuts in forces on the peninsula, as many analysts have proposed, but this will not be possible without a revival of North-South talks, a proposal on which the North continues to drag its feet.

There are two other ways to proceed. The North is seeking to replace the armistice with a new peace agreement to provide a broad security guarantee and has withdrawn (with China's support) from the Military Armistice Commission to try to force the issue. The difficulty is that the North is pursuing a new agreement while trying to exclude the South from peace negotiations, which is unacceptable to Washington and Seoul. The latter might seriously propose tripartite negotiations, which might work. But it would be most unwise of Seoul to agree to bilateral U.S.-DPRK peace talks when the real political issue is between the North and the South.

This problem has led a seemingly endless series of analysts to propose a multilateral approach to security in Northeast Asia so that a peace agreement, denuclearization, reductions in forces, and the North's security could be embedded in a larger framework.[24] The general idea makes good sense, particularly in terms of security for North Korea, but the proposals are premature. The North cannot accept a multilateral approach now because its foreign policy and its political system remain unacceptable to every other state that would participate in the security arrangement. Multilateralism would concentrate these states' objections and pressures on the North to change, hardly a welcome prospect in Pyongyang.[25] A multilateralist approach will be possible only after the North has significantly altered its concept of security, its political system, and its foreign policy. This item on the list is therefore not being provided completely.

Greater Transparency About U.S. and ROK Military Capabilities and Intentions

Until the North has a firm guarantee from Washington and Seoul of no military intervention or outright attack, having a clear view of its opponents' capabilities and intentions will be valuable. The level of openness regarding U.S.-ROK forces is vastly higher than it is for those of the North, yet the North has frequently misunderstood the intentions of those forces, as displayed in its consistent reaction to Team Spirit with expensive alerts and partial mobilization.

U.S. steps to ease North Korean concerns would require significant parallel steps by the North, steps it has refused to undertake for years. Its secrecy is a clear and large advantage that it has been unwilling to give up. The Russians were equally reluctant to give up the advantage of secrecy, except in very specified ways in arms control agreements, until they were fully committed to end the Cold War. The Chinese have similarly savored this advantage and remain reluctant to part with it. In both cases, an important objective of the secrecy was, not to facilitate preparations for a surprise attack, *but to hide significant national, including military, shortcomings.* Seldom mentioned in Western analyses, this objective is quite likely true for North Korea today.

Such a motivation greatly complicates matters. The hiding of weaknesses makes sense if it is believed that the opponent will try to exploit them or that a display of weakness will tempt the opponent to abandon efforts at conciliation and be more demanding. Such suspicions invite serious misperceptions about the enemy, but steps by the enemy to improve relations will be either mistrusted or readily discounted if the result would be the uncovering of one's weaknesses. This dilemma beset all Communist states during the Cold War; North Korea has not escaped it.

The key to emerging from such a situation is for the more accessible side to be as transparent as is prudent to demonstrate benign intentions, helping erode the other's feeling that secrecy is vital while denying the opponent some important benefits because it remains opaque. This plan is not guaranteed to work, but at least its incentives follow the right direction. U.S. and ROK invitations to the North to send observers to Team Spirit are a good idea. Efforts to have the North inspect U.S. bases in the South should continue. Informing the North in advance about any major changes in U.S. military plans and deployments on the peninsula would be good.

Unfortunately, thinking along these lines has led to a huge outpouring of analyses on the possible utility of confidence-building measures.[26] Nearly all of this literature is of limited value. The term "confidence building" is something of a misnomer. In a serious conflict, it is not nonconflictual interactions that build confidence; it is important *shifts in political judgment* (concerning what constitutes security, whether the other side is a threat, whether interactions will be favorable and negotiations worthwhile) that make the difference. These shifts normally precede or accompany confidence-building measures and are not a product of them.[27] Confidence-building measures are best thought of as ways to confirm that a shift in political judgment is on the right track or to institutionalize the emerging, larger realm of agreement and cooperation.

In the North-South conflict, no marked shift in political judgment has apparently yet occurred, and such a shift would have to occur in the North to make the pursuit of greater transparency work. The North will have to alter its image of South Korea and the United States as enemies so that secrecy becomes less critical as a security asset, for "there is a limit to what can be accomplished if great antipathy still drives the relationship."[28] But this new perception would undermine one of the psychological pillars of the DPRK regime and the political system—the grave external threat that necessitates strict national unity and control.

Thus, we can conclude that the United States and South Korea have taken some steps but could do more to offer the North sufficient transparency to fulfill this third security item. But the impact of greater transparency would be contained by the North's perceptions and policies, and it could not increase until such perceptions and policies change.

Better Relations with and
Official Recognition from the United States

Better political relations with the United States would convey greater legitimacy, making the DPRK regime more equivalent to that of the South, and would also lead to more benefits from other interactions (trade, investment, and technology). As noted earlier, establishing relations is a sharp departure from classic containment. Assuming that the Agreed Framework is carried out, this prerequisite for the North's security will be provided shortly; the two governments have been picking out sites for their embassies.

The stumbling block is the United States' desire and the ROK's insistence that fulfillment of the Agreed Framework should include progress in North-South relations. At a minimum, this means resumption of high-level contacts and negotiations, but once that occurs, some movement on specific issues will also have to take place. The United States must virtually insist on North-South talks. It promised to do so as part of the earlier negotiations[29] and then reversed itself, greatly angering Seoul. Thus, Washington has to press on this issue now for the sake of the U.S.-ROK alliance, and it is publicly saying it will do so.[30]

Still, it is quite unclear whether the North is ready for such talks.[31] It may be, and it is delaying now only to get the maximum benefit from dealing with the United States alone. Or it may not be, hoping that the United States will give way on this issue as it did before. Evidence on the positive side includes the precedents of prior North-South negotiations and agreements and the North's acceptance of the Agreed Framework provisions that it "will consistently take steps to implement the North-South Joint Declaration on the Denuclearization of the Korean Peninsula" and "will engage in North-South dialogue." Other evidence is that at one time (1989–1992) the North took numerous steps to promote trade and investment from the South.[32] On the negative side are the North's initial resistance to accepting light-water reactors from South Korea, its continued anti-South rhetoric, and its pursuit of a separate peace agreement without the South's involvement.

Retention of an Alliance with China

Ideally, an alliance with China would include protection by China's nuclear forces. Like the South, the North has always wanted a major patron for deterrence, military resources, and direct assistance in the event of war. China has filled this role, especially with the collapse of DPRK-Russian relations, but only to a degree.

It has long been debated whether a patron bolsters the North's lack of cooperation with others or gives it the security necessary to try cooperation. Recent evidence indicates that a steady decline in its relationship with China has moved the North to pursue, very gingerly, a more cooperative path. Thus, a vigorous attempt by China to renew the alliance might cut the North's cooperation short unless the Chinese attempt was conditioned on the North's cooperating anyway. It is also possible that the alliance, having helped the North sustain isolation in the past, can now work the other way. The North has abandoned its nuclear weapons program in exchange for payoffs from the United States. A healthy relationship with a nuclear power can be a satisfying substitute.

It is unclear whether such an alliance will be fully available, but it seems unlikely. China has never been in the business of extended nuclear deterrence and probably does not want to start now. China's promised support will likely be confined to non-nuclear levels—though, of course, a nuclear-armed state carries a measure of existential deterrence with respect to its allies. Thus, this security item is available to the North but in an attenuated fashion, providing significant but not complete satisfaction. The United States can do little about this issue other than not to object to the alliance.

A Supportive Association with Russia

In principle, an improved relationship with Russia could extend to nuclear deterrence and the opportunity for the North to acquire advanced weaponry. Although the North may not want to rely heavily on Russia, particularly in view of the Russian government's recent behavior, it should find an association with Russia rewarding both in itself and as a form of insurance (in case things go badly with China, cooperative security has to be abandoned, or Japan moves to become a first-class military power).

Such an alliance is not currently available to the North, and the United States cannot change that. Russia is already using resolution of the nuclear issue and an improvement in U.S.-DPRK (and Japan-DPRK) relations as good reasons to seek more normal ties with North Korea. But it does not want an alliance, for a host of reasons, and instead consistently expresses interest in a multilateral approach to security in Northeast Asia. Russia does not want anything to get in the way of satisfactory relations with the other great powers and South Korea. The best the North can expect from Russia is the comfort of having normal relations with a great power, and the DPRK will not pursue relations vigorously until its link with the United States develops further. Thus, this security item is not being provided, but control over when and how it develops lies in the North's hands.

A More Normal Relationship with Japan

In its pursuit of security, the DPRK could develop a more normal and economically beneficial relationship with Japan by being less obstreperous and isolated. Pyongyang should seek balances in its relations with each of the great powers for economic, if not for security, reasons. Like Russia, Japan is not now contributing to the security problems of the North, and this is due in large part to North Korea. A more normal and economically beneficial relationship with Japan would contribute to North Korean security. The United States appears quite willing to see such a relationship develop between the two countries.

Adequate Military Forces for Deterrence and Defense

In the past, the North's definition of "adequate" forces has been extreme, inviting the view that it was interested in attacking instead of defending. Just how adequate its forces are now, in the regime's concept of security, is not clear. The North does not have the military ability to conquer the South; it does have the ability to defend itself, but how well is uncertain. In the short run, it would do well, but its long-term combat capability is questionable. Its massive forces should be able to deter any foreseeable threats on the ground. However, it might well have been unable to deter or defend against a determined, selective U.S. attack on its nuclear program facilities. Its deterrent was a threat to attack the South in response, which carried with it the risk of jeopardizing its own regime.

Obviously, the adequacy of a nation's forces depends on the challenges it wants to be able to mount or defeat. A reduction in prospective military challenges can enhance security as much as or more than boosting the nation's relative military strength. If the North pursues more cooperative relationships, the adequacy of its existing forces would grow, and it could retain a satisfactory capability at a lower level of effort as outside threats declined. In this way it would be possible to reduce forces on the peninsula greatly.

There is persistent speculation that the North finds its military situation quite unsatisfactory, believes that it cannot keep up with the South in over-all military spending, and fears that the South is seeking either to gain military superiority or to so burden the North's economy that the regime collapses. A common explanation for the North's nuclear weapons program has been that it would be a cheaper route to security in this competition.[33] There are repeated suggestions that the North is paranoid and has a siege mentality, not only about the United States and South Korea but about Japan. If this is true, the North may resist cutting the burden of defense spending, thus inhibiting the possibilities for marked reductions in forces that would sustain the North's sense of security. There is also the possibility that the regime has become increasingly dependent on the armed forces politically and that the military's influence has grown under Kim Jong Il. This possibility would also inhibit the North from seeking security via cooperation and reduced military expenditures.

There is little the United States can do other than to suggest or support suggestions for making major mutual cuts in forces while increasing the various levels of satisfactory interaction with the North.

Elimination or Absorption of South Korea

On any wish list for security for the North, elimination of the South Korean state would be the ultimate item. For years the North has regarded the continued existence of South Korea as the ultimate threat to its regime both as a competitor for legitimate rule of the nation and as the base for the U.S. presence in Korean affairs. Many analysts, particularly in South Korea, believe that elimination of the South remains the North's primary goal. The present efforts of the United States and South Korea assume that the North has abandoned this goal as unfeasible. If it has not, then DPRK military capabilities are inadequate for security and will almost certainly remain so. If the North has not abandoned or does not abandon a desire, plans, and the pursuit of capabilities to overwhelm the South militarily, the United States can do little to add to the North's security.

The North's security goals vis-à-vis other states are listed in Table 8.1.

Table 8.1 National Security Balance Sheet, External Dimension

Component	Availability	U.S. Contribution
No nuclear attack	Yes	Major
No other attack	No	Modest
Enemy transparency	Yes	Modest
Relations with United States	Yes	Major
China alliance	Partial	None
Russia association	Potential	None
Relations with Japan	Potential	Modest
Adequate forces	Partial	Modest
End of South Korea	No	Negative

Internal Security Concerns

The other obvious dimension of the North's security concerns is internal, and the degree to which the United States has some responsibility for the North's internal security must be assessed. Let us begin by reviewing the paramount characteristics of North Korea's internal security arrangement. The first is that security of the regime is deemed essential, worthy of vast risks and burdens and considered far more important than the security of the nation. The regime has imposed enormous sacrifices on the population, in peace and war, and has often placed the people at great risk in its determination to rule how it wishes and to stay in power.

Second, the regime has long defined internal security primarily as retaining ideological purity, sustaining a way of life the regime considers the only acceptable one, and thus requiring retention of absolute control over the society. This goal was reinforced by the collapse of communism elsewhere. The North drew the conclusion that the collapse had occurred because inadequate attention had been given to ideological and political control, and it thus redoubled its efforts to prevent collapse from occurring in the North.

Third, the North has long been considered a "strong state" among less developed states, primarily for its ability to get the population to do what it wants and its low vulnerability to internal unrest and rebellion.[34] However, the collapse of communism suggests that North Korea is, instead, subject to what Fukuyama has called the "enormous weaknesses at the core of the world's seemingly strongest dictatorships."[35] Under this conception, the mechanisms and resources that have led it to be considered a strong state— massive security and ideological controls, isolation of the population—are reflections of its inability to compete and thus the fragility of its legitimacy and political support.

Fourth, the regime (like other Communist regimes) has long based its internal appeal on two elements that are increasingly perilous: the insistence that it is constructing a superior way of life, far advanced in comparison with other societies, and the belief that it faces a constant, severe threat from the outside. The erosion of both concepts directly threatens domestic security. The first was damaged some time ago and the second may be now. The regime needs big successes and enemies; it has none of the former and may now lose the latter. As one analyst has suggested, these developments can add up to a profound identity crisis as the core threat to the regime domestically.[36]

We can list the regime's prerequisites for security to aid in our analysis. These requirements are almost certainly considered of great importance in Pyongyang.

Successful Political Succession

A smooth passing of political power is an obvious prerequisite for internal security. The regime began trying to ensure a peaceful succession many years ago. It is widely assumed in the West that in the short run there has been no problem in this regard, but this view is worth challenging. Kim Jong Il has not assumed several key titles and positions that would normally have come to an unchallenged leader, he continues to make only rare public appearances, and some analysts are beginning to doubt that he has completed the succession successfully. He has strongly catered to the armed forces while in office, so much so as to suggest that he has been either placating significant opposition in the military or building his power base there because he is at odds with the party and state sectors of the leadership.[37] Political succession has sometimes gone quite badly in Communist states, resulting in severe disruption of plans laid down carefully beforehand. This was true after Stalin's death and again after Mao's.

What should the United States contribute to this situation? There has been debate over the Agreed Framework on just this point. Critics contend that the agreement contributes to the legitimacy of the Kim Jong Il regime and that it will strengthen his chances of survival. Kim Jong Il must show, among other things, that he can improve the regime's chances, and the Agreed Framework makes an important contribution to the regime's improvement. The opposing view is that the regime has survived thus far in the face of isolation and containment and has been a constant threat to stability and peace in the region, and that only if reversing its obstreperous behavior can be made to appear compatible with the survival of the regime, will this be adopted. Thus, the temporary strengthening of the regime is an acceptable price to pay for moving toward a viable regional security situation and drawing the North into more normal relationships. And only the United States is in a position to offer such rewards.

The Clinton administration has decided to adopt the latter view. Contributing to the regime's stability, including the succession, is acceptable in exchange for progress on the nuclear issue and the possibility of productive discussions on other regional security issues. Whether this will work depends on whether a good succession requires the North's continued isolation and rigid security posture or the ability of Kim and his supporters to demonstrate that a moderate policy of engagement can bring important payoffs. That in turn depends on whether Kim is, as some suggest, not really interested in major changes or, to the contrary, associated with those who see change as the only way the regime can survive.

Thus, if the perspective offered here is correct, this security item has not yet been provided, but the United States may be contributing to it.

Retention of Regime Solidarity and Control

Long associated with discussions between North and South is a pledge not to interfere in each other's domestic system, a promise often honored but seldom kept. Still, South Korea some time ago moved toward trying to embrace the North rather than isolate it, accepting the existence of its regime (though currently this approach is being held in abeyance). ROK proposals for unification now envision an extended confederation in which the North would continue to exist for a while. The United States has also, by implication, now agreed not to attempt to undermine the North's solidarity and control.

The problem is that an undermining of regime solidarity and control may be inherent in any normal relationship between the North and both the United States and the South. The latter cannot offer North Korea security from the corrosive effects that greater involvement with their societies and others will have on the regime's legitimacy and survivability. The best they have to offer—increased contacts, trade, technology—may be even more threatening to the North's internal security than the worst they have offered in the past. In other words, it is the North's responsibility to manage a more normal intercourse with its enemies without eroding the regime's foundations. Adding to the problem from the North's viewpoint is that the United States and South Korea fully expect that the North cannot do this successfully.

With this in mind, the North continues to believe that it must closely confine all contacts with the outside and retain a closed society in order to avoid infection. It is hoping, for instance, to attract foreign investment but to confine it to isolated places. U.S. and other analysts believe that this cannot be done if the North is to extract the benefits it needs.

Thus, this item on the North's internal security list is not guaranteed for the years ahead, and clearly the North will continue to fear that its solidarity and control are under attack.

Retention of the Political, Economic, and Social System

Internal security in the North is now a point of contention between the view that the system must be retained to maintain the ideological goals, purity, and identity of the North and the view that the system cannot survive much longer without substantial changes because it must become more productive and competitive. In the former view, the regime must retain autarky, highly centralized economic planning and management, tight political controls, and the like. The alternative view envisions reform, decentralization, and political flexibility.

The United States has not mounted any drive to pressure the North into major political reforms, human rights shifts, or elaborate economic reforms. It is dealing with the North as it is. U.S. preferences are clear, but they are not constraints on the development of a more normal relationship. Once again, the United States is betting that the North cannot survive a more normal relationship in the long run.

It is up to the North to show that it can find a way to retain the fundamental characteristics of the regime yet still open to the outside or that it can find ways to adjust those characteristics to survive and prosper. The United States cannot have much of an impact on this challenge.

Improved Economic Development

Everyone agrees that the North is in dire straits economically. It is widely assumed that this major failing of the regime is one of the graver threats to its stability and survival. Getting outside help to rectify its economic situation is one of the North's major goals. It needs outside markets and access to outside resources and technology through trade and investment. Recently, it has needed a great deal of outside assistance just to ward off famine.

The evidence is also clear that, given the right policies, the North could make significant economic progress. It is not lacking in many necessary resources, natural or human. East Asia has demonstrated that there are routes available to rapid economic growth and giant increases in living standards. Former socialist economies in Eastern Europe—particularly Poland, the Czech Republic, and Hungary—as well as in China have converted into economies that achieve respectable progress.

In North Korea, however, economic progress almost certainly would require substantial economic and military reform. The North must find a way to maintain the fifth largest armed forces in the world, with the world's highest ratio of troops to population and probably the highest ratio of defense spending to gross national product.[38] There will be few trade and investment opportunities without big changes in the economic system. Access to outside markets may be of little avail if the North's backward economy is not improved sufficiently to produce products others need and want. It may be necessary to mount a frontal assault on fundamental tenets of the North's socialism.

The North is trying to cope in various ways. The creation of a special economic zone for foreign investment is meant to achieve some of the benefits from outside without recasting the economic system.[39] The North has allowed or fostered the emergence of a "court economy," a special sector not subject to the regular economic practices that specializes in production of goods and services for the elite and enjoys greater access to the outside.[40] This is another way to modernize to meet certain needs without rearranging the entire economic system. The North has, in effect, a separate military economic sector that operates more freely than the rest of the economy and is perhaps fueled in part by overseas sales.[41] Kim Jong Il is associated with efforts to raise ideological exhortation to workers to obtain greater production. The regime has also put more emphasis on production of consumer goods in recent years to improve worker incentives. Outside analysts universally suggest that such measures will not work and that the North will need to accept a great deal more economic reform to reverse the economic decline. Their diagnosis is that the basic economic structure is to blame and is what needs to be changed.

The United States has now offered to relax the economic constraints that were part of containment, a move Japan is likely to follow. This relaxation might be accompanied by various forms of technical assistance or U.S. support for economic infrastructure projects or the Tumen River project. The ultimate in U.S. assistance would be making the U.S. economy available for a large number of North Korean imports, something the United States has done for other economies throughout the region. But it is clear that the regime, not the United States, must initiate the key steps. All the United States can do is offer incentives for the economic evolution of North Korea.

Conclusion

After this survey of the possibilities (see Table 8.2), it seems clear that there are distinct limits on what the United States can contribute to easing the present security concerns of the North Korean regime. Not surprisingly, the United States is better positioned to bolster North Korea's security with respect to external threats than to those from inside, but it faces limits even on that score. There is quite possibly an inverse relationship between easing the North's external security concerns—via a decline in the direct threat from the United States and the establishment of more normal political, economic, and other relations for the North with the outside world—and the viability of the regime and the domestic system it seeks so intensely to sustain. Only if the North can successfully evade this contradiction, making necessary adjustments domestically, will it be able to reap the full benefits in terms of its external security, which the relaxation of containment will make possible. And only if the North's domestic security can be made compatible with a broader interchange with the outside world will the way be truly open to constructing a multilateral framework as the international basis for security management on the peninsula and in Northeast Asia as a whole. Such a framework would in turn provide a favorable international environment for the two Koreas to tackle the unification issue.

Table 8.2   Domestic Security Balance Sheet, Internal Dimension

Component	Availability	U.S. Contribution
Political succession	Uncertain	Modest
Solidarity, control	Uncertain	Modest
System retention	Questionable	Minimal
Economic development	Available	Modest

Thus, the United States would be well advised to continue to contribute to easing the North's security concerns, being alert to the limited possibilities of such a contribution and ready to make the most of them while having a healthy respect for the complexities involved. Not least among these complexities is the tension between broadening U.S.-DPRK relations and retaining a healthy U.S.-ROK alliance. We can fairly confidently predict that the better U.S. relations with the North become (and thus the less threatening the North appears), the less vital the U.S.-ROK alliance will become for both South Korea and the United States. In turn, the South will feel less dependent and will make greater efforts to reduce its focus on the United States in favor of stronger links to the other great powers in the region.[42] Hence, the recent suggestions that (1) the U.S.-ROK alliance can continue indefinitely but only if there is careful planning for the transition to a unified Korea and its impact on the alliance and that (2) adjustments in the alliance will have to come well before unification if the North's threat fades appreciably, are correct and timely.[43]

Notes

1. William Epstein, "Nuclear Security for the Korean Peninsula," *Korean Journal of Defense Analysis* 4 (Winter 1992):55–69.
2. This includes an end to the North's sale of ballistic missiles. On the North's missile program, see David Wright and Timur Kadyshev, "The North Korean Missile Program: How Advanced Is It?" *Arms Control Today* (April 1994):9–12.
3. Richard P. Cronin, "North Korea: U.S. Policy and Negotiations to Halt Its Nuclear Weapons Program: An Annotated Chronology and Analysis," *CRS Report for Congress* (Washington, D.C.: Congressional Reference Service, 1994).
4. William T. Tow, "Northeast Asia and International Security: Transforming Competition to Collaboration," *Australian Journal of International Affairs* 46 (May 1992):1–28.
5. Kenneth Waltz, "Peace, Stability, and Nuclear Weapons," IGCC Policy Paper no. 15 (San Diego: Institute on Global Conflict and Cooperation, University of California August 1995), p. 14.
6. There are reports that the North suspended plans to sell the Nodong 1 missile to Iran in 1994; see *Arms Control Today* (January–February 1994):25.

7. Assistant Secretary of State Winston Lord, in a speech in *U.S. Department of State Dispatch*, vol. 6, no. 3, January 16, 1995, mentions U.S. interest in this.

8. A good review of the disagreements is Hwang Dong Eon, "Disagreements Between Seoul and Washington over Policies Regarding North Korea: Causes and Problems," *East Asian Review* 9 (Spring 1997):35–48.

9. See the Items on these talks in *Northeast Asia Peace and Security Network Daily Report* (Berkeley: ftp://ftp.nautilus.org/napsnet/dailly_reports), April 15, May 5–8, and May 12, 1997.

10. For reports on the famine and U.S. assistance to North Korea, see *Northeast Asia Peace and Security Network Daily Report,* April 21, April 28, May 7, and May 9, 1997; *Northeast Asia Peace and Security Network Special Report,* April 16, 1997 (transcript of a briefing by State Department spokesman Nicholas Burns), and April 11, 1997 (news conference of senators on returning from North Korea).

11. On the defection, see Kang In Duk, "Party Secretary Hwang's Defection: North Korea Now on the Brink of Collapse or Change," *East Asian Review* 9 (Spring 1997):19–34; *Northeast Asia Peace and Security Network Daily Report,* April 28, 1997.

12. See Larry Niksch, "The Agreed Framework View from Washington," in Tae-Hwan Kwak and Thomas L. Wilburn, eds., *The U.S.-ROK Alliance in Transition* (Seoul: Kyungnam University Press, 1996), pp. 141–152.

13. See Edward Olsen, "Toward Korean Unification: Arms Control and Disarmament as Political Instruments," in Jay Speakman and Chae Jin-Lee, eds., *The Prospects for Korean Unification* (Claremont, Calif.: Keck Center for International and Strategic Studies, 1993), pp. 59–73.

14. Paul Monk, "Coping with the End of History: Pyongyang and the Realm of Freedom," *Korean Journal of Defense Analysis* 4 (Winter 1992):95–123.

15. In 1992–1993 the North adopted numerous laws and regulations for foreign investment, joint ventures, and so forth; see Sang-Kyom Kim, "North Korea: Prospects for Economic Opening and Inter-Korean Cooperation," in *Korea's Economy 1995* (Washington, D.C.: Korea Economic Institute of America, 1995), pp. 83–87.

16. Selig Harrison, "The North Korean Nuclear Crisis: From Stalemate to Breakthrough," *Arms Control Today* (November 1994):18–20.

17. For a similar view, specifically on Japan, see Yoo Young Ock, "Pyongyang's Efforts to Improve Relations with Washington and Tokyo, and Seoul's Position," *East Asian Review* 7 (Autumn 1995):24–42, esp. p. 34.

18. For a similar analysis, see Oh Kwan-chi, "The Anatomy of Anxiety in the Emerging East Asia Security Order," in Ralph A. Cossa, ed., *Asia Pacific Confidence and Security Building Measures* (Washington, D.C.: Center for International and Strategic Studies, 1995), pp. 41–67, esp. p. 46.

19. Thus, South Korea insists that the North remains militarily superior by roughly 30 percent. See Ministry of National Defense, *Defense White Paper, 1992–1993* (Seoul: Ministry of National Defense, 1993), p. 67. Some roughly accurate figures on the military balance are available in *Arms Control Today* (December 1994).

20. See testimony by Secretary of Defense William Perry in Senate Committee on Foreign Relations, *North Korea Nuclear Agreement,* United States Senate, January 24–25, 1995 (Washington, D.C.: Government Printing Office, 1995), p. 26.

21. Team Spirit was initiated in the 1970s. Since 1990, North Korea has been invited to send observers but has declined. See Ministry of National Defense,

Defense White Paper, 1992–1993 (Seoul: Ministry of National Defense, 1993), pp. 106–107.

22. For a recent assessment of the military balance, see Peter Hayes and Stephen Noerper, "The ROK-U.S. Alliance: Who Benefits? An Impartial View," in Tae-Hwan Kwak and Thomas L. Wilburn, eds., *The U.S.-ROK Alliance in Transition* (Seoul: Kyungnam University Press, 1996), pp. 37–71.

23. "North Korea Said to Drop Objection to U.S. Troops," *International Herald Tribune,* September 29, 1995.

24. Some examples of these proposals: Yong Whan Kihl, "Confrontation or Compromise on the Korean Peninsula: The North Korean Nuclear Issue," *Korean Journal of Defense Analysis* 7 (Winter 1991):101–129; Donald Zagoria's remarks in House Subcommittee on Asian and Pacific Affairs of the Committee on Foreign Affairs, *The Future of Communist Systems in Asia,* House of Representatives, November 22, 1991 (Washington, D.C.: Government Printing Office, 1991), pp. 29–31, 61–65; Andrew Mack, "A Nuclear Free Zone for Northeast Asia," IGCC Policy Paper no. 9 (San Diego: Institute on Global Conflict and Cooperation, University of California, August 1994); Melvin Gurtov, "Prospects for Korea-U.S.-Japan Trilateral Security Relations," *Asian Perspective* 17 (Spring–Summer 1993):659–688; David Youtz and Paul Mitford, "A Northeast Asian Security Regime: Prospects After the Cold War," Institute for East-West Studies, Public Policy Paper no. 5 (Boulder, Colo.: Westview Press, 1992); Kim Kook Chin, "An Approach to Multilateral Security Regimes in Northeast Asia—with a Focus on the South Korean Perspective," *East Asian Review* 6 (Winter 1994):3–16; James E. Goodby, "The Context of Korean Unification: The Case for a Multilateral Security Structure," in Phil Williams et al., eds., *Security in Korea: War, Stalemate, and Negotiation* (Boulder, Colo.: Westview Press, 1994), pp. 233–249.

25. See a similar comment in Tsuyoishi Kawasaki, "The Logic of Japanese Multilateralism for Asia Pacific Security," Working Paper no. 8 (Institute of International Relations, University of British Columbia, December 1994).

26. Some examples: Young Koo Cha and Kang Choi, "Land-Based Confidence Building Measures in Northeast Asia: A South Korean Perspective," IGCC Policy Paper no. 9 (San Diego: Institute on Global Conflict and Cooperation, University of California, August 1994); various chapters in Ralph A. Cossa, ed., *Asia Pacific Confidence and Security Building Measures* (Washington, D.C.: Center for International and Strategic Studies, 1995); several chapters in Andrew Mack and John Ravenhill, *Pacific Cooperation: Building Economic and Security Regimes in the Asia-Pacific Region* (Boulder, Colo.: Westview Press, 1995).

27. For an excellent discussion, see James Macintosh, "A Confidence-Building Framework for the Korean Peninsula," *Korean Journal of Defense Analysis* 7 (Summer 1995):155–181.

28. Ibid., p. 179.

29. See remarks by Undersecretary of State for International Security Affairs Lynn Davis in Senate Subcommittee on East Asian and Pacific Affairs of the Committee on Foreign Relations, *U.S. Policy Toward North Korea,* U.S. Senate, March 3, 1994 (Washington, D.C.: Government Printing Office, 1994).

30. See the remarks by Secretary of State Warren Christopher in *U.S. Department of State Dispatch,* vol. 6, no. 7, February 13, 1995; and his testimony in *North Korea Nuclear Agreement;* and also Thomas C. Hubbard (deputy assistant secretary of state), "Prospects for Peace and Security on the Korean Peninsula," *Korea Economic Update* 6 (April 1995).

31. During Jimmy Carter's visit in June 1994, Kim Il Sung agreed to meet with Kim Young Sam "without any conditions." When Carter conveyed this to

President Kim Young Sam, he accepted. Preliminary talks were held to prepare for the meeting, which was planned for July 25–27, but plans were suspended after Kim Il Sung's death on July 8 and have remained so; see Young Whan Kihl, "Confrontation or Compromise."

32. John Merrill, "The Regional Political Context of Inter-Korean Economic Cooperation," in *Korea's Economy 1994* (Washington, D.C.: Korea Economic Institute, 1994), pp. 75–83.

33. See, e.g., Hak Joon Kim, "North Korea's Nuclear Development Program and the Future," in *U.S.-Korean Relations at a Time of Change* (Seoul: Research Institute for National Unification, 1994), pp. 53–79, especially p. 67; Sang Hoon Park, "North Korea and the Challenge to the U.S.–South Korean Alliance," *Survival* 36 (Summer 1994):78–91.

34. See the discussion in Brian L. Job, "The Insecurity Dilemma: National, Regime, and State Securities in the Third World," in Job, ed., *The Insecurity Dilemma: National Security of Third World States* (Boulder, Colo.: Lynne Rienner, 1992), pp. 11–35.

35. Quoted in Monk, "Coping with the End of History," p. 95.

36. Oh, "Anatomy of Anxiety," pp. 48–51.

37. In April 1997 Kim Jong Il promoted 123 high-level officers, the third time in the past year that he had done so. A total of 800 officers have been advanced since he took office in December 1991. See *Vantage Point* 20 (April 1997):20–21; also *Northeast Asia Peace and Security Network Daily Report,* April 15, 1997. A fascinating document in which Kim praises the armed forces' work and berates the party and state officials for their mistakes is "Remarks Made December 7, 1996 by Great General Kim Jong Il," excerpts in *Vantage Point* 20 (April 1997):40–44. A recent assessment of the domestic political situation in the North is Amos A. Jordan and Jae H. Ku, "Prospects for North Korea: Facing a Regime Crisis and Regime Collapse?" in Tae Hwan Ok and Gerrit W. Gong, eds., *Change and Challenge on the Korean Peninsula: Past, Present, and Future,* vol. 6 (Seoul: Research Institute for National Unification, 1996), pp. 18–41.

38. Nicholas Eberstadt, "North Korea: Reform, Muddling Through, or Collapse?" *NBR Analysis* 4 (September 1993).

39. The limits of this zone are explored in Lee Chan Woo, "The Outcome and Prospects of the Rajin-Sonbong Investment Forum," *East Asian Review* 9 (Spring 1997):88–109.

40. Chong-Sik Lee, "The Political Economy of North Korea, 1994," *NBR Analysis* 5 (September 1994).

41. Marcus Noland, "The North Korean Economy," *Korean Economic Update* 6 (July 1995).

42. An example of just this sort of thinking is found in Park Chong Chul, "Seoul's Policies Toward Washington and Pyongyang: After the Establishment of the U.S.–North Korea Liaison Offices," *East Asian Review* 7 (Winter 1995):48–67, esp. p. 63.

43. See Jonathan D. Pollack and Young Koo Cha, *A New Alliance for the Next Century: The Future of U.S.-Korean Security Cooperation* (Santa Monica, Calif.: RAND Corporation, 1996).

PART 4

External Relations of North Korea

9

China and North Korea: An Uncertain Relationship

Chae-Jin Lee

The Democratic People's Republic of Korea (DPRK) has faced a serious challenge in its foreign affairs because of its diminishing capacity and leverage in competing with the Republic of Korea (ROK) and in dealing with the four major powers—the United States, Russia, China, and Japan. In addition to its grave economic situation, North Korea is hard put to protect its *chuch'e* ideology against pressures for structural reform and an open-door policy, pressures that destroyed one-party dictatorships in Eastern Europe and the Soviet Union. It has also been ineffective in pursuing its self-styled crusade against capitalism and imperialism in the Third World. Most recently, the North Koreans failed to keep China's one-Korea policy intact and to normalize diplomatic and economic relations with the United States and Japan. They appear to be stymied by the complex crosscurrents that characterize their external environment.

Now that the Soviet Union has disintegrated and Russia is in disarray, the People's Republic of China (PRC) is the only major country on which the North Koreans can rely in world politics. In the post–Cold War era, China and North Korea share common or parallel interests in several important areas.[1] First, in view of the successive demise of many socialist regimes, the leaders of North Korea and China have a sense of urgency in defending their socialist systems, particularly the preeminent status of the Workers' Party of Korea (WPK) and the Chinese Communist Party (CCP). The two parties are equally opposed to the concepts of multiparty rule and the "peaceful evolution" of a socialist system.

Second, as the victims of economic sanctions and diplomatic isolation, both North Korea and China have a natural inclination to sympathize with each other's external predicament and to favor a policy of mutual aid in diplomatic and economic spheres. The two allies have cooperated for some time in joint economic activities such as hydroelectric power plants, railway transportation, and border trade, and they are interested in the Tumen River Area Development Project. The Chinese hope that

North Korea will study and emulate their model for economic modernization.

Third, since the leaders of North Korea and China are fiercely nationalistic and proud of their respective heritage and sovereignty, they reject any form of outside interference in their domestic affairs. For example, North Korea and China support each other in resisting the U.S.-led campaign for human rights. And both countries seem to share the strategic perspective that it is important to maintain a military balance between North and South Korea. For this reason North Korea allocates a great proportion of its budget to national defense, and China, unlike Russia, continues to uphold its mutual security treaty with North Korea.

In spite of many shared interests, however, China and North Korea have shown an increasingly serious cleavage in their overall policy orientations during the 1990s. In contrast to the North Koreans, who remain reluctant to outgrow the constraints of their stubborn ideological commitments and to accommodate the changing international reality, the Chinese have decisively transcended Maoist prescriptions and have successfully pursued a pragmatic open-door policy inspired by Deng Xiaoping. The legacy of the Korean War is no longer dominant in cementing the bond between the two allies, nor is the traditional rhetoric of "militant friendship" and "proletarian internationalism." At a time when the North Koreans are engaged in the transition of political leadership from Kim Il Sung to Kim Jong Il, they face the difficult task of charting the uncertain future of political, economic, and military relations with China.

Political Relations

The end of the worldwide Cold War confrontation ushered in a dramatic realignment of the international forces in East Asia. In particular, the establishment of diplomatic relations between China and South Korea in August 1992 was an unmistakable setback for Kim Il Sung, who had regarded China as his most reliable ally and patron since the Korean War. The North Koreans were bitter about this betrayal and abandonment by China, and in protest they limited cultural exchange programs with China and drew up a "black list" of Chinese officials and scholars regarded as pro-Seoul.[2] Yet the North Koreans refrained from publicly expressing displeasure toward China, as they had done toward the Soviet Union, mainly because they could not afford to alienate China. It was perhaps of some consolation to Kim Il Sung that China's top leaders, especially President Yang Shangkun and Foreign Minister Qian Qichen, came to Pyongyang to explain their diplomatic intentions in advance and to reiterate their respect and support for his policies. Their tactful handling of Kim's strong ego softened the impact of China's new two-Korea diplomacy on North Korea. Kim undoubtedly missed the bygone days when he could maximize his interests by playing off China against the Soviet Union.

The political relationship between China and North Korea improved appreciably during 1993, in part because North Korea required Chinese diplomatic support for its nuclear policy stance before the UN Security Council and the International Atomic Energy Agency (IAEA). In an attempt to soothe Kim Il Sung's wounded feelings, the Chinese designated a rising political star, Hu Jintao (a member of the Standing Committee of the CCP Political Bureau and the Secretariat), to lead the well-publicized ceremonies commemorating the fortieth anniversary of the Korean Armistice Agreement. On July 25, 1993, Hu presided over the opening of the impressive Memorial Hall for the Resist-America and Aid-Korea War at Dandong, a border city on the Yalu River. Calligraphy by Deng Xiaoping was unveiled, and Chi Haotian (minister of national defense), Hong Xuezhi (vice-chairman of the Chinese People's Political Consultative Conference), Chen Muhua (vice-chairman of the Standing Committee of the National People's Congress), and other high-level Chinese leaders were present.

In his speech, Hu praised the Korean War as a "great and just war against the aggressors."[3] In the following few days, Hu, accompanied by Chi Haotian, a Korean War veteran, met with Kim Il Sung and Kim Jong Il in Pyongyang, where he stressed the continuity of their traditional friendship and attended the Korean Armistice Agreement celebration. Kim Il Sung was placated by reassurances of China's uninterrupted high regard for the Sino–North Korean solidarity forged during the Korean War and by the close rapport between Hu Jintao and Kim Jong Il, who are close in age. Kim Il Sung was also pleased by the appointment of a new Chinese ambassador to Pyongyang—Qiao Zonghuai, a son of the late Qiao Guanhua (who had participated in the Panmunjom negotiations and had defended North Korean diplomatic interests at the UN in the early 1970s). Compared with the United States and Japan, both of which lacked a diplomatic presence in North Korea, and Russia, which had difficult relations with North Korea, China enjoyed the best of two worlds—retaining the old framework of political and military ties with North Korea while entering into a new economic and diplomatic partnership with South Korea.

On the death of Kim Il Sung in July 1994, Deng Xiaoping issued a message of condolence to the WPK Central Committee and expressed his "deep grief" at the loss of a "close comrade-in-arms" (*qinmide zhanyou*).[4] Deng sent a wreath to the North Korean embassy in Beijing and gave instructions to lower the flags to half mast in Kim's memory at Tiananmen Square and elsewhere. Other top Chinese leaders—President Jiang Zemin, Premier Li Peng, and Qiao Shi (chairman of the Standing Committee of the National People's Congress)—jointly stated:

Comrade Kim Il Sung always strove to preserve and promote the traditional friendship of the peoples of China and Korea with great zeal. He
maintained deep friendship with the older generation of Chinese revolu-
tionaries and incessantly pushed forward the friendly and co-operative
relations between the two countries. Though Comrade Kim Il Sung is
dead, his lofty image will always remain in the hearts of the Korean people. The Chinese people will always remember him. It is our strong belief
that the Korean people will surely carry out his behest, unite closely
around the Workers' Party of Korea led by Comrade Kim Jong Il, and continue their efforts in building their country well and achieving a lasting
peace for the Korean Peninsula.[5]

In addition, Jiang, Li, Qiao, and many other Chinese leaders visited the
North Korean embassy in Beijing to express condolences. The Chinese
promptly recognized Kim Jong Il as the new supreme leader in North
Korea in an attempt to ensure a smooth transition of power in Pyongyang.
They concluded that Kim Jong Il had accumulated sufficient internal sup-
port in North Korea, but they were concerned about his illnesses.[6] And
China agreed to donate 100,000 tons of grain to North Korea.

The death of Kim Il Sung marked a turning point, and henceforth
Chinese policy toward North Korea would go beyond consideration of
Kim's intimate personal ties with China and would attempt to bring about a
more normal relationship between the two countries. Since Kim Il Sung's
forty-six-year rule was over, the Chinese hoped that his successors would
adopt a pragmatic open-door foreign policy and improve inter-Korean relations. It is conceivable that Jiang Zemin and Li Peng conveyed this hope to
Vice President Yi Chong-ok, who went to Beijing to celebrate the forty-
fifth anniversary of the PRC's founding on September 27, 1994.[7] Jiang
Zemin and Kim Jong Il exchanged messages of greetings for the anniversary; the North Koreans hosted a banquet at the People's Palace of Culture
in Pyongyang for the PRC.[8]

A month thereafter, on October 31, 1994, Premier Li Peng began a
five-day official visit to Seoul. Prior to his Seoul trip, Li had proposed to
visit Pyongyang first; in addition to attempting to placate North Korea, Li
wanted to ascertain the precise condition of Kim Jong Il's health. The
North Koreans did not, however, welcome Li's visit at that time, not only
because Kim Jong Il was in mourning but also because they were unhappy
with China's growing economic and diplomatic cooperation with South
Korea.

In his meeting with President Kim Young Sam in Seoul, Li stated that
China wished to develop good-neighbor relations with both South Korea
and North Korea and that such relations would be conducive to regional
and global peace.[9] He also suggested that the two Korean governments
resume high-level dialogues and settle all questions, including nuclear
issues, by peaceful means. In turn, President Kim explained that political

stability and economic recovery in North Korea were important to peace on the Korean peninsula and to the development of Sino–South Korean cooperation. He asked for China's assistance to ensure that North Korea would fully implement the Geneva agreement on nuclear issues.[10]

After his return from Seoul, Li Peng evidently submitted a glowing report on South Korea to the Political Bureau of the CCP. He apparently recommended that China transcend its obsessive reluctance to incur a negative response from North Korea and aggressively expand its relations with South Korea in all areas, including military affairs.[11] The exchange of top-level leaders between China and South Korea continued in 1995; notably, Qiao Shi went to Seoul in April and South Korean prime minister Yi Hong-gu visited Beijing in May. Yi received an extraordinarily warm and enthusiastic red-carpet treatment in China, where he met with Jiang Zemin, Li Peng, Qiao Shi, and other Chinese leaders. Jiang accepted Yi's invitation to visit South Korea in the fall of 1995.

China and North Korea also made concerted efforts throughout 1995 to improve their strained relations and to demonstrate the continuing validity of their traditional friendship and cooperation. In spite of their obvious disappointment, the North Koreans adopted a realistic approach toward China's growing linkage with South Korea and sought China's diplomatic and economic assistance as much as possible. Likewise, the Chinese took every opportunity to recognize and praise Kim Jong Il's "wisdom and achievements," and the CCP Central Committee sent flowers to Kim on his fifty-third birthday in February 1995. In his meeting with Hwang Chang-yop, Chinese ambassador Qiao Zonghuai declared that Kim had tirelessly worked for the party and the state, as well as for the happiness of the Korean people and the dignity of the nation.[12] Li Shuzheng (director of the CCP's international liaison department), Tang Jiaxuan (vice-minister for foreign affairs), Li Jing (deputy chief of the People's Liberation Army's [PLA's] general staff), and other Chinese leaders attended a commemorative banquet at the North Korean embassy in Beijing. On the first anniversary of Kim Il Sung's death, Hu Jintao, accompanied by Wang Bingqian (vice chairman of the Standing Committee of the National People's Congress and a former finance minister) and Wu Xueqian (vice-chairman of the National Committee of the Chinese People's Political Consultative Conference and a former foreign minister), visited the North Korean embassy in Beijing and presented a bouquet on behalf of the CCP Central Committee.[13] Other Chinese leaders, such as Li Shuzheng and Zhang Wannian (chief of the PLA's general staff), participated in a memorial service held at the embassy.

To iron out China's policy differences with North Korea, the vice-minister of foreign affairs, Tang Jiaxuan, led a delegation to Pyongyang in June 1995 and met with Vice-Premier Kim Yong-nam.[14] One of Tang's missions was, reportedly, to ensure the North Koreans that China would maintain the level of its supply of crude oil and weapons (including tanks and missiles) to North Korea.[15] He also strongly protested and warned his North Korean counterparts about North Korea's increasing ties with Taiwan.[16] The Chinese were angered by North Korea's manipulation of the "Taiwan card" as a device to counterbalance China's relations with South Korea. One example of North Korea's thinly veiled maneuvering was its endorsement of the Taiwanese city of Kaohsiung as a venue for the 2002 Asian Games; China supported Pusan. Ultimately, however, the two sides reaffirmed that, no matter what happened globally or on the Korean peninsula, China and North Korea would continue their friendly relations.

On several occasions in the latter half of 1995, Jiang Zemin and Kim Jong Il exchanged congratulatory messages. On the forty-seventh anniversary of the DPRK's founding in September 1995, Jiang sent a warm message addressed to Kim as "Chairman of the Korean National Defense Committee and Supreme Commander of the Korean People's Army": "Ever since President Kim Il Sung regrettably passed away, the DPRK people have firmly rallied around the WPK Central Committee headed by you, and continuously worked to achieve the country's prosperity and enrichment and its peaceful and independent reunification by replacing sorrow with strength and following the footsteps of President Kim Il Sung." An equally enthusiastic editorial in *Renmin ribao* applauded the WPK's revolutionary achievements. The Chinese overture was properly reciprocated by Kim Jong Il's message of September 30, on the forty-sixth anniversary of the PRC's founding, and by an editorial in *Nodong sinmun.* Among other things, the North Koreans acknowledged that Kim Il Sung had personally nurtured a "precious friendship" with both Mao Zedong and Zhou Enlai.[17]

On the fiftieth anniversary of the WPK's founding in October, the Chinese made extraordinarily friendly gestures to Kim Jong Il; they were even prepared to dispatch a high-level delegation to Pyongyang in the event of his accession as general secretary of the WPK or as president of the DPRK. Attending a commemorative banquet held at the North Korean embassy in Beijing, Jiang Zemin lauded the WPK's ability to overcome manifold hardships in recent years and stated: "The Chinese Communist Party and people are as happy with the victories and achievements of the WPK and the Korean people as they are with their own, and hope that under the leadership of Comrade Kim Jong Il, they will make even greater accomplishments in domestic and foreign affairs."[18] The same message was reiterated in Jiang's long letter addressed to "Respected Comrade Kim Jong Il of the Standing Committee of the Political Bureau of the WPK Central Committee."[19] Jiang stressed Kim Jong Il's contribution to promoting the goals of socialist construction and peaceful reunification and safeguarding the peace and stability on the Korean peninsula.

In return for Presidents Roh Tae Woo's and Kim Young Sam's earlier visits to Beijing, Jiang Zemin at last made a five-day state visit to South Korea in November 1995. As the first Chinese head of state to travel to Seoul, he reaffirmed China's intention to develop friendly, good-neighbor relations with both South and North Korea and to encourage the resumption of inter-Korean dialogue and cooperation.[20] Even though he had proposed visiting Pyongyang either before or after his Seoul trip, the North Koreans refused to accommodate his wish. Moreover, Kim Jong Il did not accept Jiang's invitation to visit China publicly or secretly.[21] Jiang's journey to Seoul served as a clear illustration of China's objectives: to sustain the convenient formality of its two-Korea policy but to aggressively pursue economic relations with South Korea.

There is without doubt a sharp difference between China's economic relations with South and North Korea. Whereas China's trade with South Korea skyrocketed to $16.5 billion per year by the end of 1995, its trade with North Korea decreased to $550 million during the same year. Yet China's relative importance for North Korea's economic survival is undeniable. The North Koreans conducted about one-third of their foreign trade with China during 1995 and relied heavily on China for imports of crude oil, grains, coal/coke, textiles, chemicals, and machinery.[22] Since North Korea was unable to pay its cumulative trade deficit, the Chinese either rescheduled or forgave many of its debts. And the Chinese agreed to provide food aid (120,000 tons in 1996 and 70,000 tons by mid-1997) to help ease a massive famine in North Korea.[23] As China has outgrown its ideologically prescribed economic policy and adopted a "socialist market economy," the gap between the economic orientations of China and North Korea has widened.

The North Koreans hesitate to follow the Chinese model of economic modernization entirely precisely because they suspect that it might compromise their *chuch'e* ideology and might ignite political problems similar to those that led to the Tiananmen Square incident. They are aware of the adverse social consequences of a capitalistic system in Shenzhen. They do not have a large enough territory to insulate free economic and trade zones from the rest of North Korea. Hence, they are likely to undertake only a highly selective, cautious, and experimental emulation of the Chinese model. Even though the Chinese cannot fully satisfy North Korea's economic requests and diplomatic interests, they will help North Korea as much as they can for the sake of preventing a collapse of its system or military instability. When Hwang Chang-yop, a senior North Korean theoretician, defected to the South Korean consulate at Beijing in February 1997, the Chinese made every effort not to aggravate tension on the Korean peninsula. They carefully and adroitly resolved this five-week diplomatic crisis by making a face-saving gesture toward North Korea and sending Hwang by a Chinese plane to the Philippines.

Military Affairs

In contrast to the considerable degree of flexibility shown in their diplomatic and economic activities toward the Korean peninsula, the Chinese have been slow to modify their military alliance with North Korea. After Kim Il Sung's meeting with Deng Xiaoping in October 1991, the Chinese reportedly agreed to make up, at least partially, for the loss of Moscow's earlier support by offering a package of economic and military assistance to North Korea. In this way, they hoped to maintain a military balance in the peninsula and to bolster North Korea's defense capability after the collapse of the Soviet Union. This gesture suggests the seriousness of the Chinese desire to stave off a sense of insecurity and isolation by North Korea, which might have a dangerous consequence on the Korean peninsula.

The Chinese frequently reassured their North Korean counterparts that China would honor the Treaty of Friendship, Cooperation and Mutual Assistance with North Korea and would maintain the spirit of friendship cemented by blood between the two allies. On the thirtieth anniversary of the security treaty in July 1991, for example, Jiang Zemin, Yang Shangkun, and Li Peng jointly sent a message to Kim Il Sung, in which they stressed the "strong vitality" (*qiangdade shengmingli*) of the treaty and the "common destiny" (*gongtongde mingyun*) between the two countries.[24] In Beijing, North Korean ambassador Chu Ch'ang-jun sponsored a banquet to celebrate the occasion; China's vice president, Wang Zhen, attended and Defense Minister Qin Jiwei delivered a congratulatory speech. On the same day, the North Koreans held a banquet in Pyongyang hosted by Prime Minister Yon Hyong-muk, organized a military rally, and began the Pyongyang-Beijing "friendship week." The North Koreans were undoubtedly much more enthusiastic about the treaty with China than with the Soviet Union.

In October 1991, on the forty-first anniversary of China's entry into the Korean War, Ambassador Chu held a reception in Beijing for Defense Minister Qin and other Chinese dignitaries, and Ch'oe Kwang (chief of the general staff of the Korean People's Army [KPA]) hosted a similar reception in Pyongyang. About the same time, China's navy commander, Zhang Lianzhong, and Qu Zhenmou (commander of the Beihai fleet) visited North Korea, where they were decorated by Kim Il Sung. With the collapse of the Soviet Union under way in December 1991, Defense Minister O Chin-u hurried to Beijing for consultations with Yang Shangkun, Qin Jiwei, and Liu Huaqing (vice-chairman of the Central Military Commission).[25] Evidently, the two sides discussed the crisis in the Soviet Union, U.S.-DPRK talks, and the progress of inter-Korean military negotiations.

In his capacity as chairman of the Central Military Commission, Jiang Zemin sent a warm congratulatory message to Kim Jong Il for his appointment as the KPA supreme commander. The Chinese sent Zhang Wannian (commander of the Jinan Military Region) and Zhao Shufeng (deputy chief of staff of the Shenyang Military Region) to Pyongyang in April 1992 to celebrate the sixtieth anniversary of the KPA's founding. Another military delegation led by Yang Baibing (secretary-general of the Central Military Commission and director of the PLA General Political Department) went to Pyongyang in June 1992; Yang had a series of meetings with Kim Il Sung, Kim Jong Il, O Chin-u, and Ch'oe Kwang.[26] Even after China's diplomatic normalization with South Korea, there was no immediate sign of appreciable change in China's security commitment toward North Korea.

The Chinese took an ambivalent stand on the issue of North Korea's nuclear program during 1991 and 1992. On the one hand, they publicly rebuffed U.S. secretary of state James Baker's proposal in November 1991 that the United States, China, Russia, and Japan team up in a multilateral action to stop North Korea's nuclear weapons program. Foreign Minister Qian Qichen stated that "we do not wish to see any international pressure" on North Korea and said that the world should leave it primarily up to North and South Korea to work out their problems.[27] On the other hand, the Chinese opposed the further proliferation of nuclear weapons, especially on the Korean peninsula, and privately indicated that they would persuade North Korea to accept the IAEA's inspection of its nuclear facilities.

In March 1992, China finally acceded to the Treaty on the Non-Proliferation of Nuclear Weapons (NPT), which they had earlier denounced as a hoax perpetuated by the United States and the Soviet Union. Foreign Minister Qian expressed China's adherence to the treaty's objective of preventing nuclear proliferation but proposed that "all nuclear-weapons states undertake not to be the first to use nuclear weapons at any time and under any circumstances . . . [and] undertake to support the proposition of establishing nuclear weapon–free zones."[28] This position was similar to North Korea's demand on the United States.

It was very difficult, however, for China to apply its non-nuclear policy to the Korean peninsula, primarily because North Korea adamantly refused to fully accept the IAEA's special inspections of its suspected nuclear dump sites in Yongbyon. When North Korea announced its intention to withdraw from the NPT regime in March 1993, the Chinese faced a delicate situation. They made it clear that China definitely favored a denuclearized Korea and a negotiated resolution of the North Korean nuclear issue. They also opposed any UN-sponsored economic sanctions against North Korea or a surgical air strike against North Korean nuclear facilities because they felt that either action might lead to a serious military confrontation on the Korean peninsula. Qian stated that "we support patient consultations to reach an appropriate solution."[29]

In response to the draft resolution that the United States and other

Western powers introduced to the UN Security Council in regard to the North Korean nuclear issue, Chinese ambassador Li Zhaoxing stated on May 11, 1993:

> China, as a State party to the Treaty on the Non-Proliferation of Nuclear Weapons, has all along opposed nuclear proliferation and supported denuclearization of the Korean peninsula. China does not wish to see nuclear weapons on the peninsula, whether in the North or in the South, or to have them introduced there by a third party. In our view, the nuclear issue concerning the Democratic People's Republic of Korea is mainly a matter between the Democratic People's Republic of Korea and the International Atomic Energy Agency (IAEA), between the Democratic People's Republic of Korea and the United States, and between the Democratic People's Republic of Korea and the Republic of Korea. It should therefore be settled properly through direct dialogue and consultation between the Democratic People's Republic of Korea and the three other parties concerned, respectively. In this connection, China opposes the practice of imposing pressure.[30]

The resolution passed, however, by a vote of 13–0, with China and Pakistan abstaining. China urged North Korea to reaffirm its adherence to the NPT and to comply with its safeguards agreement with the IAEA.

While the Chinese continued to protect North Korean interests at the UN and the IAEA, they tactfully suggested that North Korea cooperate with the IAEA, and they encouraged the high-level negotiations between the United States and North Korea in New York and Geneva. They also maintained close consultations with the United States, Japan, and South Korea. For this purpose, the foreign ministers of China, Qian, and South Korea, Han Sung-ju, visited each other's capital in May and October 1993. And the nuclear issue was high on the agenda at the summit meeting between Presidents Jiang Zemin and Kim Young Sam in March 1994.

At the UN Security Council, China played a decisive role in blocking another U.S.-sponsored resolution on the North Korean nuclear question and in reaching a consensus statement to be issued by the president of the Council on March 31, 1994. Once again the statement called on North Korea to allow IAEA inspections of its nuclear facilities and to renew its discussions with South Korea for the implementation of the Joint Declaration on the Denuclearization of the Korean Peninsula. In spite of China's painstaking diplomatic activities, North Korea angrily rejected the statement as containing "unjustifiable demands," thus causing diplomatic embarrassment to China.[31]

As the nuclear crisis reached a potentially explosive level in May and June 1994, when the United States prepared a draft UN resolution to impose a concrete list of economic and diplomatic sanctions against North Korea, the Chinese were compelled to assume a more active diplomatic role toward Korea than ever before. This activism was also prompted by

U.S. president Bill Clinton's decision to extend most-favored-nation status to China without linking it to the issue of human rights; in explaining his decision, Clinton noted that the United States and China shared an "important interest" in a nuclear-free Korean peninsula.[32] Annoyed by North Korea's recalcitrant position and saber-rattling rhetoric, the Chinese attempted to moderate their ally's policy during Ch'oe Kwang's visit to Beijing.[33] In the aftermath of South Korean foreign minister Han's visit to China, the Chinese also subtly changed their posture at the UN—from the old formula of "opposing economic sanctions" against North Korea to the new position of "not favoring economic sanctions" against North Korea. This change implied that the Chinese might not veto the UN sanctions resolution but would just abstain from voting on it. They counseled all parties concerned to exercise the maximum degree of self-restraint and persuaded Kim Il Sung to negotiate with the United States in good faith.[34] In this sense, China contributed to an important breakthrough made during Jimmy Carter's meetings with Kim Il Sung in June 1994 at Pyongyang.

When the United States and North Korea reached a comprehensive agreement on nuclear issues at Geneva on October 21, 1994, a spokesman for the Chinese Ministry of Foreign Affairs enthusiastically welcomed it:

> This outcome shows that dialogue and consultation are the only effective ways to solve the Korean nuclear issue. The implementation of the agreement will help an early realization of denuclearization on the Korean peninsula, the maintenance of peace and stability there and the improvement of relations among the countries concerned. We hope that the parties concerned will continue their constructive efforts to ensure a smooth implementation of the agreement.[35]

At the Asia Pacific Economic Cooperation summit meeting held in Indonesia in November 1994, President Clinton was "pleasantly surprised" by the vigor of President Jiang's support for the Geneva agreement.[36] The two leaders promised to cooperate so that it would be effectively implemented. In view of their continuing security interests in Korea, the Chinese not only sighed in relief but also were satisfied that their patient and constructive mediatory efforts had met with success. They had defused the escalating military crisis on the Korean peninsula and assisted North Korea's rapprochement with the United States. Yet China decided not to take part in the Korean Peninsula Energy Development Organization (KEDO), an international consortium to provide light-water nuclear reactors to North Korea.

Meanwhile, China decided not to impede maneuvers for transforming the Korean Armistice Agreement into a more permanent structure for peace. In response to an explicit request from North Korea, Vice-Minister of Foreign Affairs Tang Jiaxuan announced on August 30, 1994, that China would recall its delegates from the Military Armistice Commission at

Panmunjom, which consisted of China, North Korea, and the UN Command.[37] It was probably difficult for Tang to reject the North Korean request because China regarded itself as a guest in Korea. Shen Guofeng, a spokesman for the Chinese Ministry of Foreign Affairs, explained during Li Peng's Seoul visit that it would be abnormal to have the Military Armistice Commission in Korea now that the Cold War was over.[38] Ever since a South Korean general had replaced a U.S. general as the representative of the UN Command at the commission in 1991, North Korea had boycotted the commission's meetings and attempted to abolish it. In fact, North Korea wanted to nullify the Korean Armistice Agreement altogether and to negotiate a peace treaty with the United States without South Korea's participation.

The Chinese hoped, however, that "all relevant parties" would continue to abide by the Korean Armistice Agreement until a new peace system was set up.[39] On the last day of his five-day visit to South Korea in November 1994, Premier Li Peng made it clear that China favored the change from the Korean Armistice Agreement to a peace treaty and that "all relevant parties," including North and South Korea, should take part in the negotiations for that change.[40] Li's view differed from the positions held by the two Korean governments. Whereas North Korea intended to exclude South Korea from the negotiations, South Korea preferred that both North and South Korea reach an agreement through direct negotiations and then seek its guarantee by the United States and China. In September 1995, South Korean minister of foreign affairs Kong No-myong revealed to the press that the Chinese regarded North Korea's proposal for a peace treaty with the United States as "impossible, unrealistic, and irrational," presumably because it excluded South Korea (and China as well) from the peace negotiations.[41]

Even though Russia notified North Korea in 1995 that their mutual security treaty should be abrogated or amended in 1996, neither China nor North Korea has indicated any desire to change their mutual security treaty. According to Article 7 of the treaty, neither party can nullify or revise it without mutual agreement. The normalization of diplomatic relations between China and South Korea has undoubtedly eroded the political basis of the Sino–North Korean treaty, and the Chinese have made it clear that their security commitment is effective only if North Korea comes under attack by another country. In July 1995 no messages of congratulations or reassurances were exchanged between Jiang Zemin and Kim Jong Il on the thirty-fourth anniversary of the treaty's signing, but celebrations took place in Beijing and Pyongyang. Chinese ambassador Qiao Zonghuai hosted a banquet at Pyongyang and reaffirmed China's support for North Korea's policies; present were Vice-President Yi Chong-ok and other North Korean leaders. The North Korean embassy in Beijing sponsored a similar meeting in which Chen Muhua (vice-chairman of the Standing Committee of the National People's Congress) and other Chinese guests participated.

Moreover, in October 1995 Kim Jong Il himself paid special attention to the forty-fifth anniversary of China's entry into the Korean War when he sent wreaths to the grave of Mao Anying, one of Mao Zedong's sons, and to the Chinese People's Volunteers (CPV) cemeteries in Hoech'ang County, South P'yongan Province.[42] An editorial in *Nodong sinmun* declared:

> The CPV's entry into the Korean War was a clear demonstration of the internationalist ties between the peoples of the DPRK and China in the cause of defending peace and security of the world and peace and security in Northeast Asia, in particular.[43]

At a party given by the North Korean embassy in Beijing, Minister of National Defense Chi Haotian praised the "heroic" joint struggles of North Korea and China against U.S. aggressors:

> To consolidate and develop the traditional friendship between China and the DPRK under the current complicated international situation not only confirms the fundamental interests of the two countries and peoples of China and the DPRK, but also is good for peace and security on the Korean peninsula and in Northeast Asia and the world.[44]

The public reassurances of Sino–North Korean security ties continued throughout 1996, particularly in conjunction with the thirty-fifth anniversary of the mutual security treaty. In a message to Jiang Zemin on July 10, 1996, Kim Jong Il said that "the treaty will remain conducive to defending the socialist cause in the two countries and defending peace and stability in the region." Responding to the message from Kim, Jiang emphasized the continuity of traditional friendship and cooperation between the two countries, stating:

> We are pleased to see that the fraternal Korean people, under the correct leadership of the Workers' Party of Korea headed by you, are steadily promoting the building of Korean socialism and the independent and peaceful reunification of the country, true to the intentions of President Kim Il Sung. We sincerely hope that progress will be made in all fields, the country will prosper and the people live a happy life in Korea under the leadership of Comrade Kim Jong Il.[45]

While North Korean vice-premier Kim Yun-hyok led a friendship delegation to Beijing, Luo Gan (state councilor and secretary general of the Chinese State Council) took part in the celebrations held at Pyongyang. Luo announced a Chinese decision to donate 100,000 tons of food to North Korea. When the North Korean submarine incident took place on the South

Korean coast in September 1996, the Chinese played a positive role in preventing the crisis from escalating in Korea.

While the Chinese continue to adhere to their security treaty with
North Korea, they have cautiously explored preliminary consultations with
South Korea in regard to military affairs. At a meeting on May 10, 1995, in
Beijing, Premier Li Peng and South Korean prime minister Yi Hong-gu
agreed to begin a bilateral military exchange and to promote multilateral
confidence-building measures in the Asia Pacific region.[46] Moreover, the
two leaders emphasized the importance of inter-Korean dialogue as the
most effective way to resolve military issues, such as nuclear nonproliferation and the status of the Korean Armistice Agreement. It is clear that
China intends, in a subtle but unmistakable fashion, to distance itself gradually from North Korea's recalcitrant strategic positions and to play a constructive role in reducing military tensions on the Korean peninsula.

Conclusion

The making of China's two-Korea policy initially strained its political relations with North Korea, but the North Koreans attempted to conceal their
profound disillusionment and grudgingly adjusted themselves to China's
intense economic linkage with South Korea. The Chinese endorse Kim
Jong Il's political succession, and Kim seems to feel that one of his father's
legacies is to cherish the tradition of North Korean friendship and cooperation with China. Upon the death of Deng Xiaoping in February 1997, Kim
Jong Il sent a message of condolence to Jiang Zemin and noted that Deng
had forged a "special intimacy" with Kim Il Sung and had made "strenuous
efforts" to strengthen the traditional friendship between China and North
Korea.[47] Yet the unabashed pursuit of each country's vital national interests
overshadows the rhetoric of ideological and revolutionary solidarity in
determining the substance of Beijing-Pyongyang relations.

In the next few years, the North Koreans are most likely to sustain a
generally cordial and correct state-to-state relationship with China while
they improve and normalize their relations with the United States and Japan
as a way to lessen their dependence on China. No sudden political or diplomatic rupture is anticipated between China and North Korea, unless North
Korea irresponsibly pushes the "Taiwan card" to an extreme.[48] Even though
the Chinese are aware of the possibility that the diplomatic presence of the
United States and Japan in Pyongyang might undermine their influence,
they expect that a system of cross-recognition by all four major powers
would restore a semblance of international balance on the Korean peninsula, promote the interests of its peace and stability, and reduce China's economic burden vis-à-vis North Korea. Meanwhile, the North Koreans will

continue to study the progress of China's modernization programs and to diversify the range of their external economic partners.

The Chinese hope that both Korean governments will resume their dialogue and implement the Agreement on Reconciliation, Nonaggression and Exchanges and Cooperation and the Joint Declaration on the Denuclearization of the Korean Peninsula and that the Agreed Framework and the KEDO arrangements will eventually lead to a peaceful resolution of North Korea's nuclear issue. They prefer to maintain the mutual defense treaty with North Korea as a useful instrument to provide North Korea with a sense of security, but they are careful not to give blanket support for Kim Jong Il's unpredictable military policy. If the four-party talks on the Korean question continue, the Chinese are most likely to assume an active role in transforming the Korean Armistice Agreement to a more permanent system for peace and stability in Korea.[49]

The North Koreans recognize the unreliable drift of their military association with China, but they see no option except to keep their bilateral treaty relationship as long as military tensions persist in Korea. The Chinese do not wish to confront a precipitous reunification of Korea by either military or peaceful means any time soon, but they will not be in a position to obstruct the gradual process of inter-Korean integration. The long-range future of political and military relations between China and North Korea remains uncertain, but it will probably depend less on China's two-Korea policy than on North Korea's success in maintaining its system and willingness to adapt to new international circumstances.

Notes

1. A substantial portion of this paper is based on Chae-Jin Lee, *China and Korea: Dynamic Relations* (Stanford, Calif.: Hoover Institution Press, 1996).

2. Interview by author with Chinese scholars, December 1991.

3. Hu Jintao was born in Anhui Province in 1942 and graduated from Qinghua University with a degree in hydraulic engineering. He served as CCP secretary in Gansu Province and Tibet. For his activities in Dandong and Pyongyang, see *Renmin ribao,* July 27–31, 1993.

4. See the text of Deng's message in *Renmin ribao,* July 11, 1994. Deng was probably notified of the death of Kim Il Sung before it was publicly announced.

5. *China Daily,* July 11, 1994.

6. Interview by author with Chinese scholars, March 1995. See Banning Garrett and Bonnie Glaser, "Looking Across the Yalu: Chinese Assessments of North Korea," *Asian Survey* 35, no. 6 (June 1995):530.

7. For Yi's meeting with Jiang Zemin and Li Peng, see *Renmin ribao,* September 30 and October 1, 1994.

8. See *People's Korea,* October 8, 1994.

9. *Beijing Review,* November 14–20, 1994, p. 4.

10. *Han'guk ilbo,* November 1, 1994.

11. Interview by author with Chinese scholars, March 1995.

12. See *Foreign Broadcast Information Service, East Asia* (*FBIS, EAS*), February 15, 1995, pp. 16–17.

13. *Renmin ribao,* July 8, 1995.

14. Ibid., July 14, 1995.

15. *Seoul sinmun,* June 8, 1995.

16. Interview by author with Chinese scholars, October 1995.

17. See Jiang's message in *FBIS, EAS,* September 8, 1995, p. 34, and *Renmin ribao,* September 1, 1995. Also see *Nodong sinmun,* October 2, 1995.

18. *Renmin ribao,* October 7, 1995.

19. See the text in *Renmin ribao,* October 10, 1995.

20. See *Beijing Review,* December 4–10, 1995, pp. 6–8.

21. Interview by author, October 1995.

22. For North Korea's economic dependency on China, see Chong-Sik Lee, *The Political Economy of North Korea* (Seattle, Wash.: National Bureau of Asian Research, 1994).

23. See *China Daily,* April 23, 1997.

24. *Renmin ribao,* July 11, 1991.

25. Ibid., December 13, 1991.

26. Ibid., June 6, 1992.

27. *Los Angeles Times,* November 15, 1991.

28. *China Daily,* March 13, 1993.

29. *New York Times,* March 4, 1993.

30. The Verbatim Record of the UN Security Council, May 11, 1993 (S/PV.3212), pp. 42–43.

31. *New York Times,* April 5, 1994.

32. For the text of Clinton's statement made on May 26, 1994, see *U.S. Department of State Dispatch* 5, no. 22, May 30, 1994, pp. 345–346.

33. For Ch'oe Kwang (KPA chief of staff), see *Renmin ribao,* June 8 and 14, 1994. This bilateral discussion probably continued when Kim Il Sung met with Wang Ke (commander of the Shenyang Military Region) on June 28, 1994, in Pyongyang; see *Renmin ribao,* July 1, 1994.

34. See the statement by a spokesman of the Ministry of Foreign Affairs in *Renmin ribao,* June 16, 1994, and *Los Angeles Times,* June 13–29, 1994.

35. *China Daily,* October 24, 1994. The North Koreans did not closely consult with the Chinese in regard to the progress of the Geneva negotiations, but the United States had regular consultations about ongoing developments with all permanent member states of the UN Security Council. Interviews by author, March and April 1995.

36. *Washington Post,* November 4, 1994.

37. For a meeting between Tang and DPRK vice-minister of foreign affairs Song Ho-gyong, see *Renmin ribao,* September 2, 1994, and *New York Times,* September 3, 1994. It was suggested that after receiving a precious North Korean gift from Song Ho-gyong, Deng Xiaoping decided to withdraw from the Military Armistice Commission without full consultation with the Chinese Ministry of Foreign Affairs. Interview by author, March 1995.

38. *Korea Herald,* November 1, 1994.

39. See Foreign Minister Qian's remarks in *China Daily,* September 2, 1994.

40. For Premier Li's news conference on November 4, 1994, see *Han'guk ilbo,* September 5, 1994.

41. *Korea Herald,* September 26, 1995.

42. *FBIS, EAS,* October 30, 1995, p. 21.

43. *Nodong sinmun,* October 25, 1995.

44. *FBIS, EAS,* October 25, 1995, p. 33.

45. For the English texts of Kim's and Jiang's messages, see *FBIS, EAS,* July 11, 1996, pp. 26–27, or *People's Korea,* July 20, 1996.

46. See *Han'guk ilbo,* May 11, 1995. In February 1995 a South Korean military delegation led by Lieutenant General Cho Song-t'ae (assistant minister of national defense) visited Beijing and met with Chinese military leaders; see *Korea Herald,* February 24, 1995. A Chinese military delegation headed by General Ruo Bin visited Seoul in December 1996; see *Chungang ilbo,* December 9 and 13, 1996.

47. See *Renmin ribao,* February 21, 1997.

48. For example, the Chinese were concerned about Pyongyang's agreement to store nuclear wastes from Taiwan in North Korea. For China's official reaction, see *Renmin ribao,* January 31, 1997.

49. For Chinese positions, see *Renmin ribao,* February 20 and March 8, 1997.

10

North Korean Relations with Japan

Richard Halloran

For half a century North Korean leaders in Pyongyang have missed numerous opportunities in dealing with Japan that might have been to its political and economic advantage. Efforts from Tokyo to establish normal relations with Pyongyang have been sporadic and half-hearted, slowly degenerating into apathy. By mid-1997, relations between the two neighbors across what the North Koreans call the East Sea and the Japanese the Sea of Japan varied from rancorous to nil.

The North Korean economy, from all accounts that have seeped out of that closed country, is in a "crisis,"[1] a situation that the U.S. Central Intelligence Agency (CIA) has perhaps understated as "stagnant."[2] The economy has been in decline since about 1990, per capita income has dropped, industrial production has slipped, and food has been in short supply. Natural disasters have made conditions worse. Foreign trade has slumped, especially trade with Russia after the demise of the Soviet Union. North Korea's credit abroad has become practically nonexistent because Pyongyang has reneged on its debts, and even barter exchange has been hard to come by.

The Democratic People's Republic of Korea (DPRK) has been almost isolated internationally. Russia, long its economic and military patron, has been consumed with its own troubles and has nearly abandoned North Korea; Moscow did not renew its security treaty with Pyongyang when it expired in September 1995. China, with which North Korea has had even longer connections, has been a bit more supportive but has shifted attention to Pyongyang's archrival in Seoul as a more promising economic partner. North Korea's efforts to acquire diplomatic relations with the United States have slumped as Washington has tired of Pyongyang's brinkmanship, threats of war, and testy negotiating style. North Korean relations with South Korea have been belligerent; a pledge in 1994 to open a new dialogue with Seoul has been blithely ignored. North Korea has been able to count few friends in the Third World.

211

Vis-à-vis Japan, North Korea has ruptured one chance after another to obtain economic assistance, trade, and investment, not to mention food for its hungry people. Japan could have become a channel for political communication to the rest of the world if Pyongyang had normalized relations with Tokyo. Until early 1996, Pyongyang had an opportunity to deal with socialist prime minister Tomi'ichi Murayama, who headed a party in which several strong factions favored normalizing relations between Japan and North Korea. That chance seems to have slipped away with the election of conservative prime minister Ryutaro Hashimoto.

Instead of pursuing better relations with Japan in its own national interests, North Korea has mounted a vituperative campaign in which invective has been continuously heaped on Japan, much of it rooted in the colonial days of 1910–1945 when Japan ruled Korea. A spokesman for North Korea who lives in Japan, Kim Myong-ch'ol, captured the essence of North Korea's attitude toward Japan in a statement about the strategic goals of Kim Jong Il, who has evidently succeeded his late father, Kim Il Sung, as the leader of North Korea: "The late Kim Il Sung beat two imperialist giants, first Japan and then the United States, but left the historic tasks unaccomplished to be completed by the son of Mt. Paekdu and his successor, Marshal Kim Jong Il: to officially settle the scores with Japan and the United States and reunify Korea on the terms of *chuch'e*."[3] *Chuch'e* is generally translated as "self-reliance" and is the ideology—some say religion—propounded over the years by Kim Il Sung.

North Korea has sought to block the UN from no longer declaring Japan a "former enemy" state despite the support that proposal has had among other members.[4] According to the official party newspaper *Nodong sinmun*, officials in Pyongyang have repeatedly asserted that "Japan seeks to clear the way for itself to begin new aggression and, upon seizing the opportunity, to restore its colonial control over the Korean peninsula." Japanese efforts to resume talks intended to establish diplomatic relations have been rebuffed or have proceeded desultorily. Pyongyang has test-fired missiles toward Japan into the East Sea/Sea of Japan, and it has rejected proposals by the Japanese and others that a security dialogue be initiated in Northeast Asia. Altogether, it appears that North Korea has given distinctly second priority to its relations with Japan as it has concentrated, with questionable success, on establishing relations with the United States.

Thus, despite the benefits from Japan that could have accrued to North Korea had relations been civil, Pyongyang has adopted an attitude of hostility. In the subtle tone for which the Japanese are noted, scholar Hajime Izumi has written: "It may be safe to say that North Korea is able to wait longer than we imagined, and that worries about the economic situation and isolation do not always have direct influence upon the DPRK's policy toward Japan."[5]

From the other side, the Japanese have been united on a few aspects of their relations with North Korea but have been divided or unclear on almost all others. At the top of the Japanese list of anxieties has been a fear that war might break out on the Korean peninsula. Japanese worry that they might be dragged into such a conflict because of the mutual security treaties Japan and South Korea have signed with the United States, which has 37,000 troops in South Korea. Whether Japan's constitution, government policy, or public opinion would permit Japan's forces to enter such a fray is debatable. When U.S. president Bill Clinton met with Prime Minister Hashimoto in Tokyo in April 1996, the Japanese prime minister pledged limited logistic support to U.S. forces engaged in contingency operations in Asia. From Tokyo's point of view, the Japanese have been concerned that hostilities in Korea would produce a flood of boat people and other refugees headed for Japan; the Japanese government and people have appeared to be at a loss as to how they would respond to such an influx.

The issue of normalized relations between Tokyo and Pyongyang has split Japanese politicians. For the most part, socialists have been ready to move ahead with little regard for the positions of South Korea or the United States. Most conservatives have favored moving cautiously in concert with Seoul and Washington. A critical question in Tokyo's negotiations with Pyongyang will be the compensation the North demands. North Koreans want reparations for Japan's colonial rule from 1910 to 1945 and compensation for what they contend are damages suffered at the hands of Japan since liberation in 1945. Tokyo has indicated that it would be willing to pay a sum similar to that given to South Korea when relations were normalized in 1965, which was in the form of reparations for colonial days. Japan has so far refused to consider sums beyond that amount.

After several months in office, the government of Prime Minister Hashimoto seemed ready to continue Japan's cautious policy toward North Korea. Hashimoto's conservative rival Ichiro Ozawa has written: "On the Korean peninsula, we must maintain our close relations with South Korea. We must also advance normalization of relations with North Korea and help create an environment that will encourage the peaceful reunification of the two Koreas."[6]

In the realm of Japan's national security, the Self-Defense Agency's 1995 white paper on defense pointed to North Korea as a leading threat: "Moves by North Korea have heightened military tensions on the Korean peninsula, which has thus become a seriously destabilizing element in the security of Japan and the rest of East Asia."[7] As with other questions about North Korea, that assessment may not be shared by all Japanese. Similarly, Japanese have been divided over the alleged threat generated by North Korea's nuclear ambitions. Some Japanese and many Western journalists contend that a North Korea armed with nuclear missiles would be a direct threat to Japan and could cause Japan to reconsider its policy of eschewing nuclear weapons. Other Japanese, however, assert that they have lived for decades with Russian and Chinese nuclear arms in their neighborhood. They contend that North Korea would pose no threat as long as Japan was confident that the U.S. nuclear deterrent remained in place to defend Japan.[8]

On the issue of Korean reunification, Japanese *tatemae* and *honne* have swiftly come into play. The *tatemae,* or "facade," holds that Japan favors reunification as long as it is peaceful and accomplished by agreement among the Koreans themselves. A senior official of the foreign ministry was quoted in late 1995 press reports as saying that a unified Korean peninsula would never threaten Japan, unless it were a Communist government. The Japanese government's public position and the view on the street is that a unified Korea would allow Japan and Korea to share peaceful prosperity.

The *honne,* or "real thing," however, is ambivalent, with many Japanese indicating that they are not at all sure they would like to see Korea reunified. A report from a conference in May 1995 at the University of California at San Diego noted that "the collapse of the DPRK and its absorption by the ROK [Republic of Korea] could be a disturbing scenario for Japan. . . . Whether Japan wants reunification of Korea under any circumstance is yet another question."[9] Behind this attitude lie an ancient fear that Korea is a dagger pointed at the heart of Japan and a modern anxiety that a unified Korea would become a potent economic and political competitor. Mun Chong-in of Yonsei University in Seoul has written: "Japan does not simply oppose, but [is] fearful of a unified Korea. A delicate synergy of historical distrust, guilt about its militaristic past and concern about future relations all feed Japan's distrust of Korea."[10] David Arase of Pomona College in California agrees: "Whether reunification occurred quickly through conflict, or slowly through absorption, Japan would still face the long-term problem of a heavily armed reunified Korean nation that has historical as well as current economic grievances to settle with Japan."[11]

An unusual, perhaps unique, but surely complicating element in the DPRK-Japan equation has been the presence of 700,000 ethnic Koreans living in Japan. Some are the grandchildren of laborers brought to Japan during the colonial period; others are immigrants. Many are not Japanese citizens and at best have been only partly assimilated into Japanese society. An estimated 30–40 percent of these Koreans belong to a pro-Pyongyang association called Choch'ongnyon in Korean and Chosen Soren in Japanese. This organization is a state within a state, a community with its own political structure, social organizations, schools and university, banks and businesses, newspapers, and an informal system of policing its members and collecting taxes.

Politically and diplomatically, Choch'ongnyon has provided a channel of communication between Japan and North Korea. Sometimes the association has been a formal, open channel between the Japanese and North Korean governments, with the association's Tokyo office acting as the North Korean embassy. At other times Choch'ongnyon has provided cover for North Korea's subversive operations. The Japanese government has estimated that six hundred North Korean agents, some of them trained terrorists, live and operate in Japan.[12] These agents have coerced ethnic Koreans in Japan by threatening relatives in North Korea.[13] Pyongyang has warned Japan several times to expect reprisals, possibly violent, if Japan imposes economic sanctions on North Korea, an act that Pyongyang has said would be the equivalent of a declaration of war.[14] In less belligerent terms, Choch'ongnyon is a back channel for communications between Japanese political factions of all stripes and North Korean leaders in Pyongyang. Here the complication sets in: Japan's Ministry of Foreign Affairs cannot control the contacts and communications to North Korea through the Choch'ongnyon and thus has been cut out of some private diplomacy. This has permitted the North Korean regime to play one Japanese faction against another and to conduct quasi-official relations with many groups in Japan whether the Japanese government likes it or not.

Moreover, Choch'ongnyon is a critical economic link between Japan and North Korea, having become a major source of foreign exchange and hard currency for Pyongyang. Estimates of the amount transmitted from Japan to North Korea each year have run from $100 million to $800 million, mostly in Japanese yen; experienced economists consider the lower number to be closer to the mark.[15] Most of the funds have been sent to Pyongyang by bank wire transfers from one of about eighteen banks authorized to deal with North Korea, or they have been carried by visitors traveling by ship from Niigata on the northwest coast of Japan to Wonsan or another port on the east coast of North Korea. Some funds are believed to have been carried by Japanese or Koreans traveling through Hong Kong and China into North Korea.[16]

In sum, North Korea's political intentions toward Japan have been murky, and Japan's objectives in dealing with North Korea have been less than precise. The role of Choch'ongnyon as an autonomous entity allied with North Korea but present in Japan has made relations even more convoluted.

Political Relations 1945–1994

North Korea's relations with Japan today are rooted in the wars of a century ago. Japan defeated China in 1895 and Russia in 1905, partly to establish a Japanese sphere of influence over Korea. Japan annexed Korea in 1910 and sought, sometimes ruthlessly, to integrate Korea into the Japanese empire. That pursuit ended with the Japanese surrender in World War II and the liberation of Korea in 1945 but left a bitter legacy that is nurtured to this day in both South and North Korea. A U.S. visitor to Pyongyang in January 1995, for instance, saw "columns of children marching to 'imbibe the spirit of the anti-Japanese struggle.'"[17]

After the division of Korea by the United States and the Soviet Union, Tokyo had little to do with North Korea for five years because Japan was under U.S. occupation. When North Korea invaded South Korea in 1950, the United States turned Japan into a staging area and a source of supply for U.S. forces fighting North Korean and Chinese forces. What was known as offshore procurement helped revive the Japanese economy and lay the foundation of Japan's prosperity today, a gain the North Koreans appear to have neither forgotten nor forgiven.

From the end of the Korean War in 1953 until 1990, Japan recognized the Republic of Korea in Seoul as the only legitimate government of Korea; that position was confirmed when Japan and South Korea signed a treaty in 1965 to normalize relations. Nonetheless, informal contacts with North Korea were made through Choch'ongnyon and a modest amount of trade was generated. As the United States reached détente with the Soviet Union and Washington and Beijing made contact in the early 1970s, Japan and North Korea increased informal contact. That came to naught, however, as South Vietnam fell, the Soviet Union invaded Afghanistan and shot down a Korean Airlines passenger plane, and North Korea mounted terrorist attacks on South Koreans. Trade continued at a low level until the mid-1980s, when North Korea was unable to pay its international debts. The debts mounted, and today Pyongyang owes Japan an estimated $700 million. Even as trade slowed, however, Korean residents of Japan began investing in small joint ventures in North Korea.

Contemporary DPRK-Japan relations began in September 1990, with the visit to Pyongyang of a Japanese delegation led by the late Shin Kanemaru, then vice president of the ruling Liberal Democratic Party, and Makoto Tanabe, a leader of what was then the Japan Socialist Party, now called the Social Democratic Party of Japan. The Japanese went to Pyongyang expecting to discuss Japan-DPRK relations in general and to seek the release of the *18 Fujisanmaru,* a fishing boat whose crew of two the North Koreans had accused of spying. The North Koreans, however, surprised the Japanese by proposing early normalization of relations between Tokyo and Pyongyang. The proposal implied acceptance of "two Koreas," a concept Pyongyang had heretofore shunned in its claim to be the legitimate ruler of all Korea. The North Koreans also wanted to settle the issue of compensation—in their favor—as quickly as possible and to set up liaison offices in Pyongyang and Tokyo to facilitate further diplomatic contacts. At North Korean insistence, the joint declaration issued at the end of the visit stated that "negotiations between governments toward normalizing diplomatic relations would begin in November."[18]

Kanemaru, Tanabe, and their delegation ran into strong criticism when they returned to Japan. Members of the ruling party criticized Kanemaru for indulging in private diplomacy without consulting the party or the government. In particular, he came under fire for agreeing that Japan must compensate North Korea for the years of colonialism and perhaps for the postwar period. South Korean officials were also angry because they had been informed that the Kanemaru-Tanabe delegation's mission was to be limited to securing the release of the Japanese fishermen and holding a general discussion with North Korean leaders. The U.S. government, too, was unhappy and urged that inspection of North Korean nuclear facilities, by then suspected of producing material for nuclear arms, be a condition for continuing the talks.

From November 1990 to November 1992, Japanese and North Koreans held nine meetings, the first in Beijing, the second in Pyongyang, the third in Tokyo, and the rest in Beijing. The negotiations centered on five issues: (1) diplomatic relations; (2) Japanese compensation to North Korea; (3) international inspection of North Korea's nuclear facilities; (4) dialogue between South and North Korea; and (5) other questions such as the visits to Japan of Japanese living in North Korea. During the meetings, both sides presented hardened positions, including Japan's demand that North Korea open its nuclear facilities to inspection, and little agreement was reached. In the midst of the talks, the Japanese brought up the fate of a Japanese woman (whose name is variously given), Yi Un-hye. Yi was alleged to have been abducted from Japan to North Korea to teach Japanese to a North Korean terrorist later accused of blowing up a Korean Airlines passenger plane. The North Koreans heatedly denied the charge, threatened to break off the negotiations, and did so in a meeting in November 1992. Masao Okonogi of Keio University in Tokyo has written: "The Yi Un-hye issue was thus the catalyst for suspending the Japan–North Korea negotiations twice. On both occasions, the North Koreans, angered by the stagnant negotiations, used it as the excuse for ending the negotiations. However, the real cause of the rupture in the talks was clearly the nuclear inspection issue."[19]

For the next two years, Pyongyang and Tokyo kept each other at arm's distance but quarreled over several issues. The nuclear question took top priority. The Japanese demanded that North Korea permit international inspections of its nuclear plants for evidence of nuclear arms; the North Koreans adamantly refused. Tokyo urged the Chinese to exert influence on the North Koreans and made the same plea to Moscow. Japan welcomed U.S. negotiations with North Korea over the nuclear issue, especially after news leaks from Washington suggested that the Clinton administration was considering military action against North Korea. Japan said that it would support the United States on sanctions against Pyongyang if North Korea continued to reject the inspections, but it was dubious about military action.

The United States, in turn, urged the Japanese to slow the flow of funds from Choch'ongnyon to North Korea, because those funds helped Pyongyang build nuclear plants; Tokyo appears not to have heeded the United States' request.

A second issue was North Korea's test-firing of its Nodong 1 intermediate-range ballistic missile into the Sea of Japan; intelligence reports revealed that it could reach many Japanese cities and would be ready by the end of 1994.[20] The Japan Self-Defense Agency emphasized the threat in its 1993 white paper. Tokyo and Washington agreed to set up a joint working group to assess the North Korean missile threat, and the United States further urged Japan to agree to joint development of a missile defense. Self-Defense Agency officials agreed that Japan's missile defense was inadequate. The North Korean foreign ministry criticized Japan for protesting what Pyongyang called a "normal missile launch test." The Self-Defense Agency further reported a North Korean military buildup along the Demilitarized Zone, which divides the peninsula near the 38th parallel.

A third theme was the barrage of anti-Japanese blasts from Pyongyang. The North Koreans repeatedly asserted that Japan was not qualified to be a permanent member of the UN Security Council. Tokyo had begun a campaign to win that permanent seat, contending that Japan's economic strength entitled it to such recognition. The North Koreans sought to block a revision of the UN charter, which originally named Japan and Germany as enemy states. That effort eventually failed, but not before Pyongyang had made its point. The North Koreans, however, welcomed Prime Minister Morihiro Hosokawa's statement that World War II was a war of Japanese aggression. A few months later, Radio Pyongyang was back on track, accusing Japan of seeking "nuclear armament" with the launch of an H-2 rocket.

The Japan Socialist Party sought to move negotiations off dead center by proposing a mission to Pyongyang in early 1993 to discuss nuclear inspection by the International Atomic Energy Agency. It was dissuaded by Choch'ongnyon officials who indicated that Pyongyang was adamant about not allowing inspections. In June, Pyongyang closed the country to most foreigners and to Korean residents of Japan for reasons unclear; the ban lasted until late August.[21]

Finally, the issue of "comfort women"—Korean and other Asian women allegedly forced into prostitution for Japanese troops abroad during World War II—heated up. Pyongyang expressed dissatisfaction with Japanese investigations and for failing to propose an acceptable solution and compensation. *Nodong sinmun,* the party newspaper in Pyongyang, demanded that Japan apologize in the UN for its wartime actions and insisted that the Japanese Diet pass a resolution acknowledging the crime.

In sum, political relations between North Korea and Japan have a long and troubled history, one charged with emotions that are rarely more than a centimeter beneath the surface in North Korea. In contrast, Japanese feelings about North Korea seem to be apathetic and occasionally disdainful. Couple these sentiments with different political systems and vast differences in stages of economic development, and the result is two nations with little in common. Little in history appears to motivate either side to make an effort to improve relations with the other.

Political Relations, Summer 1994 to Spring 1997

In the summer and fall of 1994, three events opened a new phase in North Korean relations with Japan and the world. In June, Tomi'ichi Murayama, a socialist who might look with favor on North Korea, became prime minister of Japan atop a coalition government. In July, Kim Il Sung died after having ruled North Korea with undisputed power since the founding of his country. His death brought Pyongyang to a halt while a transition of power began to his son, Kim Jong Il. In October, after months of tedious negotiation, North Korea and the United States signed a nuclear accord that suspended Pyongyang's nuclear program. In return, North Korea was promised oil supplies, two light-water reactors that would produce less weapons-grade material, and negotiations intended to lead to diplomatic relations between Pyongyang and Washington.[22] The optimism generated by the nuclear accord led some Japanese to believe that the time had come for Tokyo to make a fresh effort to establish normal relations with Pyongyang.

It quickly became evident that this was not to be. The coalition in Tokyo proposed sending a delegation to Pyongyang to negotiate a resumption of the talks broken off in 1992. The three Japanese parties, however, could not agree on an agenda, and Pyongyang would not guarantee a meeting with Kim Jong Il. Moreover, the North Koreans wanted the Japanese to agree before the visit that Japan would compensate North Korea for thirty-five years of colonialism and fifty years of postwar grievances. The Japanese foreign ministry insisted that the delegation discuss North Korea's nuclear ambitions and the fate of Yi Un-hye. With those conflicts, the proposed visit was canceled.[23]

After clandestine contacts between Tokyo and Pyongyang in the spring of 1995, a new meeting was arranged. A delegation of eleven representatives from the coalition led by former Japanese foreign minister Michio Watanabe visited Pyongyang. Even that mission was late getting started because of friction within the coalition, notably over the issue of compensation. Most Liberal Democrats were adamantly opposed to compensating North Korea for anything after 1945. Watanabe denied that Japan was responsible for the Korean War and asserted, "We cannot compensate every wartime enemy."[24] The socialists were miffed because the coalition had gotten ahead of the party that considered Japanese relations with North Korea to be its province. The South Koreans were also opposed to the visit; President Kim Young Sam cautioned Prime Minister Murayama during a meeting in Copenhagen not to let Japan get out ahead of South Korea. Murayama promised to give "proper consideration" to South Korean views.[25]

During a brief two-day visit, an agreement was reached to resume discussions intended to bring about diplomatic relations; no conditions were to be set before the talks.[26] After the Japanese returned to Tokyo, a senior official of the Workers' Party of Korea (WPK), Kim Yong-sun, said in a press conference that the agreement "makes clear the principled demand for Japan to make an apology and compensation for the fabulous damages and disaster inflicted upon the Korean people in the past." Kim insisted that the new talks be limited to the issue of diplomatic recognition and that Japan not bring up nuclear issues or the question of Yi Un-hye.[27] After that, the two sides eyed each other warily.

Nor did discussions between the United States and North Korea go well over the nuclear issue. Japan did not take part in the negotiations in Berlin during the spring of 1995, but it was kept informed because Tokyo had pledged to contribute part of the $4 billion needed to replace the North's nuclear reactors. The Japanese public was none too pleased with the nuclear accord of October 1994. An opinion poll by the Japanese newspaper *Yomiuri shimbun* showed that 41 percent of those queried opposed Japan helping finance new reactors for North Korea, while 44 percent said stoically *shikataganai* (it could not be helped). More than half of those who responded to the poll said Japan should go slow on extending diplomatic recognition to Pyongyang.[28]

The Japanese government was equally dubious. Foreign Minister Yohei Kono told the Diet that North Korea must eliminate suspicions about its nuclear program before Japan would contribute to funding two new reactors. "If the other side will fail to conduct its implementation, the matter is suspended," Kono was quoted by the Associated Press.[29] *Korea Times* reported that Japan would ask North Korea to sign a written pledge that it would not divert fuel or equipment from its new light-water reactors to military use, another indication of Japanese mistrust. North Korea did not agree to either request. More signs of Japanese discomfort came from foreign ministry officials who questioned whether North Korea really needed light-water reactors to generate electricity or whether it would be better off replacing obsolete oil-fueled electrical generators.

South Korea, the United States, and Japan agreed in March 1995 to establish the Korean Peninsula Energy Development Organization (KEDO), to implement the nuclear provisions of the 1994 accord. KEDO began operating in late July, and by October it had taken over the tedious negotiations with the North Koreans over providing the light-water reactors. South Korea, the United States, and Japan insisted that the reactors come from South Korea as agreed in 1994; North Korea insisted that they come from anywhere but South Korea. After months of twisting and turning and threatening to renege on the agreement, in December the North Koreans agreed to accept South Korean reactors—if KEDO and its members came up with an additional $500 million for facilities connected with the reactors.[30] The ink was not dry on the new agreement before North Korean diplomat Ho Chong said North Korea would "automatically" resume its nuclear program if the light-water reactor project was not completed.[31]

Pyongyang's belligerence toward Japan was highlighted when it again sought to stop the UN from striking a reference to "former enemy" states from its charter. The list included Japan, Germany, Italy, Finland, Bulgaria, Romania, and Hungary. In one of the rare occasions when South and North Korea agreed on anything, 139 South Korean civic leaders called on the ROK government to withdraw its support of Japan's bid to become a permanent member of the UN Security Council.[32]

North Korea continued to hammer away on the theme of Japanese brutality during World War II. A spokesman for the foreign ministry in Pyongyang asserted that a Diet resolution did not go far enough in acknowledging Japan's crimes in World War II or in promising not to launch another war.[33] Pyongyang continued to demand that Tokyo make public facts about "comfort women" from Korea who were forced into sexual slavery by the Japanese Imperial Army. *Nodong sinmun* denounced Japan for increasing military expenditures with the intent of expanding abroad even though the North Korean armed force is the world's fourth largest and Japan's ranks twenty-fourth.[34] A politically tactless remark by Prime Minister Murayama asserting that Japan had annexed Korea with a legal treaty in 1910 sent editorial writers in both Pyongyang and Seoul into a frenzy.[35] Pyongyang asserted several times that Japan sought to restore its colonial rule in Korea. According to *Nodong sinmun*, "Japanese militarists have not yet discarded the ambition to launch an invasion once again."[36] Pyongyang asserted that Japan's 1995 white paper on defense was mistaken in naming North Korea, with its new ballistic missiles, its suspected biochemical weapons, and its nuclear research, as the biggest threat to Japan.[37]

The shadow of Seoul fell over every contact between Pyongyang and Tokyo. South Koreans scrutinized each move to make sure that Tokyo did not get ahead of Seoul or agree to something Seoul saw as inimical to South Korean interests. While North Korea and the United States were negotiating over light-water reactors in the spring of 1995, ROK prime minister Yi Hong-gu said that Japan should take care not to "give North Korea the wrong message at a time when North Korea must make important decisions."[38] Before the Watanabe delegation visited Pyongyang, Vice Foreign Minister Yi Si-yong called on Ambassador Shintaro Yamashita to urge the delegation to convey to Pyongyang a firm stance on the issue of South Korean reactors.[39]

After the North Koreans and Japanese agreed to resume negotiations over diplomatic relations, South Korean officials told the *Wall Street Journal* that they were worried that North Korea might "exploit apparent divisions within the US-Japan–South Korean alliance." When the question of food aid to North Korea arose, President Kim Young Sam complained to *Nihon keizai shimbun* that Japan had proceeded without adequately consulting with Seoul.[40] President Kim avoided a meeting with Prime Minister Murayama during the Asia Pacific Economic Cooperation forum in Osaka in October 1995. Later, Kim said if Tokyo established diplomatic relations with Pyongyang without Seoul's permission, that would show Japan's unwillingness to see Korea reunified. Japan made amends to some extent in November, when Murayama published three principles with which Tokyo would deal with Pyongyang: (1) Tokyo would not pursue relations with Pyongyang at the expense of Seoul; (2) Japan would link the pace of normalizing relations with Pyongyang to progress in inter-Korean relations; and (3) Tokyo would refrain from extending economic assistance to North Korea before opening diplomatic relations.[41]

In the spring of 1995, North Korea was forced to ask for food because economic mismanagement had substantially reduced harvests. That problem was compounded in the summer by disastrous floods. By late fall, UN agricultural specialists were warning that North Korea faced famine. At first, South Korea, Japan, and the United States responded with alacrity. ROK deputy prime minister Na Ung-bae said that Seoul was ready to provide emergency food aid without political conditions, a policy that was applauded in much of the South Korean press.[42] Tokyo consulted with Seoul and agreed to ship 300,000 tons of rice to help meet North Korea's request for 1 million tons, provided that the rice not be diverted to Pyongyang's military forces.[43] The North Koreans, instead of expressing gratitude, once again demonstrated clumsy manners. Kim Yong-sun, secretary of the WPK, asserted that Japan offered the rice as an apology for its past crimes.[44] Another senior North Korean, to cover the humiliation of having North Korean citizens learn that their government had asked for rice from abroad, said that Japan had taken the initiative in offering the rice. Then Pyongyang, apparently fearing Japan would cut off further aid, retracted the remarks and sent a letter of appreciation to the Japanese.[45]

Over the summer, Seoul changed tactics and sought to widen discussions with North Korea into a dialogue over economic cooperation. Seoul sought to resolve some of the bitter differences that have haunted North and South Korea since 1945. Japan indicated that it would like to proceed with negotiations leading to diplomatic relations. The North Korean response was unequivocal and hostile: No. Instead, Pyongyang's abuse of Tokyo continued. When Pyongyang later asked for more help, the new Japanese foreign minister, Yukihiko Ikeda, said the Japanese did not think that this was the time to consider additional aid. A meeting of senior South Korean, Japanese, and U.S. officials in Honolulu in late January 1996 came to the same conclusion, largely on Seoul's insistence that North Korea had to live up to its pledges on dialogue first.[46] The Korean Central News Agency stated that the ill-intentioned move of the "puppets" was designed to harm the dignity of the DPRK.

Over the next year, relations continued to deteriorate. North Korea repeatedly attacked Japan with propaganda, and at one point it was discovered that it had sailed a ship into a Japanese port with a cargo of illicit drugs. For its part, the Japanese government hardened its refusal to send more food aid to North Korea. The Japanese, who for more than half a century have not been noted for tough stands on security issues, said publicly that they would render no more aid until North Korea had accounted for ten people it was accused of having kidnapped from Japan. Pyongyang denied the allegations. Privately, Japanese officials said there was no point in giving food to North Korea until Pyongyang came up with a plan to reform its agriculture with proper fertilizer, crop rotation, and care of the land and to open the economy to market forces. These officials contended that natural disasters have worsened the situation in North Korea but were not the primary cause of the current shortages. "If they don't come up with their own plan of reform, with set times to make the reforms work," said a senior official in Tokyo, "we will be feeding them forever."[47]

Despite the optimistic start of this period and occasional intense contacts between Japanese and North Korean leaders, at the end of the day, there was not much to show for it. One conclusion stands out: The North Koreans have placed low priority on their relations with Japan, even though the Japanese stood ready to render economic and food assistance. Evidently, Pyongyang considers its relationship with the United States to be the one worth pursuing, thinking if that works, Japan will fall into place.

Economics and Trade

For much of its existence, North Korea's economic policy has been heavily influenced by the doctrine of *chuch'e,* or self-reliance, and has thus been autarkic (see Chapter 2). Trade has been given low priority. Initially, the regime relented enough to permit limited trade with Russia and China. Later, Pyongyang relented a bit more to allow trade with Japan and the Third World as long as its trading partners respected DPRK sovereignty. In Pyongyang, trade with Japan has ranked second or third in total volume in recent years; in Tokyo, trade with North Korea has been a blip on the screen, accounting for less than 0.3 percent of Japan's worldwide trade. Overall, North Korea's foreign trade totaled $2.64 billion in 1993, dropped to $1.8 billion in 1994, and rose slightly to $2.06 billion in 1995. Japan was North Korea's largest trading partner, with a volume worth $590 million. China was right behind at $550 million, and Russia trailed at $60 million. In contrast, South Korea's worldwide trade in 1994 totaled nearly $200 billion and Japan's came to $670 billion.

Shortly after the Korean War, North Korea started to trade with Japan through Manchuria, with shipments disguised as trade with China. Later, trade was conducted through Hong Kong. During the 1960s, several agreements were reached; normal trade patterns began in the 1970s as North Korea launched a six-year economic development plan. Pyongyang imported large- and small-scale plants and obtained capital loans from Japan and Western Europe.[48]

This situation did not last long; in the mid-1970s, North Korea began to default on import and loan payments. That surprised Japan and Western trading partners, because other Communist nations paid debts on time and maintained their credit ratings. North Korea had negotiated several deferred payment agreements but was not reliable in abiding by them. Accordingly, Pyongyang come to be considered a high risk, and the nation's external relations have been largely frozen because Western creditors have become pessimistic about getting paid.

North Korea's trade with Japan has been something of an exception even though the debt is a dark cloud. In 1971, total trade between Japan and North Korea came to $59 million; in 1972 it jumped to $130 million, in 1973 to $170 million, and in 1974 to $360 million. Thereafter it fluctuated, with a peak of $550 million in 1980, another of $560 million in 1988, and $590 million in 1995. North Korea ran a surplus in 1971, then deficits until 1987, when it returned to a surplus for the ensuing years.

The expansion of trade with Japan occurred as the United States and China normalized diplomatic relations and as Japan and China did the same. When Japanese terrorists known as the Red Army hijacked a Japan Air Lines plane to North Korea in the 1970s, the North Koreans returned the plane and passengers, which improved relations.

In the summer of 1974, even as plant imports from Japan continued, warning signs appeared as North Koreans failed to make payments. Even so, Japanese traders sought to keep North Korea afloat. In December 1976 a delegation of Japanese creditors and a North Korean trade bank agreed to deferred payments for two to three years. But the North Koreans again reneged, and in the fall of 1979 a second deferred agreement was signed in Tokyo, with North Korea agreeing to pay in full in ten years, beginning in 1980. North Korea paid off principal and interest for three years from the end of 1979 to June 1983, but in the spring of 1983 it requested that reduced payments be accepted until 1986. Thus, a third deferred payment agreement was concluded.

In the fall of 1983, North Korean terrorists set off a bomb that killed several senior South Korean officials in Rangoon, Burma. The Japanese government determined that Pyongyang had instigated the terrorism and imposed economic sanctions against North Korea. In retaliation, North Korea refused to make scheduled interest payments and has continued to withhold payments ever since. The accumulated North Korean debt to Japan, including principal and interest, had reached 80 billion yen by 1994.

North Korea has asserted that it could not pay its debts because of the 1973 oil shock and the difficulty in securing cargo ships for exports. It has claimed that the world recession brought on by the oil crisis reduced North Korean exports of nonferrous metals and minerals. From the Japanese point of view, North Korea's economic plan was unrealistic in calling for large purchases of equipment that required large bank loans. North Korea's optimistic forecasts that imported plants would generate exports and would thus reduce Pyongyang's debt turned out to be mistaken because so many North Korean products were shoddy.

Much of the trade between North Korea and Japan is carried on by Korean residents in Japan. The Japan External Trade Organization (JETRO) has estimated that 80–90 percent of Japan's trade with North Koreans is conducted by affiliates of Choch'ongnyon. They export raw materials and equipment to joint ventures in textiles between North Korea and North Korean residents of Japan and import finished apparel—suits and coats. That trade is larger than the general merchandise trade in machinery, electronics, vehicles, and steel plate.

A North Korean joint venture law was adopted in September 1984 "to help North Korean residents of Japan who are struggling in the worsening economic climate of Japan and a high yen recession." North Koreans contend that the law is mutually beneficial, because Korean residents in Japan can transfer technology to North Korea and North Korea can use its raw materials to manufacture goods for export. Relations between North Korea and Korean residents in Japan are based, according to this law, on "contribution to the motherland" and "concern for our comrades in Japan." But that attitude has distorted business transactions as North Koreans neglected the rules of trade or insisted on superior-subordinate personal relations. In reality, North Korean trade with Japan has been much more local than international. By mid-1995, according to the National Unification Ministry in Seoul, 149 foreign companies were operating in North Korea; capital for 131 of those joint ventures came from Japan, mostly with funds from ethnic Koreans.

Until 1992, North Korean trade with Japan was settled with U.S. dollars, Japanese yen, German marks, and British pounds. Then North Korea refused to accept contracts in U.S. dollars, with officials citing worsening U.S.-DPRK relations as the reason. Japanese banks often have not bought North Korean letters of credit but have sought to collect payments themselves. Therefore, many Japanese exporters include in prices interest on deferred payments, meaning that North Korean buyers must pay higher prices.

Another problem for Japanese or Korean residents importing from North Korea has been frequent delays in delivery. Cargo ships have been delayed in departing from North Korea, which has disrupted schedules and pushed up transport costs. The clog at North Korean ports has been attributed to inefficient cargo assembly and loading. When foreign currency exchange rates fluctuate, buyers cannot foresee future rates because they don't know when North Koreans will deliver. In addition, the quality of North Korean exports has sometimes not matched samples shown when a contract is drawn. Agricultural and fishery goods have been poorly maintained during transport, which has resulted in the delivery of inedible foodstuffs that importers have had to dump. These problems could happen anywhere, but they would be covered by international rules on claims. North Koreans, however, have not responded to claims, and few problems have been resolved.

North Korea's policy in 1984 was to emphasize trade with developing nations. Kim Il Sung stated at the Supreme People's Assembly that North Korea planned to diversify its trade to lessen its dependence on socialist countries. As that trade took hold, DPRK imports from Japan declined, as did exports to Japan when measured in yen. In 1985, North Korea exported 43.2 billion yen worth of goods to Japan and imported 59 billion yen worth. Then exports dropped to the range of 25–35 billion yen, and imports from Japan slumped to 25–30 billion yen. In JETRO's view, this shift was due to, among other reasons, high prices of Japan's quality goods and demands by Japanese importers that deliveries be timely, their quality ensured, and international commercial regulations observed.

The political negotiations between Pyongyang and Tokyo in recent years have had little effect on trade. It has become easier, however, for Japanese to travel to North Korea on regular passports. Lines of telecommunication have been increased to make telephone calls and facsimile transmission easier, and charter flights between Tokyo and Pyongyang have been permitted.

One Japanese export to North Korea that has experienced a rapid increase has been used cars and trucks, many of which are sent on to China. Sales of used cars to North Korea in 1992 were estimated at 2.2 billion yen, and nearly nine thousand passenger cars worth 4.6 billion yen were shipped to North Korea in 1993. The used cars were bought from Japanese dealers at an average price of $3,500 each and sold to Chinese dealers for $8,000. China has strong demand for cars, but import controls and high tariffs have been obstacles; used car sales evade such barriers.

Since the issue of North Korean nuclear arms surfaced, the Japanese have debated whether economic sanctions should be imposed. The possibility that war might break out or that the North Korean economy might collapse has been argued in Japan's mass media, with the United States, and in the UN Security Council. In the spring of 1994, a right-wing group in Tokyo stormed the offices of the Council on East Asian Trade and demanded that trade with North Korea be stopped. The group asserted: "Exporting goods and payments for imports from North Korea is helping North Korea to develop nuclear weapons and produce missiles that would target Japan. Japan–North Korea trade is against our national interest. Those who are engaged in such trade are traitors."[49]

After North Korean food shortages arose, Pyongyang sought stable supplies of food from rice-exporting nations in Southeast Asia before asking for assistance from South Korea, Japan, the United States, and others. In the spring of 1995, Pyongyang agreed with Bangkok to import 300,000 tons of rice in exchange for hot-rolled steel plate. In another agreement, North Korea would import 100,000 tons of rice from Vietnam in exchange for cement. The DPRK Committee for the Promotion of International Trade invited Japan's Council on East Asian Trade to send a delegation to North Korea in November 1995 to look for ways to develop trade, apparently seeking a way around political obstacles. By mid-1997, however, nothing much had come of those efforts and two-way trade amounted to no more than a trickle.

In summary, North Korea's economic and trade relations with Japan do not amount to much, and the outlook for the foreseeable future is for little change. The curious aspect of this relationship is that it makes little difference to the Japanese but could make a great deal of difference to the limping North Korean economy.

Conclusion

From the start of the DPRK until today, there has been a nearly unremitting hostility on the part of Pyongyang toward Japan. Even though a glimmer of light occasionally slips through the gloom, the prospects for the future are not bright. It appears that change is likely only if the rulers in Pyongyang come to see that a sound and civil relationship with Japan is in the best interests of North Korea. Even though such a relationship would seem to be in Pyongyang's best interests, the North Koreans are caught up in emotions, ideology, and a history of hostile relations that goes back nearly a century. For the Japanese, North Korea appears to be of minor importance as long as a war on the peninsula is precluded and a flow of refugees is averted. Beyond that, the Japanese are not eager to see a reunification of the two Koreas, because that might pose a new political, economic, and possibly military threat to Japan. The status quo thus seems quite acceptable.

Notes

1. *Far Eastern Economic Review,* Asia 1996 Yearbook, p. 149.
2. Central Intelligence Agency, *World Factbook 1995* (Washington, D.C.), p. 231.
3. Kim Myong-ch'ol, September 5, 1995, Northeast Asia Peace and Security Network Daily Report (NAPS).
4. *Yomiuri shimbun, Japan Times, Kyodo News Agency,* November 24–27, 1994, NAPS.
5. Hajime Izumi, "Tokyo's Policy Toward North Korea and Korean Reunification," in Garret W. Gong, Seizaburo Sato, and Tae Hwan Ok, eds., *Korean Peninsula Developments and U.S.-Japan–South Korea Relations,* vol. 1 (Washington, D.C.: Center for Strategic and International Studies, 1993), p. 41.
6. Ichiro Ozawa, *Blueprint for a New Japan: The Rethinking of a Nation* (Tokyo: Kodansha International, 1994), p. 134.
7. *Boei hakusho, heisei nananenkan* [Defense of Japan 1995] (Tokyo: Self-Defense Agency, 1995), p. 57.
8. Interview by the author with a senior Japanese official in Honolulu, spring 1995.
9. *North Korea and Prospects for Korean Unification,* Conference Report, Graduate School of International Relations and Pacific Studies, University of California, San Diego, May 25–27, 1995, p. 7
10. Mun Chong-in as quoted in Jennifer Lind, "Gambling with Globalism: Japanese Financial Flows to North Korea and the Sanctions Policy Option," unpublished paper, University of California, San Diego, 1995.
11. David Arase, as quoted in ibid.
12. Terauki Ueno, June 9, 1994, as quoted in ibid.
13. David Hamilton, *Wall Street Journal,* June 10, 1994.
14. As seen in *Nodong sinmun* and Korean Central News Agency dispatches.
15. See *North Korea and Prospects for Korean Unification,* and Lind, "Gambling with Globalism."
16. Lind, "Gambling with Globalism."
17. Torkel Patterson, "North Korea: First Impressions," PacNet, Pacific Forum, Honolulu, April 6, 1995.
18. Masao Okonogi, "Japan's Policy Toward North Korea: Developments in the Korean Peninsula, the United States, and Japan," background paper for the Shimoda '94 conference, Shimoda, Japan, p. 3.
19. Ibid., pp. 3, 4, 8.
20. *Kankoku-Kita Chosen yoran, 1994* [South Korea–North Korea Handbook, 1994] (Tokyo: Sekai seikei chosakai, 1994), May 1, June 11 and 14, July 30, August 18, September 26, 1993, and February 6, 1994.
21. Ibid., March 16, June 4, August 9 and 25, 1993.
22. For text, see *Arms Control Today* (December 1994):19
23. See *Japan Times* and *Korea Times,* from November 22 to December 2, 1994.
24. *Asahi shimbun,* April 2, 1995, NAPS.
25. *Nihon keizai shimbun,* March 12, 1995, NAPS.
26. *Asahi shimbun,* March 31, 1995, NAPS.
27. *Korea Report,* April 1995, p. 5, NAPS.
28. *Yomiuri shimbun,* November 26, 1994, NAPS.
29. Associated Press, February 22, 1995. See also *Korea Times,* February 22, 1995.

30. Associated Press, December 15, 1995.

31. *Washington Times,* December 16, 1995, p. A8, NAPS.

32. *Korea Times,* February 2, 1995, p. 2, NAPS.

33. *Jiefang Daily,* June 25, 1995, p. A4, NAPS.

34. See *Military Balance, 1995–96* (London: Institute for International and Strategic Studies, 1996).

35. *Jiefang Daily,* October 10, 1995, p. A4, NAPS.

36. Ibid., March 22, 1995, p. A4, NAPS.

37. Ibid., July 22, 1995, p. A4, NAPS.

38. *Korea Times,* March 25, 1995, p. 1, NAPS.

39. *Korea Herald,* March 26, 1995, p. 2, NAPS.

40. *Nihon keizai shimbun,* October 10, 1995, p. 1, NAPS.

41. *Korea Herald,* November 19, 1995, p. 1, NAPS.

42. "Rice for North Koreans," *Korea Herald,* May 30, 1995, p. 6, NAPS.

43. *Asahi shimbun,* June 29, 1995, p. 1, NAPS.

44. *Yomiuri shimbun,* August 19, 1995.

45. *Asahi shimbun,* September 14, 1995, p. 1, NAPS.

46. Reporting by the author, Honolulu, January 25–27, 1996.

47. Author's discussions with Japanese officials in Tokyo, April 1997.

48. *Kita Chosen no keizai to boeki no tempo, 1992 nenkan* (Tokyo: Nihon boeki shinkyokai, kaigai keizai joho senta, 1992). Economic and trade data and statistics in this section are taken from the 1992 and subsequent yearbooks, unless otherwise noted.

49. Ibid.

11

North and South Korean Confrontation in the Nuclear Age

Chong-Sik Lee

The Kim Young Sam puppet regime, engrossed in treachery and irregularities, is doomed to destruction as the successive rulers of South Korea went to ruin, while seeking confrontation with the fellow countrymen in the North and "unification by invading the North," estranged from the people. The South Korean puppet clique, who are driven into a tight corner, rejected within and without, are desperately trying to find a way out of their catastrophic crisis in North-South confrontation and war provocation. Their allegation about "the North's threat" is nothing but talk for invading the North. If the United States and the South Korean puppet clique persistently seek confrontation and war, the situation will be further aggravated and brought to a hopeless phase. We cannot remain an onlooker to it, nor will we allow any provocation. The reunification of the country is the cause of the nation and the supreme task to which Comrade Kim Il Sung devoted all efforts until he passed away.[1]

This quotation from the New Year's joint editorial of North Korean government organs epitomizes North Korea's attitude toward South Korea in early 1996. The North Korean leadership not only finds the Kim Young Sam regime unsuitable as a collaborative partner for unification but sees it as an antagonistic and hostile regime doomed to destruction.

The intensity of hostility displayed by the North Korean editorial stands in sharp contrast to the spirit of cooperation shown by North and South Korea between 1990 and 1992. The premiers of the two regimes met numerous times in those years, and on December 13, 1991, the two sides signed an Agreement on Reconciliation, Nonaggression, and Exchanges and Cooperation that was sweeping and far-reaching in scope. The two sides agreed, for example, that they would respect each other's political and social systems and would not slander and vilify each other. They also agreed not to attempt in any manner to sabotage or subvert each other, to cease confrontation on the international stage, and to cooperate to promote national interests and esteem. North and South Korea followed up this agreement by issuing a joint declaration on non-nuclearization of the

Korean peninsula and by agreeing to establish a nuclear control commission.

Why the Renewed Hostility?

The immediate cause of the renewed hostility lies in the conflict over North Korea's nuclear program.[2] To encourage North Korea to take a more conciliatory attitude toward the nuclear issue, South Korea and the United States suspended the Team Spirit exercise in 1992 and instead carried out the smaller-scale Hwarang and Toksuri exercises in November of that year. North Korea found these exercises offensive nonetheless and returned to the old practice of calling the South Korean government and the United States puppets and American imperialists.[3] As expected, North Korea intensified its bellicose verbiage when South Korea and the United States resumed the Team Spirit exercise in March 1993.

Neither the conflict over the nuclear issue nor the Team Spirit exercise, however, adequately explains the hostile North-South relations, since North Korea has been eager to improve its relations with the United States, the principal partner of South Korea in the Team Spirit exercise. The suspension of the exercises between 1994 and 1996 had no effect on North Korea's behavior toward South Korea. North Korea's enmity toward the Kim Young Sam regime in Seoul betrays deeper causes.

Several factors can account for North Korea's unmitigated hostility against President Kim Young Sam and his government. One is North Korea's vulnerability. Kim Young Sam happened to be occupying South Korea's presidency when North Korea was at its most vulnerable. A second factor is North Korea's perception that President Kim Young Sam actively seeks to destroy the North Korean political system or to pressure North Korea to submit to South Korea's demands. None of his predecessors, of course, had exhibited affinity with the regime in North Korea, but neither had any leader, at least after Syngman Rhee, taken any action that materially jeopardized the very existence of the North Korean political system. A third factor is the South Korean regime's desecration of the late president Kim Il Sung on the occasion of his death. It is difficult to know which of the last two factors the North Korean elites find more repugnant, but the combination of these factors has certainly left no room for a dialogue with South Korea.

North Korea's Crises

North Korea's vulnerability derives from a combination of economic, diplomatic, and leadership crises.[4] The economic crisis is in part the result of North Korea's inability to modernize and diversify its coal-based and heavy-industry-oriented industrial structure. In the early 1970s North Korea took important steps toward modernization by purchasing industrial facilities from abroad, but the oil shock of 1973 thwarted these efforts and led the North to default on its payments, which erected a major roadblock for its international transactions. Unable to attract foreign capital or to import needed foreign technology, North Korea was forced to maintain its inefficient and largely outmoded coal-dependent industrial structure. Its efforts since 1984 to attract foreign capital by adopting foreign investment laws have produced no tangible results. As coal production began to decline, electric power supply dwindled, severely affecting transportation and industrial production. Much of North Korea's transportation is dependent on railways running on electricity, which in turn depends on coal.

The unprecedented floods of 1995 and 1996 severely aggravated North Korea's agricultural sector, but its problem has deeper roots. The collectivized farms have been stagnant for many years in spite of repeated ideological campaigns. Simply put, the soil and labor have been exhausted through overuse. When the industrial sector failed to supply the needed fertilizers and pesticides, crops suffered. Overcultivation of the land in the mountainous country left the soil more vulnerable to floods.

Events abroad aggravated North Korea's economic problems. The North drastically increased its trade with the Soviet Union after President Kim Il Sung's celebrated journey to the Soviet Union and Eastern Europe in 1984, but President Mikhail Gorbachev's 1989 decision to demand hard currency for Soviet products severely curtailed North Korea's imports from the Soviet Union, which had included 20 percent of the North's oil requirements. The fall of the Soviet Union in 1991 meant the loss of North Korea's major trade partner, which had supplied over half its imports.

Gorbachev's new policies also dealt a severe blow to North Korea on the diplomatic and security fronts. His decision to establish diplomatic relations with the Republic of Korea (ROK) in 1990 in effect nullified the Soviet–North Korean defense treaty, which had facilitated a nuclear shield. It is not surprising, then, that when informed of the Soviet decision to establish diplomatic relations with South Korea, the North Korean foreign minister responded by saying that North Korea must produce nuclear weapons on its own.[5]

Not only did North Korea lose its principal ally, the Soviet Union, but the Chinese attitude toward the North began to change, culminating in the establishment of China's diplomatic relations with South Korea in August 1992. Since then, South Korea has quickly become one of China's biggest trade partners, the trade volume surpassing that between China and North Korea by several fold. Although China still maintains diplomatic, economic, and military ties with the Democratic People's Republic of Korea

(DPRK) and continues to provide it some economic assistance, it is no longer the dependable ally in the North Korean struggle against South Korea.

All of these events naturally heightened Pyongyang's sense of vulnerability, which had an immediate effect on its relations with South Korea. The South Korean government celebrated each of these developments as a great victory that would contribute to the moderation of North Korea's behavior, but North Korea turned in the opposite direction. A conciliatory attitude toward South Korea under the circumstances would have been interpreted as a sign of weakness that South Korea was likely to exploit. It was not simply a question of pride; North Korea's survival required a hard-line attitude.

The Death of President Kim Il Sung

The death of President Kim Il Sung could not have happened at a worse juncture for North-South relations. Just a month before his death in July 1994, North and South Korea had been preparing for an unprecedented summit meeting between the two presidents. All indications were that the two leaders would remove or begin to remove the obstacles lying between the two states and earnestly seek ways to improve relations. Anticipation was high because Kim Il Sung was no ordinary leader. He had ruled for half a century with an iron hand, and his words were the law in his domain. He alone was in a position to surmount the rivalry among his underlings and set a new course in inter-Korean relations. President Kim Young Sam of South Korea, the first civilian head of state in three decades, did not have as much latitude or the power to chart a new course, but any reasonable agreement reached at the summit would have enhanced his stature, which in turn would have enhanced his ability to implement the agreement. Even if the summit failed to produce concrete results, the meeting itself, if held and concluded in a cordial atmosphere, would have eased the tension that had prevailed. Kim Il Sung's death, therefore, had a significant impact on both sides. Not only did the summit meeting fail to materialize, but the two sides fell into an abyss of uncertainty and hostility.

The announcement of the summit had been preceded by a warlike atmosphere on the Korean peninsula. North Korea's refusal to permit the International Atomic Energy Agency (IAEA) to inspect suspected nuclear installations had precipitated an international crisis, with the United States calling for UN sanctions against North Korea. In March 1993 North Korea's announcement of its intent to withdraw from the Treaty on the Non-Proliferation of Nuclear Weapons (NPT) and a North Korean delegate's comment that "if a war breaks out, Seoul would turn into a sea of fire" led the South Korean government to place its armed forces on high alert.

The tension abated in early June when North Korea invited Selig Harrison of the Carnegie Foundation to Pyongyang and indicated its willingness to negotiate. Former U.S. president Jimmy Carter visited Pyongyang on June 15, with the Clinton administration's blessing, and returned with not only a confirmation of the DPRK's willingness to negotiate but an expression of the North Korean president's willingness to meet with his South Korean counterpart. Kim Young Sam had already expressed his wish to speak with Kim Il Sung when Carter stopped over in Seoul before his journey to Pyongyang. It is reasonable to assume that both sides sought to find short- and long-term solutions through the summit talks.

President Kim Young Sam and North Korea

What happened in South Korea after Kim Il Sung's death graphically revealed the effect of five decades of continued hostility between North and South Korea. President Kim Young Sam had astounded many in Korea and abroad by saying at his inaugural ceremony on February 25, 1993, that "no ally can be more important [or better] than the *minjok,* the nation" and calling for a summit meeting with the North Korean president. He was reportedly ecstatic at the prospect of the summit meeting.[6] But after Kim Il Sung's death, the South Korean government issued statements and took actions that could not have angered the North Korean elites more. On July 18, ten days after Kim's death, the South Korean government issued a statement declaring that the leader has been "responsible for such unfortunate events as the perpetuation of the national division and the internecine war" and that the government would enforce the law that prohibited contact with North Korea.[7] The South Korean government clamped down on the radical members of the Federation of Korean Student Councils who had set up altars to mourn the North Korean leader and arrested thousands of students who tried to march to Panmunjom to meet their northern counterparts. The North Korean mass media maligned the South Korean president in the vilest language.

Other actions by Seoul aggravated the situation even further. On July 27, the South Korean intelligence agency produced an alleged North Korean defector who claimed to be a son-in-law of the North Korean premier, Kang Song-san. Even more, the defector claimed to know that North Korea had already produced five nuclear bombs. On August 8, the ROK vice-premier in charge of unification referred to the possibility of "unification by absorption" in the event of North Korea's collapse, as well as the government's determination to insist on improvement of human rights in North Korea and the release of South Koreans kidnapped by North Korea.[8] The war of words was on.

Given the crises North Korea faced in 1994, the talk of "unification by absorption" was nothing short of a declaration of war, but President Kim

Young Sam's statement on October 8 to a *New York Times* correspondent went a step further. In that interview, Kim lashed out against Washington for its "naive and overly flexible" negotiations at Geneva with a government that "was on the verge of economic and political crises that could sweep it from power." In his view, Washington was "led on by North Korean manipulations."[9] Kim wanted the United States to apply more pressure on North Korea to open its two suspected nuclear waste storage sites for inspection, facilities at which the U.S. intelligence community had long suspected the North Koreans of concealing weapons-grade plutonium.

One may wonder why the Kim Young Sam regime took ten days after Kim Il Sung's death to issue a hostile statement toward the deceased and why the South Korean president did not simply publish the text of the speech he had intended to deliver at the summit meeting, which, presumably, would have been more conciliatory. Why did the South Korean government choose instead to denigrate the deceased and slam the door against North Korea?

Kim Young Sam's October 8 statement to the *New York Times* provides a possible answer. In his view North Korea "was on the verge of economic and political crises that could sweep it from power" and could not survive long without Kim Il Sung; hence, there was no need for reconciliation. All North Korea needed was a little pressure before it would collapse. Most South Korean pundits supported this reasoning.[10]

It is also possible that Kim Young Sam feared adverse political repercussions for taking a moderate stance toward North Korea. His government had been ridiculed and criticized in South Korea for making juvenile assumptions about North Korea's behavior. An example of such disapproval occurred during the initial months of his administration when, as a goodwill gesture, South Korea repatriated a former North Korean war correspondent, Yi In-mo, who had been a prisoner in South Korea since the days of the Korean War. The Kim government evidently hoped that North Korea would make a reciprocal gesture, but the North Korean regime instead launched an intense propaganda campaign to exalt Yi In-mo and to denounce South Korea's barbarity in holding the prisoner so long. Kim was placed in an untenable position, and he replaced the deputy premier in charge of the unification board. Thus, Kim Young Sam had to pay a heavy political price for his first official action as president vis-à-vis North Korea, a lesson he could not forget. Kim had to face adversaries not only in North Korea but within South Korea as well.

Driving a Wedge Between the United States and South Korea

The South Korean government's actions after the death of President Kim Il Sung made it virtually impossible for the new North Korean leadership to resume talks with South Korea. For them, the resumption of talks would have been tantamount to committing lèse-majesté. Furthermore, as noted earlier, the North was in too weak a position to resume negotiations with the South.

A dissonance of views between the United States and South Korea at this juncture eliminated whatever incentive the North Koreans may have had to engage in talks with South Korea. Although the United States and South Korea agreed on the need to stop North Korea's graphite-core nuclear projects, they followed different strategies for North Korea because they had different priorities. The Clinton administration, which had been accused of being weak on the foreign policy front, wanted North Korea to remain a member of the NPT system and abide by the rules of the IAEA. North Korea's membership in the NPT was critical, particularly because the treaty was up for renewal in 1995; the system had already been widely criticized from many quarters, and North Korea's withdrawal from it would have been a fatal blow. Hence, the United States was more willing to accommodate North Korean demands than was South Korea.

The most critical issue for South Korea was the immediate removal from North Korea of all nuclear materials that could be developed into weapons. The ROK wanted North Korea's nuclear project to be terminated and its suspected nuclear waste sites to be inspected immediately, as the IAEA demanded. Postponement was unacceptable to the South.

North Koreans also discovered a wide gap between the United States and South Korea in their attitudes toward the death of Kim Il Sung. To the South Koreans, particularly those of the older generation who had suffered so much from the Korean War, an expression of condolence would have meant the whitewashing of past crimes. Kim Il Sung had been the archenemy responsible for the war and had offered no accounting for the excruciating events of the past. An expression of condolence would have also meant the recognition of the legitimacy of the North Korean regime, an act that would have required a revision of the ROK constitution. Even though both North and South Korea had joined the UN in 1991, neither of their constitutions had addressed the possibility of another regime on the Korean peninsula. The death of Kim Il Sung thus brought forth many difficult political and legal questions to the South Korean regime. This probably explains why the South Korean government waited ten long days to issue a statement regarding Kim's death.

The United States, however, did not need to agonize over such an issue. Messages of condolence were only perfunctory diplomatic gestures that carried no great political significance. As it happened, President Kim Il Sung died as U.S. officials were engaged in negotiations with the North Korean representatives in Geneva, and the U.S. side was eager to facilitate an agreement that would include the opening of U.S. diplomatic relations with North Korea. When the North Korean delegation insisted that a presidential message of condolence would materially improve the chance of reaching an accord, the U.S. side readily agreed. On the conclusion of the Geneva accord in October 1994, U.S. president Bill Clinton dispatched a letter to the "Supreme Leader of North Korea, Kim Jong Il" pledging that the United States would abide by the content of the agreement.[11] Significantly, the U.S. side received no similar pledge from the North.

North Korea must have been elated to receive these messages from the United States, particularly in light of the sharp contrast between U.S. and South Korean attitudes. Whereas the South Korean government denounced Kim Il Sung as a war criminal, the United States joined in mourning him. Whereas South Korea talked of North Korea's imminent collapse, President Clinton not only recognized Kim Jong Il as North Korea's supreme leader but unilaterally pledged himself to abide by the agreement. Clinton may not have recognized it, but he had clearly handed North Korea a resounding victory in the diplomatic contest. There is no doubt that North and South Korea interpreted the two messages as a blow to South Korea.

As President Kim Young Sam would indicate to the *New York Times* less than two weeks before the agreement was reached, the Geneva accord itself was not to South Korea's liking. (It should be noted that his remark was published on October 8, 1994.) The Agreed Framework called for the immediate suspension of ongoing North Korean nuclear projects but post-poned the inspection of suspected storage sites for five years. In the mean-time, the United States would supply North Korea with 500,000 metric tons of oil a year (50,000 tons during the first year) to compensate for the elec-tricity that would no longer be produced by the scrapped nuclear power plants, and it would construct—at no cost to North Korea—two light-water nuclear reactors that would produce as much electricity as the scuttled graphite-moderated reactors had. The United States would also take steps to establish diplomatic relations with Pyongyang, beginning with the exchange of liaison offices.[12]

Thus, North Korea had used its image of a rogue and volatile state to win a major victory. The United States had long refused to engage in direct talks with North Korea, insisting on the improvement of North-South rela-tions as a prerequisite. Now, however, the United States not only engaged in high-level talks with North Korea but agreed to establish diplomatic rela-tions. And it agreed to provide North Korea not only with new light-water nuclear reactors but also with badly needed oil for ten years. Above all, the United States ignored repeated protestation from Seoul.

North Korea attached symbolic importance to Clinton's messages in 1994, but Jimmy Carter's visit to Pyongyang in March 1993 was particular-ly significant to the North. Carter, of course, was not an incumbent presi-dent of the United States, and, as far as the United States was concerned, his visit was strictly in a private capacity. But for both North and South

Korea, his former title carried much more weight than the West presumed, and his trip enormously bolstered the image of the DPRK. His visit and the cordiality he displayed to President Kim Il Sung removed from Kim the stigma of being the head of a pariah state and accorded him the legitimacy he had long sought. North Korean mass media did not apply to Carter the language they had used to characterize President Richard Nixon during his trip to Beijing in 1972—that is, as the imperialist chieftain holding a white flag in hand—but it would not be surprising if North Koreans drew a parallel. Carter's visit was probably the best gift the United States had sent to President Kim Il Sung before his death.

The actions taken by the United States and South Korea after President Kim Il Sung's death thus intensified North Korea's resolve to ignore the South Korean government. To add salt to the wound, President Kim Young Sam, who had objected to the Geneva accord, was obliged to assume much of the cost of building the light-water reactors for North Korea. At this point there was no need for North Korea to negotiate with the South.

Ignoring the South Korean government, however, did not mean terminating economic interaction; North Korea evidently opted for a policy of separating politics from economics. The South Korean government attempted to salvage its position in the aftermath of the Geneva accord by announcing the lift of its ban against investment in the North and encouraging the business community to apply for permission to conduct business with the North. The North Koreans snubbed the South Korean government by rejecting its offer. Korean Central News Agency said in a dispatch that "cooperation and confrontation are incompatible."[13] At the same time, however, North Korea continued to encourage South Korean business groups to send trade missions, and such business groups as Samsung, Hyundai, Ssangyong, and Lucky Goldstar were eager to comply.[14] Inter-Korean trade through third countries, in the meantime, has continued to increase.

Japan, South Korea, and Rice for North Korea

Pyongyang employed the same pattern of diplomacy it had previously followed to obtain much-needed rice from South Korea. In the summer of 1995, the North Koreans approached the Japanese government for 300,000 tons of rice; Japan was more than willing to dispose of the excess supply it had previously imported from Southeast Asia. The Japanese government also thought that providing rice might favorably affect the pending diplomatic negotiations with North Korea. The news of North Korean negotiations with Japan, of course, put the South Korean government in an awkward position because it could be accused of ignoring its desperate compatriots in the North. Accordingly, the South Korean government requested that the Japanese delay their negotiations until the South had provided the North with 150,000 tons of rice.

The final result was that North Korea obtained rice from both Japan and South Korea. Pyongyang did not express appreciation for the South's assistance; instead, it scoffed at the government's motive. Pyongyang went to the extent of holding a South Korean ship that had transported the rice because one of its crew members had taken photographs at the Ch'ongjin port. The ROK government, in order to obtain the ship's release, was forced to apologize for the crew member's indiscretion.[15] After this incident, Pyongyang continued to hold the South Korean government in disdain. It was determined not to deal directly with Seoul and insisted that negotiations concerning additional supply of rice be handled by representatives of nongovernmental organizations. North Korea's actions, of course, made it impossible for South Korea to provide additional aid. The South Korean public was indignant at the treatment accorded to South Korean ships and dealt Kim Young Sam's party a severe blow in the June 1995 elections of municipal governors and representatives.[16]

North and South Korean Behavior in Perspective

The roots of North Korean behavior have already been analyzed. North Korean elites have been operating in a crisis atmosphere, sensing great vulnerability, and the survival of the Communist state has been at stake. In such an atmosphere, they have found the actions of the Kim Young Sam regime repugnant. North Korea's behavior is a perfect example of what John Mearsheimer characterizes as the three main patterns of state behavior: States in the international system fear each other; each state in the international system aims to guarantee its own survival; and each state in the international system aims to maximize its relative power over other states.[17]

What complicates the inter-Korean relationship is that the competition in Korea involves more than the quest for military advantage that the realist school in international relations posits. In spite of numerous exchanges of official delegations and documents signed, and in spite of the two states' memberships in the UN, neither side has yet acknowledged the legitimacy of the other, and each has been engaged in a fierce battle to win the support of the people on the opposing side as well as those abroad. Although the South Korean regimes may have abandoned their attempt to affect the North Korean population in light of the tight control the DPRK government exercises, North Korea has not slackened its efforts to win over the opposition. The relatively free political atmosphere in South Korea, including the dissension concerning the government's Northern policy, has made it imperative for Pyongyang to continue the struggle.

North Korea has been engaged in the same battle in the international arena, the discord in the North Korean strategies of the United States, South Korea, and Japan proving most fortuitous for Pyongyang. The North's strategy of snubbing "the South Korean puppet" while exacting material aid from the United States and South Korea may not have materially altered the relative power positions of North and South Korea, but there is no doubt that it has contributed significantly to guaranteeing the survival of both the North Korean state and its leadership. The North Korean leaders could claim, with considerable justification, that their brilliance put South Korea in its proper place while obtaining much needed materials. In retaliation, South Korea persuaded Japan to suspend its supply of rice to North Korea, but shipment of rice has resumed in 1996.

Kim Young Sam's North Korean strategy is a replica of early U.S. containment strategy, bearing a striking similarity to the way George Kennan, Clark Clifford, and Harry Truman saw the Soviet Union in the early days of the Cold War. To these U.S. leaders, the Soviet Union was an inherently aggressive power holding a neurotic view of world affairs, a view aggravated by a fear of more competent, more powerful, and more highly organized societies in the West. The United States, Kennan argued, had to "hunker down" for a long struggle because the goals and philosophies of the United States and the Soviet Union were irreconcilable.[18] Truman's adviser Clifford believed that a significant Soviet change of heart and probably a new set of Soviet leaders were required before an overall Soviet-U.S. agreement would be possible. Given these conditions, as long as the Soviet Union maintained its ideology, negotiations were pointless. The conflict could be settled only by a change in Soviet purposes, by the collapse of its system, or both.

Kim Young Sam is not alone in his view of North Korea. During the heated spring 1996 electoral campaign for the National Assembly, hardly a candidate referred to the North Korean issue. Nor has there been an editorial calling for a substantial change in South Korean policy toward North Korea.

The Future

The North Korean leadership played its limited hand very skillfully. It effectively used its political and economic weaknesses as weapons by making credible the threat of suicidal attack. The threat to withdraw from the NPT system forced the United States to make major concessions, ignoring or overruling the South Korean president's protestations. North Korea clearly won the first round of diplomatic battles—a victory that brought Kim Jong Il's new regime credibility in the outside world and, most likely, admiration within North Korea.

But the North Korean policy of refusing to negotiate with South Korea and of alienating South Korea from the United States and Japan cannot be a viable weapon for any length of time because no one but North Korea will suffer from it. President Kim Young Sam was clearly humiliated by the Geneva accord, but he will not suffer further adverse political consequences even if the stalemate continues. North Korea's treatment of South Korea's rice-carrying ships aroused considerable anti–North Korean sentiment within the ROK, and as a result, policies toward North Korea ceased to be an issue within South Korea. In the meantime, the South Korean, U.S., and Japanese governments are satisfied that North Korea has ceased its graphite-core nuclear projects, as are China and Russia. Improvement of relations with North Korea is clearly not a priority for any of these governments. Given the economic conditions in the DPRK, there is very little pressure from the commercial sector in any of these countries to improve relations with North Korea.

Meanwhile, the frigid relationship between North and South Korea is seriously hampering the North's economic recovery. First of all, it prevents South Korean firms from making major investments in North Korea. Second, it also prevents Japan from normalizing its relationship with North Korea. The Japanese are aware that South Korea is much more important as a political and economic partner than North Korea can ever become and thus are not likely to take steps that would alienate the South. Because the Japanese have expressed an interest in providing a substantial sum—a minimum of approximately $5 billion—to North Korea as compensation for the colonial period, the delay in normalization deprives North Korea of a major source of foreign capital. Third, the continuing confrontation between North and South Korea makes it difficult for the United States to intensify its contacts with North Korea. The United States' interest does not go much further than preventing nuclear proliferation and North Korea's implosion, an interest that South Korea shares. The United States and South Korea may differ in their choice of tactics, but there is a limit to their disagreement.

It is therefore incumbent on North Korea to change its strategy, but it is difficult to predict how and when a change will occur. Emotion plays a far more important role in North Korea than in other societies. We also know very little about Kim Jong Il's pattern of decisionmaking. The best South Korea and its allies can do under the circumstances is to create an atmosphere conducive for the North Korean leadership to change its attitude. The stability on the Korean peninsula requires it.

Notes

1. From "Let Us Advance Vigorously in the New Year, Flying the Red Flag," the joint editorial of North Korean papers *Nodong sinmun, Choson inmin'gun,* and

Nodong ch'ongnyon, on January 1, 1996, as transmitted by the Korean Central News Agency.

2. For details, see Michael J. Mazarr, *North Korea and the Bomb: A Case Study in Nonproliferation* (New York: St. Martin's Press, 1995).

3. See *Nodong sinmun* editorial of November 9, 1992.

4. I have presented my analysis of these problems in Chong-Sik Lee, "Political Economy of North Korea, 1994," *National Bureau of Asian Research* 5, no. 2 (1994).

5. *Asahi shinbun,* January 1, 1990.

6. *Tong-a ilbo,* July 5, 1994.

7. *Choson ilbo,* July 19, 1994.

8. *Tong-a ilbo,* August 10, 1994.

9. James Sterngold, "South Korean President Lashes out at U.S.," *New York Times,* October 8, 1994.

10. See, e.g., the survey conducted by *Han'guk ilbo,* June 10, 1994, pp. 6–7.

11. Ibid. For the full text of the letter, see *Japanese Economic Newswire,* October 22, 1994, in Nexus-Lexus. North Korea, of course, paid prominent attention to the letter. See the front page of *Nodong sinmun,* October 23, 1994, and *T'ong'il sinbo,* October 19, 1994.

12. Alan Riding, "U.S. and North Korea Sign Pact to End Nuclear Dispute," *New York Times,* October 22, 1994.

13. Associated Press News Release, November 11, 1994.

14. *Choson ilbo,* on November 30, 1994, reported that these groups had applied for permission from the South Korean government to send "investment missions."

15. Another South Korean ship suffered the indignity of being forced to replace the South Korean flag with a North Korean flag when it entered a North Korean port. Although this incident caused an uproar in South Korea, it was clearly a case of misunderstanding or lack of adequate communication on both sides. Representatives from both sides had previously agreed that no flag would be displayed on ships entering North Korean ports, but ship captains had not been properly informed about the agreement.

16. See B. C. Koh, "South Korea in 1995," *Asian Survey* (January 1996):53–60, esp. pp. 57–58.

17. John J. Mearsheimer, "The False Promise of International Institutions," *International Security* (Winter 1994):5–49 (at pp. 11–12).

18. For the views of Kennan, Clifford, and Truman, I use the summary provided by Henry Kissinger's recent essay "Reflections on Containment," *Foreign Affairs* (May–June 1994):113–130.

APPENDIX 1

Acronyms & Abbreviations

APEC	Asia Pacific Economic Cooperation
BOK	Bank of Korea
CCP	Chinese Communist Party
CIS	Commonwealth of Independent States
CNN	Cable News Network
COCOM	Coordinating Committee on Export Controls
CPE	centrally planned economy
DKIH	Deutsch-Koreanische Industrie- und Handelskammer
DMZ	Demilitarized Zone
DPRK	Democratic People's Republic of Korea
GATT	General Agreement on Tariffs and Trade
GDP	gross domestic product
GNP	gross national product
IAEA	International Atomic Energy Agency
IISS	International Institute for Strategic Studies
IMF	International Monetary Fund
IPU	Inter-Parliamentary Union
JETRO	Japan External Trade Organization
KEDO	Korean Peninsula Energy Development Organization
KFRAM	Korean Fatherland Restoration Association in Manchuria
KOC	Kapsan Operation Committee
KOTRA	Korean Trade Promotion Corporation
KPA	Korean People's Army
LWR	light-water reactor
MAC	Military Armistice Commission
MIA	missing in action
NPT	Treaty on the Non-Proliferation of Nuclear Weapons
OECD	Organization for Economic Cooperation and Development
PLA	People's Liberation Army
PPP	purchase power parity

PRC	People's Republic of China
ROK	Republic of Korea
SEZ	special economic zone
UNDP	United Nations Development Programme
WPK	Workers' Party of Korea
WTO	World Trade Organization

APPENDIX 2

Members and Ranks of the Funeral Committees of Kim Il Sung, O Chin-u, and Ch'oe Kwang

Key

AC	Administration Council Member
ACM	Auditing Committee Member
AFM	Minister of the People's Armed Forces
CC	Central Committee of the Workers' Party of Korea
CCM	Central Committee Member
Changes	Refers to changes after the death of Kim Il Sung
Ch'oe Kwang	Numbers refer to the rank order of the Ch'oe Kwang Funeral Committee
CIC	Commander-in-Chief
CMC	Central Military Commission
CMCC	Alternate Members of the Central Committee
CPCM	Members of the Central People's Committee
Mar.	Marshal
NDC	National Defense Council
O Chin-u	Numbers refer to the rank order of the O Chin-u Funeral Committee
P	Refers to member of the Central Committee after the Sixth Party Congress
Partisan	Kim Il Sung's partisan guerrilla fighters
PBCM	Alternate Member of the Politburo of the Workers' Party of Korea
PBM	Member of the Politburo of the Workers' Party of Korea
PCCM	Members elected to the Central Committee after 1980
PCMCC	Alternate Members elected to the Central Committee after 1980
Position	Position held at the time of the death of Kim Il Sung
Prem.	Premier
Record #	Numbers indicate the rank order in the Kim Il Sung Funeral Committee
Sec.	Secretary of the Secretariat of the Workers' Party of Korea
SPA	Supreme People's Assembly
VP	Vice-President
VPr.	Vice-Premier
3456p	Numbers refer to the party congresses where member was elected to the Central Committee. 3456 stands for Central Committee membership at the Third, Fourth, Fifth, and Sixth Central

	Committees; p stands for membership in the Central Committee after the Sixth Party Congress
456p	Refers to membership in the Fourth, Fifth, and Sixth Central Committees and remained member of the committee after the Sixth Party Congress
456	Refers to membership in the Fourth, Fifth, and Sixth Central Committee but was not mentioned after the Sixth Party Congress
6p	Refers to membership in the Sixth Central Committee and remained member of the committee after the Sixth Party Congress

Name	Position	Record #	O Chin-u	Ch'oe Kwang	Changes
Kim Jong Il	CIC Sec. 56p	1	1	1	
O Chin-u	PBM Mar. 3456p	2	0	0	died 2/25/95
Kang Song-san	PBM Prem. 56p	3	2	0	resigned 2/97
Yi Chong-ok	PBM VP 3456p	4	3	2	
Pak Song-ch'ol	PBM VP 456p	5	4	3	
Kim Yong-ju	PBM VP 456p	6	5	4	
Kim Pyong-sik	VP	7	21	0	from 7 to 21
Kim Yong-nam	PBM VPr. 56p	8	6	5	
Ch'oe Kwang	PBM AFM 346p	9	7	0	died 2/21/97
Kye Ung-t'ae	PBM Sec. 56p	10	8	9	
Chon Pyong-ho	PBM Sec. 56p	11	9	10	
Han Song-yong	PBM Sec. 6p	12	10	11	
So Yun-sok	PBM CPCM 56p	13	11	0	
Kim Ch'ol-man	PBCM Gen. 56p	14	12	12	
Ch'oe T'ae-bok	PBCM Sec. p	15	13	13	
Ch'oe Yong-nim	PBCM VPr. 56p	16	14	0	
Hong Song-nam	PBM VPr. 6p	17	15	16	
Kang Hwi-won	PBCM VPr. 456	18	0	0	died 7/28/94
Yang Hyong-sop	PBCM SPA 56p	19	16	14	
Hong Sok-hyong	PBCM CPCM p	20	17	17	
Yon Hyong-muk	PBCM CPCM 56p	21	18	0	
Yi Son-sil	PBCM 6p	22	19	0	
Kim Ch'ol-su	Unknown	23	20	0	
Kim Ki-nam	Sec. 6p	24	23	19	
Kim Kuk-t'ae	Sec. 56p	25	24	18	
Hwang Chang-yop	Sec. 56	26	25	0	defected 2/12/97
Kim Chung-nin	Sec. 456p	27	26	20	
So Kwan-hui	Sec. 6	28	27	0	
Kim Yong-sun	Sec. 6p	29	28	21	
Kim Hwan	VPr. 6p	30	29	0	
Kim Pok-sin	VPr. p	31	30	0	
Kim Ch'ang-ju	VPr.	32	31	0	
Kim Yun-hyok	VPr. 6	33	32	0	
Chang Ch'ol	VPr. 56p	34	33	0	
Kong Chin-t'ae	VPr. 6p	35	34	0	
Yun Ki-bok	Sec. 56p	36	35	22	
Pak Nam-gi	Sec. p	37	36	0	
Chon Mun-sop	Military 456	38	37	15	
Yu Mi-yong	Ch'ondogyo	39	22	0	from 39 to 22
Hyon Chun-guk	News Media 6p	40	38	0	
Won Tong-gu	Dept. Head 6	41	39	0	
Yi Ha-il	Vice-Mar. 6	42	40	0	
Kim Ik-hyon	Dept. Head 5p	43	41	25	
Yi Ch'ang-son	Dept. Head 6	44	42	0	

Name	Position	Record #	O Chin-u	Ch'oe Kwang	Changes
O Kuk-yol	Military 56	45	43	0	
Kwon Hui-gyong	Dept. Head 6p	46	44	0	
Kim Kyong-hui	Daughter p	47	45	0	
Kang Sok-sung	Dept. Head 6	48	121	0	from 48 to 121
Ch'ae Hui-jong	Former Sec. 46p	49	46	0	
No Myong-gun	Dept. Head 6	50	47	0	
Chon Ha-ch'ol	Dept. Head 56p	51	48	0	
Kim Tu-nam	Former PBCM 6p	52	49	85	
Paek Hak-nim	Vice-Mar. 456	53	50	24	
Chi Ch'ang-ik	CMC NDC 6p	54	51	0	
Yi Yong-mu	CMC AC 5p	55	52	0	
Yi Chi-ch'an	AC 23456	56	53	0	
Ch'oe Pok-yon	AC p	57	0	0	died 11/15/94
Kim Ch'ang-ho	AC 6p	58	54	0	died 11/26/95
Yi Sok	AC p	59	55	0	died 7/13/96
Pak Yong-sok	AC 56	60	56`	0	
Yi Ch'ol-bong	AC 56p	61	57	0	
Chong Chun-gi	News Media 56	62	58	0	
Hwang Sun-hui	Rev. Museum 456	63	59	28	
Sin Sang-gyun	6PCCM	64	60	0	died 8/7/97
Chong Ha-ch'ol	6PCCM	65	61	0	
Kim Ki-ryong	6PCCM	66	62	0	
Kang Hyon-su	Local Sec. 56	67	63	0	
Pak Sung-il	Local Sec. p	68	64	0	
Kim Hak-bong	Local Sec. p	69	65	0	
Paek Pom-su	Local Sec. 56	70	66	0	died 9/15/95
Ch'oe Mun-son	Local Sec. 6	71	67	0	
Yim Hyong-gu	Local Sec. 56	72	68	0	
Yi Kun-mo	Local Sec. 456p	73	69	0	
Hyon Ch'ol-gyu	Local Sec. 5	74	70	0	
Yi Kil-song	Local Sec. 6	75	71	0	
Yim Su-man	Local Sec. 56p	76	72	0	
Yi Ul-sol	Mar. 56	77	73	6	
Kim Pong-yul	Military 36p	78	74	0	died 7/19/95
Kim Kwang-jin	Vice-Mar p	79	75	23	died 2/27/97
Kim Chong-gak	Military p.	80	77	32	
O Yong-bang	Military 56p	81	78	33	
Kim Myong-guk	Military p	82	79	44	
Won Ung-hui	Military p	83	80	39	
Kim Kyok-sik	Military p	84	81	45	
Chang Song-u	Military 6	85	82	46	
Chon Chin-su	Military 6p	86	83	47	
Chu Sang-song	Military p	87	84	48	
Kim Yong-ch'un	Vice-Mar. 6p	88	85	8	
Cho Myong-nok	Vice-Mar. 6	89	86	7	
Kim Il-ch'ol	Vice-Mar. 6	90	87	49	
Paek Ch'ang-sik	Military p	91	0	0	died 10/13/94
Kim Yong-un	Col. Gen. 6	92	0	53	
Kang Tong-yun	Military p	93	88	50	
Pak Ki-so	Vice-Mar. 56p	94	89	51	
Han In-sul	Military p	95	90	0	
Kim Ha-gyu	Military p	96	91	37	
Nam Sang-nak	Military p	97	92	0	
Hyon Ch'ol-hae	Military p	98	95	38	
Yi Pong-won	Military 56	99	96	0	
Kim Pyong-yul	56CCM	100	97	0	

Name	Position	Record #	O Chin-u	Ch'oe Kwang	Changes
Chu Song-il	PCMCC	101	98	0	
Ch'oe Yong-hae	PCCM	102	99	0	
Ch'oe Song-suk	PCCM	103	100	29	
Kim Song-ae	56CCM	104	101	0	
Paek In-jun	PCCM	105	102	0	
Yi Mong-ho	PCCM	106	103	0	
Mun Song-sul	6CCM	107	104	0	
Yom Ki-sun	6PCCM	108	105	0	
Yi Yong-ch'ol	PCCM	109	106	52	
Chang Song-t'aek	PCCM	110	107	0	
Kim Si-hak	56CCM	111	108	0	
Kim Ch'ung-il	PCCM	112	109	0	
Pak Song-bong	PCCM	113	110	0	
Kang Kwan-ju	Unknown	114	111	0	
Kim Yong-ch'ae	6CCM	115	112	0	
Hong Song-yong	PBCM 6PCCM	116	113	0	
Cho Sun-baek	6CCM	117	0	0	
Yu Chong-suk	56CCM	118	114	0	
Chon Hui-jong	6CCM	119	115	0	
Kim Yong-yong	PCCM	120	116	62	
Kang Sok-chu	PCCM	121	117	0	
Son Song-p'il	56PCCM	122	118	0	
Chu Ch'ang-jun	PCCM	123	119	0	
Kim Kuk-hun	456CCM	124	120	0	
Cho Se-ung	PBCM 6CCM	125	122	0	
Ch'a Yong-jin	PCCM	126	123	0	
Chu Kyu-ch'ang	56PCCM	127	124	0	
Kim Yun-sang	6CCM	128	125	0	died 10/14/96
Kim Hoe-il	3456CCM	129	126	0	died 11/3/96
Ch'oe Man-hyon	6PCCM	130	0	0	died 8/28/94
Yom T'ae-jun	456CCM	131	127	0	
Yom Chae-man	6CCM	132	128	0	
Pyon Ch'ang-bok	6CCM	133	129	0	
Ch'oe In-dok	56CCM	134	130	27	
T'ae Pyong-yol	456CCM	135	131	0	died 2/4/97
Chu Kil-bon	6CCM	136	132	0	died 6/13/96
Yun Ho-sok	6CCM	137	133	0	
Hong Si-hak	Sec. 56PCCM	138	134	0	
Ch'oe Chin-song	56CCM	139	135	0	
Kim Tal-hyon	PBCM PCCM	140	136	0	
Chong Ch'ol	6CCM	141	137	0	
Ho Kuk-song	PCCM	142	138	0	
Yi Tu-ik	56CCM	143	76	26	from 143 to 76
Yi Song-dae	PCMCC	144	139	0	
Kim Ung-sang	46CMCC	145	140	0	
Kim Won-jin	PCMCC	146	141	0	
Kim Yi-ryong	PCMCC	147	142	0	
Kwak Pom-gi	PCMCC	148	143	0	
Kim Se-yong	PCMCC	149	144	0	died 10/22/95
Pak Won-hyon	PCMCC	150	145	0	
Kim Hak-sop	PCMCC	151	146	0	
Kim Song-gu	PCMCC	152	147	0	
O Song-yol	PCMCC	153	148	0	
Ch'oe Ki-ryong	PCMCC	154	149	0	
Yi Chae-yun	45CCM	155	150	0	
Yun Ki-jong	6CMCC	156	151	0	

Name	Position	Record #	O Chin-u	Ch'oe Kwang	Changes
Kim Su-hak	PCMCC	157	152	0	
Yi Yong-sop	PCMCC	158	153	0	died 11/18/95
Pak Myong-ch'ol	PCMCC	159	154	0	
Ch'ae Kyu-bin	PCMCC	160	155	0	
Chong Song-t'aek	PCMCC	161	156	0	
Kim Chong-suk	PCMCC	162	157	0	
Yi Pyong-uk	6CMCC	163	158	34	
Chong Ch'ang-yol	PCMCC Gen.	164	159	35	
Kim Tae-sik	PCMCC	165	160	42	
Chon Chae-son	PCMCC Vice-Mar.	166	161	54	
Yo Ch'un-sok	6CMCC	167	162	55	
Kim Song-gyu	PCMCC	168	163	56	
Chong Ho-gyun	PCMCC	169	164	57	
Yo Pyong-nam	PCMCC	170	165	0	
Yi Won-jae	PCMCC	171	166	0	
Chu Sung-nam	PCMCC	172	167	0	
Won Myong-gyun	6CMCC	173	168	0	
Paek Sang-ho	PCMCC	174	169	58	
Kim Pok-mun	PCMCC	175	170	0	
Yi T'ae-ch'ol	PCMCC Col. Gen.	176	171	59	
Pak Chae-gyong	PCMCC	177	172	40	
Yim Tong-ok	PCMCC	178	173	0	
Yi Pong-ik	PCMCC	179	174	0	
Kim Chung-hyop	PCMCC	180	175	0	
Ch'ae Hyong-sik	PCMCC	181	176	0	
Yim Sang-jong	PCMCC	182	177	0	
Yi Song-bok	6PCMCC	183	178	0	
Yi Hwa-son	6CMCC	184	179	0	died 11/18/96
Hong In-bom	6CMCC	185	180	0	
Kim Ch'ol-myong	PCCM	186	181	0	
Kil Chae-gyong	6PCCM	187	182	0	
Pak Pong-ju	6CMCC	188	183	0	
Kim Yu-sun	6CMCC	189	184	0	died 8/10/96
Kim Chae-bong	6CMCC	190	0	0	died 2/14/97
Pak Chung-guk	6CMCC	191	185	0	died 10/8/96
Ko Chong-sik	6CCM	192	0	0	
Kang Sun-hui	PCCM	193	186	0	
Yi Yang-suk	46CMCC	194	0	0	
Chang Kuk-ch'an	6CCM	195	187	0	
Ch'oe Sang-yol	6CMCC	196	0	0	
Paek Se-yun	PCMCC	197	188	0	
Ok Pong-nin	6CMCC Col. Gen.	198	189	43	
Kim Yong-yon	56CMCC	199	190	30	
Chong Song-nam	6CMCC	200	191	0	
Yi Yong-gyun	PCMCC	201	192	0	
Im Nok-chae	6CMCC	202	193	0	
Yo Yon-gu	SPA	203	194	0	
Sin Chin-sun	56CMCC	204	195	0	
Kim Nak-hui	56CMCC	205	197	0	
Cho Ch'ang-dok	6CCM	206	198	0	
Ho Sun	6CMCC	207	199	0	
Hwang Sok-kyu	PCMCC	208	200	0	
Pak Su-bom	6CMCC	209	201	0	
Kim Sang-ho	PCCM	210	202	0	
Sin T'ae-rok	PCMCC	211	203	0	
Kim Hyong-muk	PCMCC	212	204	0	

Name	Position	Record #	O Chin-u	Ch'oe Kwang	Changes
Yi Won-gwan	PCMCC	213	205	0	died 2/24/97
Pak Yong-ch'an	6PCMCC	214	206	0	
Kim Chu-ho	PCMCC	215	0	0	
Ch'oe Myong-ch'ol	6CMCC	216	207	0	
Yi Yun-hup	PCMCC	217	208	0	
Yim Pong-yong	PCMCC	218	209	0	
Kim Yun-u	PCMCC	219	210	0	
Kim Pyong-p'al	PCMCC	220	211	0	
Pak Yong-sik	PCMCC	221	212	0	
Ho Min-son	6CMCC	222	213	0	
Ch'oe Pyong-ho	PCMCC	223	214	0	
Han Kyu-p'al	6CMCC	224	215	0	
Ch'oe Hyon-gi	PCMCC	225	216	0	
Yi Hyon-ho	Unknown	226	217	0	
Paek Un-sun	PCMCC	227	218	0	
Chon Yong-hun	Unknown	228	219	0	
Pak Si-hyong	6CMCC	229	220	0	
Yi Hak-sop	PCMCC	230	221	0	
Kim Kwang-su	PCMCC	231	222	0	
Yi Tae-se	PCMCC	232	223	0	
Yi Tong-song	PCMCC	233	224	0	
Kim Ung-sam	56CMCC	234	225	0	
Paek Sol-hui	Unknown	235	226	0	
Kwak Yong-ho	6CMCC	236	227	0	
Yi Nak-bin	56ACM	237	228	0	
Kim Ung-ch'ol	PACM	238	229	0	
Yun So	PACM	239	230	0	
Kim Se-yun	PACM	240	231	0	
Sin Kyong-sik	PACM	241	232	0	
Chong Tu-hwan	3456ACM	242	233	0	
Han Yong-ho	PACM	243	234	0	
Han Yun-ch'ang	PACM	244	235	0	
Han T'ae-yong	PACM	245	236	0	
Maeng T'ae-ho	PACM	246	237	0	
Song Kum-sun	56ACM	247	238	0	
Kim Ch'on-p'il	PACM	248	239	0	
Ch'oe Ch'i-son	6ACM	249	240	0	
Kim T'ae-guk	6CMCC	250	0	0	
Ch'oe Hui-jong	Unknown	251	0	0	
Kim P'yong-gil	Unknown	252	0	0	
Yi Ch'un-sok	Unknown	253	0	0	
Kim Kil-yon	Unknown	254	0	0	
Cho Yun-hui	Unknown	255	0	0	
Yi Paek-ha	Unknown	256	0	0	
Ch'oe, Won-ik	Chief Justice	257	0	0	
Chong Mun-san	Unknown	258	0	0	
Im Chong-sang	Unknown	259	0	0	
Yi Ho-hyok	6CCM	260	0	0	
Yi Chong-ju	Unknown	261	0	0	
Ch'oe Chong-gon	45CMCC	262	0	0	
Pak Yong-nam	Unknown	263	0	0	
Kim Song-hwan	Unknown	264	0	0	
Kim Ch'i-dok	Unknown	265	0	0	
Sin Il-nam	Unknown	266	0	0	
Kim Sok-hyong	Scholar	267	0	0	died 11/26/96
Yi Chi-su	Scholar	268	0	0	
Pak Kwan-o	Scholar	269	0	0	

Name	Position	Record #	O Chin-u	Ch'oe Kwang	Changes
Ch'oe Kwang-yol	2CMCC	270	0	0	
Chon Chu-nam	Unknown	271	0	0	
Kim Pyong-hun	Unknown	272	0	0	
Kang Yong-sop	Diplomat	273	0	0	
Kang Yong-ho	Col. Gen.	274	93	0	only to O Chin-u
Kim Hyong-yong	Col. Gen.	275	94	0	only to O Chin-u
Pyon Yong-nip	Col. Gen.	276	196	0	only to O Chin-u
Yi Chong-sam	Vice-Mar.	277	0	31	only to Ch'oe Kwang
Yi Yong-su	Vice-AFM			36	only to Ch'oe Kwang
O Kum-ch'ol	Col. Gen.			60	only to Ch'oe Kwang
Yi Yong-hwan	Col. Gen.			61	only to Ch'oe Kwang
Ch'oe Ki-ryon	Col. Gen.			63	only to Ch'oe Kwang
Ch'oe Sang-yo	Lt. Gen.			64	only to Ch'oe Kwang
Yi Pyong-sam	Lt. Gen.			65	only to Ch'oe Kwang
Chi Yong-ch'un	Lt. Gen.			66	only to Ch'oe Kwang
Kim Ki-son	Col. Gen.			67	only to Ch'oe Kwang
Pak Sung-won	Lt. Gen.			68	only to Ch'oe Kwang
An Pi-duk	Lt. Gen.			69	only to Ch'oe Kwang
Yi Pong-juk	Lt. Gen.			70	only to Ch'oe Kwang
Kim Sung-yon	Maj. Gen.			71	only to Ch'oe Kwang
Yi Ch'ang-han	Lt. Gen.			72	only to Ch'oe Kwang
Chong T'ae-gun	Maj. Gen.			73	only to Ch'oe Kwang
Yom Ch'ol-song	Maj. Gen.			74	only to Ch'oe Kwang
Pyon Sang-mo				75	only to Ch'oe Kwang
Kim Won-hong				76	only to Ch'oe Kwang
Yi Chu-ul	Lt. Gen.			77	only to Ch'oe Kwang
Han Pae-yon	Lt. Gen.			78	only to Ch'oe Kwang
Son Ch'ol-chu	Maj. Gen.			79	only to Ch'oe Kwang
Sim Sang-dae	Lt. Gen.			80	only to Ch'oe Kwang
Ch'oe Ho-jun	Maj. Gen.			81	only to Ch'oe Kwang
Tong Yong-il				82	only to Ch'oe Kwang

Name	Position	Record #	O Chin-u	Ch'oe Kwang	Changes
Kim Kye-nam				83	only to Ch'oe Kwang
Paek Pok-yong	Maj. Gen.			84	only to Ch'oe Kwang

APPENDIX 3

Agreed Framework on the Nuclear Issue

Delegation of the Government of the United States of America (U.S.) and the Democratic People's Republic of Korea (DPRK) held talks in Geneva from September 23 to October 17, 1994, to negotiate an overall resolution of the nuclear issue on the Korean peninsula.

Both sides reaffirmed the importance of attaining the objective contained in the August 12, 1994 Agreement between the U.S. and the DPRK and upholding the principle of the June 11, 1993 Joint Statement of the U.S. and the DPRK to achieve peace and security on a nuclear-free Korean peninsula. The U.S. and the DPRK decided to take the following actions for the resolution of the nuclear issue:

I. Both sides will cooperate to replace the DPRK's graphite-moderated reactors and related facilities with light-water reactor (LWR) power plants.

1. In accordance with the October 20, 1994 letter of assurance from the U.S. President, the U.S. will undertake to make arrangements for the provision to the DPRK of a light-water reactor project with a total generating capacity of approximately 2,000 MW(e) by a target date of 2003.

   The U.S. will organize under its leadership an international consortium to finance and supply the light-water reactor project to be provided to the DPRK. The U.S., representing the international consortium, will serve as the principal point of contact with the DPRK for the LWR project.

   The U.S., representing the consortium, will make best efforts to secure the conclusion of a supply contact with the DPRK within six months of the date of this document for the provision of the LWR project. Contract talks will begin as soon as possible after the date of this document.

   As necessary, the U.S. and the DPRK will conclude a bilateral agreement for cooperation in the field of peaceful uses of nuclear energy.

2. In accordance with the October 20, 1994 U.S. letter of assurance concerning interim energy alternatives, the U.S., representing the consortium, will make arrangements to offset the energy foregone due to the freeze of the DPRK's graphite-moderated reactors, pending completion of the first LWR unit.

   Alternative energy will be provided in the form of heavy oil for heating and electricity production.

   Deliveries of heavy oil will begin within three months of the date of this document and will reach a rate of 500,000 tons annually, in accordance with an agreed schedule of deliveries.

3. Upon receipt of U.S. assurances for the provision of light-water reactors and for arrangements for interim energy alternatives, the DPRK will freeze its graphite-moderated reactors and related facilities and will eventually dismantle these reactors and related facilities.

   The freeze on the DPRK's graphite-moderated reactors and related facilities will be fully implemented within one month of the date of this document. During this one-month period and throughout the freeze, the IAEA will be allowed to monitor this freeze, and the DPRK will provide full cooperation to the IAEA for this purpose.

   Dismantlement of the DPRK's graphite-moderated reactors and related facilities will be completed when the LWR project is completed.

   The U.S. and DPRK will cooperate in finding a method to store safely spent fuel from the 5 MW(e) experimental reactor during the construction of the LWR project, and to dispose of the fuel in a safe manner that does not involve reprocessing in the DPRK.

4. As soon as possible after the date of this document U.S. and DPRK experts will hold two sets of experts talks.

   At one set of talks, experts will discuss issues related to alternative energy and the replacement of the graphite-moderated reactor program with the LWR project.

   At the other set of talks, experts will discuss specific arrangements for spent fuel storage and ultimate disposition.

II. The two sides will move toward full normalization of political economic relations.

1. Within three months of the date of this document, both sides will reduce barriers to trade and investment, including restrictions on telecommunications services and financial transactions.

2. Each side will open a liaison office in the other's capital following resolution of consular and other technical issues through expert level discussions.

3. As progress is made on issues of concern to each side, the U.S. and DPRK will upgrade bilateral relations to the Ambassadorial level.

III. Both sides will work together for peace and security on a nuclear-free Korean peninsula.

1. The U.S. will provide formal assurance to the DPRK, against the threat or use of nuclear weapons by the U.S.

2. The DPRK will consistently take steps to implement the North-South Joint Declaration on the Denuclearization of the Korean Peninsula.

3. The DPRK will engage in North-South dialogue, as this agreed framework will help create an atmosphere that promotes such a dialogue.

IV. Both sides will work together to strengthen the international nuclear non-proliferation regime.

1. The DPRK will remain a party to the Treaty on the Non-Proliferation of Nuclear Weapons (NPT) and will allow implementation of its safeguards agreement under the Treaty.

2. Upon conclusion of the supply contract for the provision of the LWR project, ad hoc and routine inspections will resume under the DPRK's safeguards agreement with the IAEA with respect to the facilities not subject to the freeze. Pending conclusion of the supply contract, inspections required by the IAEA for the continuity of safeguards will continue at the facilities not subject to the freeze.

3. When a significant portion of the LWR project is completed, but before delivery of key nuclear components, the DPRK will come into full compliance with its safeguards agreement with the IAEA (INFCRC/403), including taking all steps that may be deemed necessary by the IAEA, following consultations with the Agency with regard to verifying the accuracy and completeness of the DPRK's initial report on all nuclear material in the DPRK.

Signed by
Robert Gallucci,
Assistant Secretary of State
for Political Military Affairs of the United States
Kang Sok-chu,
The First Vice-Minister of Foreign Affairs of the DPRK,
Geneva, October 21, 1994

BIBLIOGRAPHY

Studies of North Korea in general suffer from a paucity of scholarly works in all fields. Because the Korean peninsula is divided into ideologically disparate regimes, historical narratives and political analyses, in particular, are at times passionate condemnations of the North Korean Communist system or spirited propaganda for and outlandish justification of North Korea. Scholars who study North Korea have to deal with this problem and read the biased sources to gain access to scarce information, making the objective understanding of North Korea that much more difficult. The following is a brief list of selected scholarly books in English on North Korea; it was necessary to include a few biased studies from North and South Korea.

Baik, Bong. *Kim Il Sung: Biography.* 3 vols. Tokyo: Miraisha, 1969–1970.

Bandow, Doug. *Tripwire: Korea and U.S. Foreign Policy in a Changed World.* Washington, D.C.: Cato Institute, 1996.

Bandow, Doug, and Ted Galen Carpenter. *The US–South Korean Alliance: Time for a Change.* New Brunswick, N.J.: Transaction Publishers, 1992.

Berry, William. *North Korea's Nuclear Program: The Clinton Administration's Response.* Colorado Springs, Colo.: Institute for National Security Studies, 1995.

Byun, Dae-Ho. *North Korea's Foreign Policy: The Juche Ideology and the Challenge of Gorbachev's New Thinking.* Seoul: Research Center for Peace and Unification of Korea, 1991.

Chen, Jian. *China's Road to the Korean War: The Making of the Sino-American Confrontation.* New York: Columbia University Press, 1994.

Cho, Sung Yoon. *Law and Legal Literature of North Korea: A Guide.* Washington, D.C.: Library of Congress, 1988.

Choe, In Su. *Kim Jong Il: The People's Leader.* 2 vols. Pyongyang: Foreign Languages Publishing House, 1983 and 1985.

Cumings, Bruce. *The Origins of the Korean War.* 2 vols. Princeton, N.J.: Princeton University Press, 1981 and 1990.

———. *Korea's Place in the Sun: A Modern History.* New York: W. W. Norton & Co., 1997.

Eberstadt, Nicholas. *Korea Approaches Reunification.* Armonk, N.Y.: M. E. Sharp, 1995.

Gills, Barry. *Korea Versus Korea: Political Economy, Diplomacy and Contested Legitimacy.* New York: Routledge, 1996.

Goncharov, Sergei N., John W. Lewis, and Litai Xue. *Uncertain Partners: Stalin, Mao, and the Korean War.* Stanford, Calif.: Stanford University Press, 1993.

Henriksen, Thomas H., and Kyongsoo Lho, eds. *One Korea?* Stanford, Calif.: Hoover Institution Press, 1994.

Hwang, Eui-gak. *The Korean Economies: A Comparison of North and South.* Oxford: Clarendon Press, 1993.

Kihl, Young Whan, ed. *Korea and the World: Beyond the Cold War.* Boulder, Colo.: Westview Press, 1994.

Kim Il Sung. *Selected Works.* 10 vols. Pyongyang: Foreign Languages Publishing House, 1971–1994.

———. *With the Century: Reminiscences.* 6 vols. Pyongyang: Foreign Languages Publishing House, 1992–1995.

Kim Jong Il. *Selected Works.* 2 vols. Pyongyang: Foreign Languages Publishing House, 1992 and 1995.

Koh, Byung Chul. *The Foreign Policy Systems of North and South Korea.* Berkeley: University of California Press, 1984.

Koo, Bon-Hak. *Political Economy of Self-Reliance.* Seoul: Research Center for Peace and Unification in Korea, 1992.

Lee, Chae-Jin. *China and Korea: Dynamic Relations.* Stanford, Calif.: Hoover Institution Press, 1996.

Lee, Chong-Sik, and Se-hee Yoo, eds. *North Korea in Transition.* Berkeley, Calif.: Institute for East Asian Studies, 1991.

Lee, Suck-Ho. *Party-Military Relations in North Korea: A Comparative Analysis.* Seoul: Research Center for Peace and Unification of Korea, 1989.

Mazarr, Michael J. *North Korea and the Bomb: A Case Study in Nonproliferation.* New York: St. Martin's Press, 1995.

Merrill, John. *Korea: The Peninsular Origins of the War.* Newark: University of Delaware Press, 1989.

Ministry of National Defense. *Defense White Paper, 1996–1997.* Seoul: Ministry of National Defense, 1997.

Noland, Marcus. *The Economics of Korean Unification.* Washington, D.C.: Institute for International Economics, 1997.

Park, Jae Kyu, et al. *The Foreign Relations of North Korea: New Perspective.* Boulder, Colo.: Westview Press, 1987.

Research Institute for National Unification. *White Paper on Human Rights in North Korea, 1996.* Seoul: Research Institute for National Unification, 1996.

Research Institute of History, Academy of Sciences. *History of the Just Fatherland Liberation War of the Korean People.* Pyongyang: Foreign Languages Publishing House, 1961.

Scalapino, Robert A., and Jun-yop Kim, eds. *North Korea Today: Strategic and Domestic Issues.* Berkeley, Calif.: Institute of East Asian Studies, 1983.

Scalapino, Robert A., and Chong-Sik Lee, eds. *Communism in Korea.* 2 vols. Berkeley: University of California Press, 1972.

Scalapino, Robert A., and Hongkoo Lee, eds. *North Korea in a Regional and Global Context.* Berkeley, Calif.: Institute of East Asian Studies, 1986.

Simons, Geoff. *Korea: The Search for Sovereignty.* New York: St. Martin's Press, 1995.

Smith, Hazel, et al. *North Korea in the New World Order.* New York: St. Martin's Press, 1996.

Stueck, William. *The Korean War: An International History.* Princeton, N.J.: Princeton University Press, 1997.

Suh, Dae-Sook. *The Korean Communist Movement, 1918–1948.* Princeton, N.J.: Princeton University Press, 1967.

———. *Documents of Korean Communism, 1918–1948.* Princeton, N.J.: Princeton University Press, 1970.

———. *Korean Communism, 1945–1980: A Reference Guide to the Political System.* Honolulu: University of Hawaii Press, 1981.

———. *Kim Il Sung: The North Korean Leader.* New York: Columbia University Press, 1988.

Tak, Jin, Gang Il Kim, and Hong Je Pak. *Great Leader Kim Jong Il.* 2 vols. Tokyo: Sorinsha, 1984–1985.

U.S. Department of State. *North Korea: A Case Study in the Technique of Takeover.* Washington, D.C.: U.S. Department of State, 1961.

Van Ree, Erik. *Socialism in One Zone: Stalin's Policy in Korea, 1945–1947.* Oxford: Berg Publishers Ltd., 1989.

Williams, Phil, et al., eds., *Security in Korea: War, Stalemate, and Negotiation.* Boulder, Colo.: Westview Press, 1994.

Yang, Sung Chul. *The North and South Korean Political Systems: A Comparative Analysis.* Boulder, Colo.: Westview Press, 1994.

THE CONTRIBUTORS

Doug Bandow is a Senior Fellow at the Cato Institute, Washington, D.C., a nationally syndicated columnist with Copley News Service, and the former editor of *Inquiry* magazine. He also served as a special assistant to President Reagan. He has written and edited several books, including *Tripwire: Korea and U.S. Foreign Policy in a Changed World* (Cato Institute, 1996); *Human Resources and Defense Manpower* (National Defense University); and *The U.S.–South Korean Alliance: Time for a Change* (Transaction, 1992). He has also been widely published in such periodicals as *Foreign Policy, Harper's, National Interest,* and *Orbis.*

Richard Halloran is an independent writer who was formerly with the *New York Times* as a foreign correspondent in Asia and a military correspondent in Washington, D.C. He writes from and about Asia and U.S. relations with Asia, especially security issues, for publications in the United States and Asia. He is the author of *Japan: Images and Realities* (Knopf, 1969); *Conflict and Compromise: The Dynamics of American Foreign Policy* (John Day, 1973); *To Arm a Nation: Rebuilding America's Endangered Defenses* (Macmillan, 1986); and *Serving America: Prospects for the Volunteer Force* (Twentieth Century Fund, 1988).

Selig S. Harrison is a Guest Scholar at the Woodrow Wilson International Center for Scholars. He served as a senior associate of the Carnegie Endowment for International Peace from 1974 to 1997 and is the author of five books on Asia and U.S.-Asia policy, including *Dialogue with North Korea* (The Carnegie Endowment for International Peace, 1989). In May 1972 Harrison, representing the *Washington Post,* visited North Korea to interview Kim Il Sung. He subsequently visited Pyongyang in 1987, 1992, 1994, and 1995. In June 1994 he met Kim Il Sung and won from him agreement to the concept of a freeze and eventual dismantlement of the North Korean nuclear program in exchange for U.S. political and economic concessions. His meeting, together with former president Carter's meeting one week later, opened the way for the U.S.–North Korean nuclear agreement of October 21, 1994.

B. C. Koh is professor of political science at the University of Illinois at Chicago. He is the author of *The Foreign Policy Systems of North and South Korea* (University of California Press, 1984), *Japan's Administrative Elite* (University of California Press, 1989), and other works. He has taught at Seoul National University as a Fulbright lecturer.

Chae-Jin Lee is professor of government and director of the Keck Center for International and Strategic Studies, Claremont McKenna College. He is author of *China and Korea: Dynamic Relations; China's Korean Minority; Zhou Enlai: The Early Years; China and Japan: New Economic Diplomacy;* and *Japan Faces China;* and coauthor of *U.S. Policy Toward Japan and Korea.* He also edited or coedited *The Korean War, The Prospects for Korean Reunification,* and *Political Leadership in Korea.*

Chong-Sik Lee is professor of political science at the University of Pennsylvania. His publications include *The Politics of Korean Nationalism* (University of California Press, 1963); *Japan and Korea: The Political Dimension* (Hoover, 1985); and (coauthored with Robert A. Scalapino) the two-volume work *Communism in Korea* (University of California Press, 1973). During the past few years, he has published numerous articles on political and economic development in North and South Korea, Japanese-Korean relations, and U.S. and Soviet policies toward Korea.

Patrick M. Morgan is Tierney Professor of Peace and Conflict Studies and director of the Global Peace and Conflict Studies at the University of California at Irvine. He is the author of *Deterrence, a Conceptual Analysis* (1983), *Theories and Approaches to International Politics* (4th edition, 1987), *Security and Arms Control* (two volumes, coeditor, 1989), and other works. He has concentrated on national and international security studies. Currently he is involved in projects on the psychological dimension of foreign policy making, regional conflict, and great-power security strategies.

Marcus Noland is a Senior Fellow at the Institute for International Economics, Washington D.C. He served as a senior economist at the Council of Economic Advisers in the Executive Office of the President of the United States. His publications include *Japan in the World Economy* (coauthor with Bela Balassa); *Pacific Basin Developing Countries: Prospect for the Future; Pacific Dynamism and the International Economic System* (coeditor with C. Fred Bergsten); *Reconcilable Differences? Resolving United States–Japan Economic Conflict* (coeditor with C. Fred

Bergsten); and other scholarly works. He has also served as a consultant to the World Bank, the New York Stock Exchange, and the Advisory Committee on Trade Policy and Negotiations.

Edward A. Olsen is professor of national security affairs at the Naval Postgraduate School in Monterey, California. He is concurrently director of its Center for Northeast Asian Security Studies. He served as a Japan-Korea political analyst at the U.S. Department of State, Bureau of Intelligence and Research. In the field of Asian security, he is the editor of four volumes and the author of four books, over fifty book chapters, and more than one hundred articles.

C. Kenneth Quinones served as a foreign service officer from 1980 to 1997. He also served as a North Korean analyst in the Bureau of Intelligence and Research at the U.S. Department of State. Between August 1992 and September 1994, he was the North Korea "desk" officer in the Office of Korean Affairs, Bureau of East Asian and Pacific Affairs. At that time, he served as the main point of contact between the United States and North Korea and was a member of the U.S. delegation to the nuclear negotiations with North Korea. Since 1992, he has visited North Korea thirteen times.

Robert A. Scalapino is Robson Research Professor of Government Emeritus, a former director of the Institute of East Asian Studies, and the editor of *Asian Survey* at the University of California at Berkeley. He is a member of the American Academy of Arts and Sciences and a trustee of the Asia Foundation, Pacific Forum, and the Atlantic Council. He has written numerous books and articles on Asian politics, international relations, and foreign policy. His most recent books include *Modern China and Its Revolutionary Process* (with George T. Yu); *Asia and the Road Ahead; The Foreign Policy of Modern Japan;* and a monograph, *The Last Leninists: The Uncertain Future of Asia's Communist States.*

Dae-Sook Suh is Korea Foundation Professor of Policy Studies at the University of Hawaii at Manoa and former director of its Center for Korean Studies. He is the author of *The Korean Communist Movement, 1918–1948* (Princeton University Press, 1968), *Documents of Korean Communism, 1918–1948* (Princeton University Press, 1970); *Korean Communism, 1945–1980* (University of Hawaii Press, 1981); *Kim Il Sung: The North Korean Leader* (Columbia University Press, 1988); *Kin Nichisei to Kin shonichi* (Iwanami Shoten, 1996); and other works.

INDEX

ABOUT THE BOOK

Suh, Lee, and their contributors offer insight into the politics of a nation that has long been a source of mystery and alarm for Western powers.

Chapters on political leadership and the economy point to North Korea's attempt to move away from its extreme isolationism in foreign policy since the death of longtime leader Kim Il Sung, even as it has fallen into increasing disarray in its domestic affairs.

The authors evaluate the military capabilities of the country, explore the history, politics, and strategic issues involved in North Korea's standing within the global community and with the United States, and investigate the risks and opportunities that might arise from its current internal turmoil.

One of the book's most important contributions is the close attention it pays to the threats that North Koreans perceive about their own security and sovereignty.

Dae-Sook Suh is Korea Foundation Professor of Policy Studies at the University of Hawaii at Manoa. His books include *The Korean Communist Movement* and *Kim Il Sung: The North Korean Leader.* **Chae-Jin Lee** is director of the Keck Center for International and Strategic Studies at Claremont McKenna College. He is author of *China and Korea: Dynamic Relations* and coauthor of *U.S. Policy Toward Japan and Korea.*

DATE DUE

Demco, Inc 38-293